The Power of Curiosity

Celebrating
30 Years of Publishing
in India

Praise for *The Power of Curiosity*

'The reader is taken into a beautifully created classroom universe based on an ingenious yet in-depth grasp of the learning process! The power that curiosity wields in nurturing creativity and critical thinking is brought out with exceptional storytelling laced with humour. A must-read for all. You might just find the child inside you!'

—Nandan Nilekani, Co-Founder and Chairman, Infosys, and Founding Chairman, UIDAI (Aadhaar)

'When fiction is the outcome of creative, knowledgeable and insightful minds, it could be a precursor to a revolutionary development in the real world. This work is a very unusual approach from the unconventional thinking of a few extraordinary minds coming together. It is sure to find unprecedented response from a wide range of readers, including educationists and visionaries charting out the future trajectory of humanity with its multiple dimensions.'

—Dr K. Kasturirangan, former Chairman, Indian Space Research Organisation, and Chairman, National Education Policy 2020 Drafting Committee

'An invigorating and thought-provoking book that challenges conventional boundaries and prompts readers to rethink education. This literary work inspires individuals to explore new pathways and embrace novel ideas, offering a blueprint for the creation of a dynamic learning environment. It is a must-read for those seeking to broaden their horizons and unlock the limitless potential of education.'

—Dr Swaroop Sampat, theatre artist, film actor, producer and educationist

The Power of Curiosity

IN AND BEYOND CLASSROOMS

ANITA KARWAL | RAJNISH KUMAR | RASHI SHARMA

HarperCollins *Publishers* India

First published in India by HarperCollins *Publishers* 2023
4th Floor, Tower A, Building No. 10, DLF Cyber City,
DLF Phase II, Gurugram, Haryana – 122002
www.harpercollins.co.in

2 4 6 8 10 9 7 5 3 1

P-ISBN: 978-93-5629-667-1
E-ISBN: 978-93-5629-678-7

Typeset in 11/14 Minion Pro at
Manipal Technologies Limited, Manipal

Printed and bound at
Replika Press Pvt. Ltd.

This book is produced from independently certified FSC® paper to ensure responsible forest management.

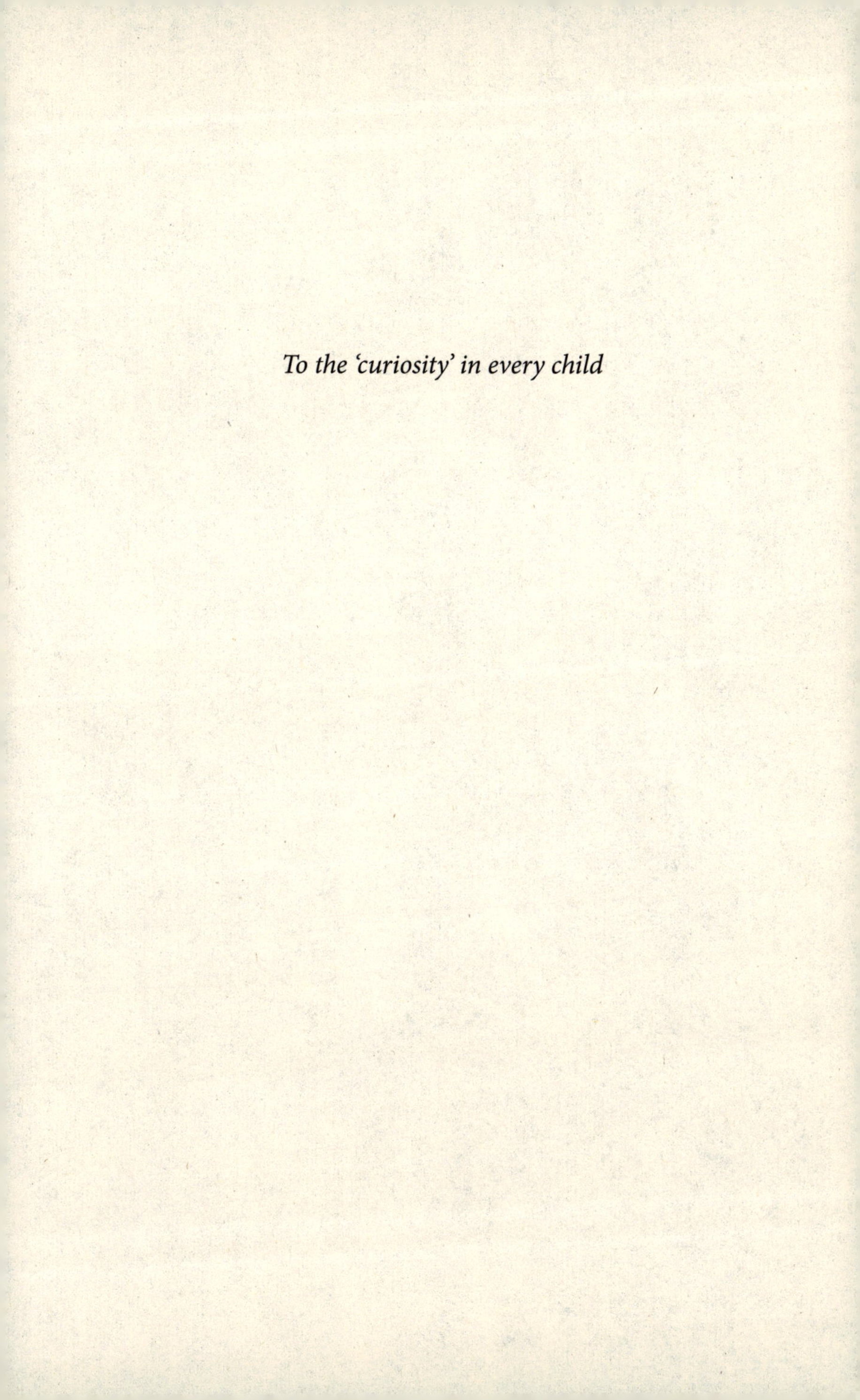

To the 'curiosity' in every child

Contents

Foreword

GLOBALIZATION AND DIGITALIZATION HAVE CONNECTED people, cities, countries and continents in ways that vastly increase our individual and collective potential. But the same forces have also made the world more volatile, more complex, more uncertain and more ambiguous. The world has seen a growing disconnect between the infinite growth imperative and the finite resources of our planet; between the financial economy and the real economy; between the wealthy and the poor; between the concept of our gross domestic product and the well-being of people; between what is technologically possible and the social needs of people; and between governance and the perceived voicelessness of people.

No one should hold education responsible for all of this, but neither should we underestimate the role that knowledge, skills, attitudes and values of people play in social, economic and cultural development. While digital technologies, globalization and climate change all have disruptive implications for our economic and social structure, those implications are not predetermined. It is the nature of our collective responses to these disruptions that determines their outcomes—the continuous interplay between the technological frontier and the cultural, social and institutional agents that we mobilize in response.

In this world, education is no longer just about teaching students something, but about helping them develop a reliable compass and the tools to navigate with confidence through an increasingly complex, volatile and uncertain world. Success in education today is about building curiosity—opening minds; it is about compassion—opening hearts; and it is about courage—mobilizing our cognitive, social and emotional resources to take action. And those are also our best weapons against the biggest threats of our times—ignorance, the closed mind; hate, the closed heart; and fear, the enemy of agency.

The kind of things that are easy to teach and test have become easy to digitize and automate. We know how to educate second-class robots, people who are good at repeating what we told them. In this age of accelerations and artificial intelligence, we need to think harder about what makes us human.

The conventional approach in school is often to break problems down into manageable bits and pieces and then to train students how to solve these bits and pieces. But modern societies create value by integrating different fields of knowledge, making connections between ideas that previously seemed unrelated, connecting the dots where the next innovation will come from.

In the past, schools were technological islands, with technology often limited to supporting and conserving existing practices, and students outpacing schools in their adoption of technology. Now schools need to use the potential of technologies to liberate learning from past conventions and connect learners in new and powerful ways, with sources of knowledge, with innovative applications and with one another.

The past was divided—with teachers and content divided by subjects and students separated by expectations of their future career prospects; with schools designed to keep students inside, and the rest of the world outside; with a lack of engagement with families; and a reluctance to partner with other schools. The future needs to be integrated—with an emphasis on the interrelation of subjects and the integration of students.

In today's schools, students typically learn individually and at the end of the school year, we certify their individual achievements. But the more interdependent the world becomes, the more we need great collaborators and orchestrators. Schools need to help students learn to be autonomous in their thinking and develop an identity that is aware of the pluralism of modern living. At work, at home and in the community, people will need a broad understanding of how others live, in different cultures and traditions, and how others think, whether as scientists or as artists. The foundations for this don't all come naturally. We are all born with 'bonding social capital', a sense of belonging to our family or other people with shared experiences, common purposes or pursuits. But it requires deliberate and continuous efforts to create the kind of 'bridging social capital' through which we can share experiences, ideas and innovation with others, and increase our radius of trust to others.

All easy to say, really hard to do. It's so much easier to educate students for our past, than for their future. Schools are inherently conservative social systems; as parents we get anxious when our children learn things we don't understand, and even more when they no longer study things that were important for us. Teachers are more comfortable to teach how they were taught, than how they were taught to teach. And policy-makers can lose elections over education issues, but rarely win elections over education, because it takes so much more than an election cycle to translate good ideas into better results.

This is where Karwal's, Kumar's and Sharma's book is truly inspirational. Rather than talking us through how to tinker with existing education systems to seek marginal improvements, it helps us reimagine education afresh, through the lens of imaginary students who are leaders for a better future, teachers who are learners and creative designers of innovative learning environments, and communities that do not conserve but transform learning opportunities.

It shows us how mastery can be developed not at the expense of student well-being, but through student well-being, agency, awareness and connectedness. It helps us cut through the educational laws, regulations, and structures that too often cloud our minds, to discover the heart of educational improvement: The capacity to listen and envision, broadening perspectives and co-creating what success means and how we can see it. The ability to learn and design, building curiosity and critical knowledge, valuing learner ownership and expecting higher order thinking. The disposition to love and connect, building relationships, fostering belonging, nurturing culture and humanity. The openness to reflect and grow, to learn, unlearn and relearn at every level of the system.

But the greatest power of the book lies in making us realize that this need not be fiction, that universal high-quality education is an attainable goal if we step back and tackle institutional structures that too often are built around the interests and habits of adults rather than those of learners. If we become better aware of how organizational policies and practices can facilitate or inhibit educational transformation. If we recognize emerging trends and turn good ideas into practice and good practice into culture. And if we use our understanding of power and influence to build the alliances and coalitions that are needed to create a better world through education. Karwal, Kumar and Sharma make us realize that it is within our means to deliver a future for millions of learners who currently do not have one, and that the task is not to make the impossible possible, but to make the possible attainable.

Andreas Schleicher
Director for Education and Skills
Organisation for Economic Co-operation and
Development (OECD), Paris

Introduction

BETWEEN THE THREE OF US, WE HAVE A COMBINED experience in administration and governance of nearly eighty years, more than an average lifetime! While Anita was the Secretary of the Department of School of Education of the Ministry of Education in Government of India until her superannuation in November 2022, Rajnish and Rashi were Directors in the same department, working as a team under Anita. The three of us, along with other team members and several experts, had worked very closely on preparing the final draft of the path-breaking National Education Policy, 2020. The discussions and heated arguments that we would have on every word put down in the policy had somehow managed to bring us closer. Now, the bureaucracy in India is a well-oiled machine, and as far as superiors and subordinates are concerned, the two maintain their distance from each other, except on official matters. Rather, it's more like—never the twain shall meet, unless ordered to do so!

Then there was another trial by fire that we underwent together, that is, handling the century's greatest disruption—the COVID-19 pandemic. We worked together with a larger team on the various guidelines, budgeting, monitoring, developing and implementing the Maintain, Restore and Grow action plan for COVID response, mitigation and continuing learning, for the entire country. The school closures across the world, including in India, had put a dent in our hearts, and we knew that the restoration of normality would not exactly be easy on the whole school ecosystem, including on the teachers, students and parents.

And then as fate would have it, along with experts and a few others, we also worked together administratively, to bring out the new National Curriculum Framework for the Foundational stage of learning.

It was the middle of 2021. The creative and restive mind of Rajnish was unable to hold itself back anymore.

'Madam, will you write a book with us on how to engage a child's learning abilities through joyful classroom transactions? A happy book is what our stakeholders need right now.'

Now, in our bureaucratic milieu, it is unusual for a junior to address his superior in such a bold manner. But then, by now, the three of us had become good friends too. Yes, Anita continued to give directions during office hours and expect all work given to them that day, to be completed by the previous day! But that did not prevent our fertile imagination from joining hands to write this book in minutes and hours stolen on rare holidays. Our professional experience was of course the factor that provided the ignition, but our personal experiences were no less. Starting with Rashi's two sons (6 and 8 years old), Rajnish's two daughters (18 and 22 years old) and Anita's two daughters (27 and 29 years old), we had the combined experience of a hundred years of mothering and fathering our children!

This book thus began as a Google Drive-based effort, where three people wrote and edited each other's work simultaneously, and ended up bringing forth all the years of our experience and learnings in the form of this fiction, that you now hold in your hands.

Although we have integrated few did-you-knows and here-is-one-way-in-which-it-could-be-done, this book is more of a sum total of our real-life experiences and our imagined view of the mind of a classroom, that we have weaved into a story. Through the medium of our three protagonists, the classroom, the teacher and a child aptly named Cuebee by her parents, standing for Question Box, we have tried to make out a case for the importance of nurturing curiosity to bring out the full creative potential of the child.

We have written this book not only for schools, teachers, parents and students, but also for every person who would like to take a dip into the fun world of learning. We have emphazised that learning is not linear for us humans. It is sometimes systematic, sometimes scattered, and often random. We believe that learning is a lifelong gift, and curiosity is a non-negotiable tool for it, at any age. We have used storytelling to the best of our abilities to bring out the nature of curiosity and our responsibility towards watering its root and fostering its growth, not only in our children, but also for the child within each of us.

Anita Karwal, Rajnish Kumar and Rashi Sharma

Characters in the Book

Alphabet Teacher: Cuebee's class teacher for Grades 4–6

Amla: The three girls, Amla, Imli and Simla, are Cuebee's classmates and good friends since Grade 1

Amygdala: One of the eight classrooms in the school. The amygdala is the part of the human brain that is responsible for emotions, memory and the fight-or-flight response

Anxy: Cuebee's classmate, a girl prone to anxiety

Arty: Cuebee's classmate, a boy artistically gifted

Arty's Mother: A nurse who appears briefly in Chapter 4

Awey: Cuebee's classmate, a boy with a tendency to get easily overawed

BeeTee: Cuebee's classmate, a boy who loves animals

Bhoora: Cuebee's pet at home

Bullie: Cuebee's classmate, a boy who initially faces adjustment issues

Brainstem: One of the eight classrooms in the school. The brainstem is located at the base of the human brain. It controls many involuntary functions of the human body like breathing, blood pressure, heart rate, etc.

Buddy Teacher: The teacher who teaches the Foundational Grades 1–3

Butterfly Teacher: Cuebee's class teacher in Grades 1–3

Cerebellum: One of the eight classrooms in the school. The cerebellum is the part of the brain that is associated with higher cognitive and emotional functions. Though the cerebellum forms only 10 per cent of the entire brain, it contains 50 per cent of the total number of neurons in the brain

Cerebrum: One of the four classrooms in Chapter 11. The cerebrum is the largest part of the human brain, controlling muscle function, reading ability, writing skills, emotions, etc.

Circle of Willis: One of the four classrooms in Chapter 11. The circle of Willis is a junction at the bottom of the human brain where several arteries that supply blood to the brain meet

Cook: One who cooks and serves hot and fresh meals for the children at school

Cuebee: A girl child, our protagonist, represents most children of her age group

Cookie: Cuebee's classmate, a quiet sort of girl

Cuebee's Father: A car mechanic by profession. He appears at several places in the story

Cuebee's Mother: A woman who takes pride in her family

Doubting Mother: A character who appears briefly in Chapter 4

Dura Mater: One of the four classrooms in Chapter 11. It is the outermost layer of tissue that covers and protects the human brain and spinal cord

Frontal: One of the eight classrooms in the school and one of our main characters. The frontal lobe is the part of the human brain that is associated with reasoning, critical thinking and problem solving, motor function, and expression including humour

Gardener: The one who looks after the kitchen garden and other flora in the school

Geekay: Cuebee's classmate, a boy with an unfamiliar diction

Gram Panchayat Members: They appear briefly in Chapter 10

Grandma: Cuebee's sprightly grandmother. She is a fabulous storyteller

Head Teacher: The administrative and pedagogical head of the school

Helper: One who helps the cook in the school kitchen and serves lunch every day

Hippocampus: One of the eight classrooms in the school. The hippocampus is the part of the human brain that provides the base on which memories are formed. It assists in neural activities that lead to a strong pattern of associative memories

Hypothalamus: One of the four classrooms in chapters 11. It is the part of the human brain that controls the stability or homoeostasis of the body

Imli: The three girls, Amla, Imli and Simla, are Cuebee's classmates and good friends since Grade 1

Jadoo: Cuebee's classmate, a boy who believes in miracles

Joy: Cuebee's little brother

Kancha: Cuebee's classmate, a playful boy

Language Teacher: She teaches Cuebee's class from Grade 4 onwards

Madam-2: The woman who was Sarpanch when Cuebee joined Grade 7. She was addressed as Madam-2, being the second woman Sarpanch of the village

Maths Teacher: She teaches Cuebee's class from Grade 7 onwards

Millie: Cuebee's classmate, a girl who loves to create instant rhymes

Mindesh: Cuebee's classmate. He is a brainy boy and very sincere in studies, but a *lakir ka fakir*

Occipital: One of the eight classrooms in the school. The occipital lobe is the part of the human brain that interprets visual stimuli and information such as colours, words, numbers, objects, etc.

Ocean: Cuebee's classmate, an ever-smiling boy

Parietal: One of the eight classrooms in the school. The parietal lobe is the part of the human brain that manages sensation, handwriting and body position

Police Officer: The Superintendent of Police of the district where the school is located

Rainbow Teacher: She teaches the Foundational Grades 1–3

Roof: The roof of the school

Sarpanch Madam: The woman who was the president of the gram panchayat when the school was built

Science Teacher: He teaches science to students in Grades 4 and upwards

Seerie: Cuebee's classmate, a boy prone to being serious and laughing less

Simla: The three girls, Amla, Imli and Simla, are Cuebee's classmates and good friends since Grade 1

Sky: Cuebee's classmate, a boy given to excessive enthusiasm

Social Science Teacher: He teaches social science to students of Grade 5 and upwards

Sports Teacher: The sports teacher of the school

Techie: Cuebee's classmate, the twin of Yoga and a girl in love with all technical/machine-based equipment

Techie's Father: A character who appears briefly in Chapter 4

Temporal: One of the eight classrooms in the school. The temporal lobe is the part of the human brain that interprets sounds and language and is associated with the formation of memories

Yoga: Cuebee's classmate and Techie's twin brother, extremely energetic at all times

Zouzou: Cuebee's classmate, a girl given to quick responses

0

Soily, Weedy and Innocuous

MOST CLASSROOMS ARE DESTINED TO PROGRESS systematically, mechanically and at a certain pace, quite often leading to their premature yet natural deaths in the minds of their occupants. But as I embark on my tour of socio-emotional endurance and agitation, I am delighted to point out that this is not the case each time. Sample this!

'So, what have you understood about the colour of an object?' asked the Science Teacher.

'The colour is all about the light that bounces off an object or gets reflected off it. And like you said, it will depend on the frequency and wavelength of the light waves,' said Cuebee.

In Grade 6, the kids did not have deep insights into the topics of frequency, wavelength, colour, etc., but their conceptual clarity was such that they were like crouching tigers ready to spring at anything dangled in front of them.

'Yes, you are right. Now here is the interesting part. We commonly think of colour as an intrinsic characteristic of an object, but the colour of the object that we see is the colour of light reflected from the object. What does it mean then?'

'It means that the colour we see does not belong to the object; in fact, it is rejected by the object,' Bullie said with a victorious smile like he had discovered America.

'And from a science point of view, white and black are not strictly colours,' the teacher said with a hint of a smile on his lips. He was finding it difficult to hide his amusement at Bullie assuming a Columbus-like air.

'I know about this, Teacher. White colour can be seen when all of the light is reflected by the object. If nothing is reflected, we see black. But what makes each object reflect a different light?' Cuebee asked with an eager look on her face.

'That is the nature of matter in the object, and the types of atoms it contains. This will sound tough right now but you will understand it gradually. Imagine that a light wave of a certain colour strikes an object. If the colour of the light wave matches with the properties of the object, all the energy will be absorbed and nothing will be reflected of that colour. Instead, all other colours will be reflected. The colour of light depends on something called frequency, which you will understand later.'

'Exactly like how dogs can absorb and hear the sound of certain frequencies which we cannot hear,' BeeTee remarked.

'The lesson in optics teaches you something about life. What do you think that is?' the teacher persisted.

'The lesson is that BeeTee has become an expert on dogs ever since he made friends with the stray outside school,'

Bullie informed the class, this time beaming winsomely at the teacher and the class while BeeTee turned a rich shade of crimson.

'But BeeTee is right,' said the teacher.

'Oh! But how would he know what the dog can or cannot hear?' Bullie had such a look of incredulousness on his face that it seemed like the boundary between his eyebrows and hairline had disappeared!

'Now, that is a subject of discussion for another class. We will surely take it up. So, does anyone else want to take a shot at the life lessons that we can derive from the study of optics?'

'Teacher, I want to explain this with my understanding of metaphors that I learnt from Butterfly Teacher. May I?' A thoughtful Cuebee piped up suddenly.

'Metaphors! Oh yes! Go, Cuebee go!' Bullie was never able to hide his *déjà vu* moments. The teacher too nodded, as if on cue.

'Thanks, Bullie. So, metaphorically speaking, what we see around us, perhaps in each other, is just the reflection, not the absorbed part!'

'Exactly! The lesson for all of us here, is to never go on the face value of things and accept things as they are. We must look deeper. Examine, understand, analyse and study the context before we accept it,' the teacher said, elaborating on the idea.

'Sorry, BeeTee. I transmitted based on reflection, not absorption,' Bullie was quick to apologize, man-to-man as he held his ears between his fingers. The class sniggered. They loved the weird yet self-effacing interjections by Bullie.

'Ha ha. It's alright,' said BeeTee generously, before turning a richer shade of crimson.

My nervous system, if I had one, would have shuffled with delight at such a classroom transaction, but all I ended up doing was to give a hollow, impassive and soundless laugh, heard by no one, except me. Given the dearth of mirth in our surroundings, and my tendency to look at humour, sarcasm and wit as life's necessity rather than as a luxury, I always yearned to join in. But in all the excitement of narration to a book-loving audience, I probably forgot to mention that I don't have a voice, or at least not one that can be heard by the 'mortal' world. However, that may not hold true for the 'mortar' world, as you shall see for yourself. You see, I am a feeling, thinking, often elated, sometimes sulking, mostly curious presence, bound by four walls, stabilized by a floor and topped by a roof. Ladies and gentlemen, I present to you, myself, the Archetypal Classroom.

The principal characteristic of a classroom is evidently 'public space', but practically—and I learnt this along the way—it is all about 'space travel' where the mind travels freely and without fear. There is a divinity that builds and shapes classrooms and connects them to their learners. And I will give you a window to view it as I proceed.

My claim to fame is that you will find every kind, structure and variety of child you can conceive, in my fold. There will be those who will stomp all over me, if only for the pleasure of hearing the sound of their feet senselessly knocking my floor out. Then, there will be others who walk so gently that they might even be startled by the sound of their own voice. Not to forget those who prefer to draw illegible lines all over me, believing that their artistic skills far surpass the need for clean walls. I have even seen those who leap from one end to another like grasshoppers imitating a Chhau dancer from Mayurbhanj, or those whose fingers are congenitally joint to their lips.

But never had I seen one who softly, curiously and happily pranced and swirled around the school clock, questioning everything that came her way as if her life depended upon it. Her enthusiasm was so infectious that it spread faster than a virus; her constant queries and wit might have put Socrates to shame; the permanent twinkle in her eye seemed as if the North Star had finally found its retirement home. Right from day one, I felt in my cement and bricks that Cuebee was different. But more about Cuebee later, for once I start on her, the entire world's wild horses may not be enough to pull me back. Permit me, dear readers, to saunter back on my memory lane and narrate to you the story of my origin.

It was the month of April, more than two decades back. The sun was piping hot, and the general populace was ducking under all kinds of shady places (pun unintended) to escape the heightened degrees of the sun's wrath. It was then that my foundation was laid by a lady addressed as Sarpanch Madam. A demure, unsure lady who quietly went about the process, in the presence of a captive male audience consisting of the village elders, youth and children. At a distance stood a motley flock of females—adults, adolescents and little girls from the village. In those days, the gender in question could be only seen at a distance at an event; they were neither permitted proximity nor the right to be heard. Reservation of the Sarpanch electoral seat for a woman for the next five years, had forced the village to choose the previous incumbent's wife as a stop-gap arrangement until the seat returned to the male bastion.

On that sunny day, she followed up the stone-laying ceremony with a nervous, rather brief and to-the-point speech.

'I am happy we are finally getting a school in our village. Now our daughters too can attend school. I am really happy. Very, very happy. I am sure all of you are happy too. We are all very happy.'

For want of more vocabulary to express her unbridled happiness, she suddenly stopped. There were just a few moments of awkward silence, until a strong male voice from the collected crowd shouted, '*Taaliyan!*' And that was the cue for the clapping and conversation that followed around the possibilities that a school in the village would create.

In an era when acuity, intellect and success—not necessarily in that order—are dependent on things such as glibness of speech, confidence in eye contact and manner of walk, Sarpanch Madam may not have scored much on her words that day. But I learnt much later that had it not been for her persistence and insistence, the district administration would have, once again, overlooked the need for a school in this village on the pretext that it was located close enough to a metropolis, which had far too many schools. Sarpanch Madam, on that scorching hot afternoon, had secured a great deal of respect for her deed, thereby hitting the winning goal for her gender in the village.

I started out that day as a muddy presence—soily, weedy and innocuous. As Sarpanch Madam appreciatively scoured my piece of land, I felt elated at the thought that I was examined and found worthy by her, the woman who brought education to the doorsteps of girl children in the village. The boys of the village were already attending school in the neighbouring village. For the girls, this school meant access to a brand-new world; for the boys, it would be a ten-minute walk from home as compared to the 10-kilometres walk to school in the neighbouring village. It was a win-win situation for both.

Now, dear reader, I need you to garner all the patience at your command while I describe myself in approximately four more paragraphs. Then, no more reminiscing about my origins!

There existed two kinds of doctrines in the village about what the upcoming school ought to look like—first, the predominantly male doctrine and second, the Sarpanch Madam doctrine. The former was keen to cover the whole land with just a series of rooms and more rooms, but the latter wanted much more—rooms, a playground, toilets, a kitchen shed and eating area, plus more. The 'pertinent' (from their point of view) questions raised by the male coterie held unconstitutional sway over the opinion-makers of the village for a fairly long time.

'Why would you want a playground, Madam, when the children can play anywhere in the village?' asked one male member.

'And pray why have separate toilets for girls and boys? Do you really believe that we want to send our girls to school?' said another.

Thereafter, it was questions galore.

'Food can as well be cooked under the open sky. The women of my family do it. Why should the school cook be treated so royally so as to get a room of her own?'

'We look upon a separate staffroom for teachers as an excuse to not teach. No, we will not allow this.'

'Whoever heard of hand-wash facilities in a school? Wash your hands once at home, and that should be enough for the day!'

'Why would a school need a boundary wall? If you are already scared of children running away from school, why have a school in the first place?'

'And this is why we prefer a male Sarpanch!'

Now consider me on oath at the witness stand as I narrate the last three-and-a-half paragraphs about how I emerged. Sarpanch Madam may have been at the receiving end of many insults, but she silently, patiently and with a sense of purpose continued to do what was needed to do to give the village a good school. Once the foundation was dug, the school building started taking shape, replete with all the amenities that she felt were necessary to attract and retain children in school. She would be at the site every day from sunrise to sunset. She literally worked, walked, talked and ate with the labourers and oversaw the placement of each brick, beam, cement, tile and fitting that went into the making of the school.

Her devotion finally made a dent in the hearts of the villagers. I overheard the menfolk talk valiantly about their Sarpanch Madam to the visiting members of the neighbouring villages. With a sense of pride hitherto unfamiliar to the male ego, they mentioned how they had made it a point to extol her virtues in block and district headquarters too. When the school building was finally completed, on one fine cold winter morning with the sun in full attendance, Sarpanch Madam asked a six-year-old girl of the village to cut the ribbon of inauguration. Drawn by the rumours of a *Jaadugarni* Sarpanch, several people, from all over the district, attended this atypical event that day. It was a riot of colours, jingling and chiming along with an uninterrupted flow of cups of *chai*, as men, women and children appeared from all corners of the village, dressed in their best finery.

The whole ceremony was a joy to the being, and I waited with bated plinth for Madam to give her speech. The last time at the foundation ceremony, she had spoken a trite too briefly, unsurely and hesitantly. But this time, she was like a breath of freshly empowered air!

'Today we are not just giving a school to the village. We are giving a doorway to a world of opportunities to our children, particularly our girl children, and a better quality of life to our people. Let us together set an example for all to see that we are committed to sending our children to school every day, that we as parents and a community will support the school in all its endeavours, and that we will leave no stones unturned to give our children the future they deserve. Remember that these classrooms shall build the foundations for our children and give them the ability to prepare their own plinths for building their life's superstructure. The classrooms will strengthen the walls of their beliefs to protect them from wrong ideas and opinions, construct the columns of their inner strength to take on the task of nation-building, expose the roof of their minds to more knowledge and diversity, and tile the floors of their being with the variety that is needed to live life holistically. These classrooms must be treated with respect and dignity by all,' she said with liquid eyes.

That was an unusual speech given by an unusual woman on a day unusually full of tears of joy. Many found themselves literally melting beyond the limits of convenience. And that is how I was born. I, the classroom, realized the huge responsibility that had been placed on me, and suddenly developed my own version of voice and vision within my quantum packets.

I soon discovered that we were an army of eight classrooms, all interconnected through walls that we considered a gift for our budding friendship. We became adept at communicating with each other through a format somewhat like Chinese whispers, and hence I am not quite sure whether the last classroom heard the sorted or the distorted words. Each of us faced the rising sun and were smitten by this object of nature. This, to us, was not just the ultimate source of all life-giving energy but also the provider of light in the classrooms, warmth in the cold winter months, and the harbinger of good tidings. The same force of nature, and yet such a multitasker!

There exists a school of thought that is headed, followed and encouraged by me. It is based on my 'school-vault' theory. Now the human brain is encased in the cranium, which is often referred to as the 'vault'. The vault protects various parts of the brain, each having its own distinctive functions. Having been exposed to several years of learning, even if rote learning, all eight of us classrooms were full of weird notions that we may well be the last word on education, and thereby on intellect. At some point in time, I happily named each one of us after a part of the brain that we best represented.

The emotional one with an elephant's memory and ready to jump at the sound of a crisis was named Amygdala, while the one that gave the appearance of doing nothing but was always steeped in action was named the Brainstem. The room that grasped anything going on in its vicinity and yearned to win prizes for its creatively weird ideas, such as classrooms are likely to grow taller as they eat chalk dust over the years, was named Cerebellum. The room whose heightened power of observation was crucial for our daily banter was named Occipital. Similarly, Parietal was named thus, because it appeared to have very artistic ideas and was a creature of sensations. Hippocampus was brought up very carefully for he was always able to remind us of things we had forgotten about, much in the nature of a diligent spouse. My friend Temporal is a great interpreter of language and hence the title. As for yours truly, I named myself Frontal, for I truly believe that I control this group and solve their conflicts with delightful wit and abundant sarcasm.

The school itself was like a vault, protecting and nurturing all of us, while the brain cells or neurons were like the children, teachers, families and community, continuously building synapses or connections. Though each of us probably looked like millions of other classrooms in the world, we felt unique because of what we called ourselves. Needless to say, we were clearly the 'brains' behind the 'vault'!

We eight would often attempt to pull each other's columns.

Cerebellum: I think the classroom is the greatest invention of mankind.

Hippocampus: That is a rather immodest proclamation, but pray, what puts that extraordinary idea into your bricks?

Cerebellum: Nothing can induce me to think otherwise.

Hippocampus: Really, how about the whole school itself? Could that not be a greater invention?

Frontal (me): Yeah! Had there been no school, would a stand-alone classroom have any worth?

Cerebellum: Of all the disconsolate words emanating from the pen or tongue, these take the crown. Exactly when I am doling out pretty words of wisdom, you have to dive in to demolish my defining moment.

Temporal: Ha! Wisdom indeed! What we do not know about inventions can fill up all the athenaeums on planet earth!

Cerebellum: Fine! Now will you continue to snigger about my conjectures the whole day?

Occipital: No, only up to sundown.

Frontal (me): Where is your ambition, Occipital? Let's go on till sunrise tomorrow!

Permit me, dear readers, to expose you to another side of us, the cerebral side—at least we believe it to be our cerebral side—where we are prone to thought-provoking arguments, analysing electrons, neutrons and protons out of anything, a sense of pathos occasionally, and mostly comparing 'those' days with 'these' days and 'this' with 'that'.

Cerebellum: I am getting new furniture this time. What about you?

Parietal: Me too. But nothing exciting about it.

Amygdala: I am getting a new green chalkboard. I am intrigued. Never seen one!

Brainstem: I am increasingly feeling like a bank! The school keeps dropping furniture, books and equipment, while my students are empty accounts for teachers to keep dropping in topics and subjects.

Frontal: Ha ha! I can almost visualize your hoarding, 'The Bank of Brain and Stem Ltd.'

Hippocampus: You are raising the bar with all that bank talk. We are just a set of drop zones!

Temporal: I do not conform to this drop-zone idea. I have yet to turn cynical. I still continue to hold the view that we are not really classrooms, we are learning spaces. I only wish for more vibrancy and a dash of creativity in the classroom.

Occipital: High hopes, Temporal! Most classrooms are born boring, some achieve boredom, while others have boredom thrust upon them. Yawn!

It has been over twenty years since the day I was born on the bedrock of respect and dignity. The gate of the school has been opening and closing for two decades, and its slow creaking movement was, perhaps, a reflection of the unhurried pace of change in the school. The classroom interactions were undertaken in such a routine manner—so dry, so soundless. Children were scared; they did not speak to avoid the unwelcome drill of being either scolded, hushed, insulted or punished for 'wasting the time of the whole class'. Even though some say it was better in our younger days, I, for one, believed that these kinds of trifling arguments are what we develop when we have lofty and unmet objectives in life.

In those years, the only occurrence that we looked forward to, used to be in the beginning of each academic session, when the new entrants to Grade 1, a group of happy, howling or excited-for-no-reason children, would create commotion and ruckus of the highest order. The cacophonic chitter-chatter of these children rushing into the school and then towards me was turf-racking yet endearing.

'School, school, this is my school!'

'This is my classroom? But why can I not sit with my older sister?'

'Oh look, blank walls! Time to get my pencil out and doodle.'

'See the bench is so strong, I can dance on it.'

'I will act as a teacher. Class, take out your textbooks and go to sleep.'

'Let us jump from table to table and play "*Oonch, Neech*".'

'That is my pencil. Teacher, Teacher, tell him to give it back to me.'

'Look, I am hanging from the door.'

'You look like a monkey.'

'Let's look for his tail.'

'Monkey! Monkey!'

But this experience would diminish exponentially and peter out within a month, by which time the teachers managed to 'discipline' the freshers and ensure pin-drop silence in the classroom. For the life of me, I could not comprehend how fingers-on-your-lips for five hours a day could be intellectually stimulating for these curious, eager minds—not to mention the closed gates throughout the nights that haunted me. No, I don't do silence. I need visible signs of animation to be displayed at all times to feel alive. With a nature like that, one could not have chosen a better place to exist than in a school, right?

Such experiences notwithstanding, I must not in any way undermine the slow but steady changes that had started taking place in the school after I turned seventeen. An energetic new Head Teacher had joined along with three new teachers, and now there were a total of eight teachers.

I ought to have been born a smug structure to part with such nuggets of information that you wouldn't imagine I knew! It is important at this stage that I clarify, that while we classrooms were indulging in relay conversation, the rest of the school building—the roof, floors, playground, kitchen, staff room, etc.—weren't leading a life of tranquil anonymity either. They too had their own circle of wall, floor and room friends, but the rooftop was commonly close to us all. It was the roof that kept us well-informed about the school's surroundings and the latest happenings. The school was situated on the highest point of the village, and the roof had front-row seats to panoramic views and sounds of the whole area.

'There is a kachcha road from the school gate that leads straight to the community hall. Yesterday, the television out there appeared to be dancing in psychedelic lights, all through the day. I think the village finally has a coloured TV.'

'Hey, I can see the rain clouds coming this way from the neighbouring village. It's bathing time, my brick-cementors!'

'There is a tiny rivulet in the distance. I can see kids splashing around.'

'Listen, all. People outside the gate are talking. Another new teacher is joining next week. She will teach grade 1 this year. Now, in our twentieth year, we will have a full contingent of eight class teachers, plus the Sports Teacher who visits twice a week, the cook, helper and the gardener. Rooms and beams, floors and walls, plinths and foundation, slabs and columns, lend me your atoms. In our twentieth year, we are finally a big school now!'

'Just outside our gate, there is an old not-in-use-anymore blue-coloured car along with its chassis and full body; it's just lying there. I have heard that the car was donated by the local scrap dealer at the request of the Head Teacher. I wonder why?'

'I have an epiphany. There must be millions of school buildings, and just like I connect you all to each other, the earth interconnects all the school buildings. The earth by now must have absorbed all knowledge of the cosmos through the floors, walls and rooftops of millions of school buildings such as ours. Therefore, earth, my friends, is the largest repository of knowledge.'

The rooftop's proclamations, peppered with its own conclusions and maxims, were heard keenly by all of us. One had no way of knowing if these were the absolute truth, but we school-parts liked to believe in the roof above our heads! It was like a timely bulletin that was meant to help us dissect the world around us and provoke our discussions.

As I embark upon the telling of the story of my life as a classroom, I plan to skip the first seventeen years, by merely stating that the greater part of this time was spent listening to the routine humdrum of teaching and learning the same textbook over and over again. But after seventeen years of 'solid' existence, things were beginning to show tiny elements of change. Rest of the school did not know it then, but a cathartic experience was imminently awaiting us all on completion of twenty years, for that is when Cuebee danced her way into our life and times.

1

Discovery of the water monster

THE SUN HAS ITS MOMENTS, PARTICULARLY IN THE MIDDLE of June, when soaring temperatures can pierce the skin through layers of clothing and resolve, with fiery aplomb. But on that day, ever so close to the longest day of the year, the sun appeared to have declared a holiday. As heavy yet shapely clouds hung over the immediate sky, I heard a tiny voice.

'And that one is shaped like Ma's *belan*.'

'And the one next to it looks like your father's head,' said an older female voice.

'Ha ha, Grandma. You are so right. Pa, does that scare you?' said the tiny voice again.

'I am petrified!' responded a mature male voice.

This was followed by squeals of laughter. I discerned one adult male hoot, an older woman's gentle laughter and a child's giggles combining together to convey a shared moment of extreme joy. That was my first encounter with Cuebee, albeit with her voice. Before I could mull over it, as is my habit, the voice began singing, as if to an audience, in full glory.

Badal, badal door ke,
Belan dikhaye door se.
Jhankey ghar ki jaali se,
Khaaye ma ki gaali re.

This was then repeated with the older female voice singing along. I was dumbstruck. Years of experience with voices had made me quite the specialist, as they say in your world, in detecting age, attitude and nature of the human being attached to the voice. The voice could not have belonged to a person more than 3-feet tall, perhaps 5-6 years old. A kid as young as that being able to develop an instantaneous situational parody based on the popular lullaby *Chanda Mama Door Ke* was too much for my sensibilities to digest.

It was the first day of school after the summer break in my twentieth year. Parents accompanying their new-admission wards and new admissions attached to parents in uncertain knots was a common sight. On the opening day in a school, you can find every type of parent conceivable. Past years may have added wear and tear to my structure, clutter to the school and a predominance of boredom to my outlook, but I could recognize the category of a parent from the moment they uttered a single word in my vicinity. The eight of us classrooms, after much deliberation, had divided parents into six categories:

- Brat-who-never-grew-up
- Restless-legs

- *Bahar-se-garam-andar-se-naram*
- Anxiety-inducers
- Disturbed-and-at-large
- Take-the-kid-off-my-back

To deal with such parents on the first day of school, teachers needed to summon a level of patience and sweetness that is mostly found among preachers and teachers! On that day in June when I first surmised the voice and laughter of Cuebee and understood her grandmother's and father's nature, I felt the need to review the above-mentioned classification and measure of success it had seen so far. I decided to add yet another type to the categorization: cheerful-to-a-fault! We classrooms jointly decided that this category had the potential to whistle past a graveyard, and hence was our one and only favourite category so far.

I felt the clouds making way and the warm glow of the sun spreading over me as the father and grandmother walked towards me. Cuebee was a sunny young girl, slightly tall for her age, slim and springy, with innocent eyes, a determined chin and a face that appeared to be manufactured for radiance and happiness. Cuebee's father was a tall and wiry man but with a strong gait and the general demeanour of a person who works with his hands. Her grandmother was a sprightly old woman with a benevolent face, replete with laughter lines embedded in the corner of her eyes and lips.

'This is your classroom, Cuebee. Do you like it?' asked the father as he stood outside my door.

'And look at those kids out there. Many of them will end up being your lifelong friends,' Grandma said while ruffling Cuebee's hair.

Cuebee peered at me with such reverence—big, inquisitive eyes moving quickly, trying to absorb everything at once. A gentle-looking lady, with the most welcoming smile that Cuebee had ever seen, came and stood at the classroom door.

'Come and join the fun world of learning, Cuebee,' she said to the little girl.

Cuebee scrutinized her with a strange and mysterious look, but only for a fleeting moment. She suddenly felt safe in the warmth of her presence.

'How do you know my name?' asked Cuebee.

'It is my job to know all names and the kids attached to those names, even before they know me,' she said.

'If that is the case, tell me more about me. Introduce me to me, please,' said Cuebee unhesitatingly with a gleam in her eyes. She loved such conversations, and she was just warming up to one.

'Ha ha. You have a sense of humour I see, and I think I am going to love it. Cuebee, allow me to introduce you to you and to the whole class once the whole class has settled down, please.'

'Fine, you have my permission,' said Cuebee with an air of dignity.

'I am delighted with your permission, little girl.'

'Mother says I must listen to you and not talk too much in class. She says that there is yet to be a box made in the world that is filled with so much chatter as this box.' Cuebee pointed to her head with a giggle.

The teacher had a hearty laugh. 'You have the gift of being able to laugh at yourself too. It is rare.' And then as if on cue, she said to Cuebee's father, 'You have brought up a fine child. You have done most of the work for me. I am indebted to every parent who nurtures the child to be a happy child. That's a great starting point for learning inputs.'

It was at this time that Cuebee noticed the aquarium in the corridor, full of colourful fishes swimming gracefully and in utter enjoyment. She ran towards it, shouting, 'Lost fish! Lost fish!'

Her father ran after her. He kneeled on the floor so they could see eye to eye, and in an attempt to cut short his daughter's proclivity for curious outbursts, he said gently, 'Cuebee, my child, they are not lost just because they are not in the river. Those are pet fishes, like Bhoora, our pet dog. Now listen to what your mother said, and keep the bonnet of your mouth shut for some time. Go and see what awaits you in the classroom.'

Grandma, with a faint smile playing on her lips, meanwhile locked her hands with Cuebee's. Cuebee looked quizzically at the teacher who obligingly pointed her towards the row of benches in the classroom. Cuebee dutifully unclasped her hand from her grandmother's tight grip and went and sat in the first row. She looked back with a dimpled grin and waved at her father and grandmother to show her comfort. Grandmother at this point took the teacher aside and almost in a whisper, said, 'I am very good at storytelling. If you ever need me to tell the class a story, I will be so glad to do it.'

'Ma, I heard what you said. You cannot just impose yourself like that. Schools are not homes where families can be invited into the classrooms,' Cuebee's father protested.

'No, that may not be entirely true. Unless the family pitches in and actively participates in the learning process of the child, there can be no holistic development of the child. Therefore, Ma ji, thank you so much for your wonderful offer.

I shall call on you soon to tell a story to our kids,' was the emphatic response of the teacher.

The grandmother seemed terribly pleased with the teacher, herself and the world in general; she touched my floor at the door of the classroom and started to leave, but not without glancing back once, with a gaze that conveyed as if she had sent her granddaughter to a place of worship, in service of the Almighty.

Cuebee settled on the bench of her choosing. While the teacher was busy welcoming more freshers at the door, Cuebee did something strange. She bent down, touched my floor and whispered softly as if directly talking to me. 'My Ma says that in this village, classrooms are to be treated with respect and dignity. I promise to take care of you, and I request you to take care of me.'

This special parlay, reserved only for me, by a child yet to see the world at large, was an entirely new experience for me. I think I must have been gushing my mortar, and I knew instantly that something special was in store that would alter the history of the classroom.

The class appeared half full already. Cuebee looked around her. She could recognize quite a few children from her *Anganwadi*, but there were several strange faces too. A few children sitting in the back row were sobbing uncontrollably. That must have been a disturbing sight for Cuebee. But on the other hand, she found a girl and a boy, gleefully yet nimbly playing hopscotch on the benches. She appeared to instantly like them. But then she probably remembered what her grandma had whispered in her ears, just before leaving. 'Help whoever you can, whenever you can, however you can.'

Cuebee got out of her seat to go check on the crying kids, when someone patted her on the back. Cuebee turned and immediately recognized her next-door neighbour, BeeTee. I gathered much later that his mother had named him thus because she felt that BeeTee had the capacity to guiltlessly transmit every word spoken in the house to all and sundry within hearing distance, exactly like a Bluetooth device! Cuebee and BeeTee often played together. They particularly loved playing hide-and-seek and also with marbles. Cuebee always beat him at both games, but BeeTee was a very graceful loser and a generous friend. Cuebee sensed a feeling of relief on BeeTee's face when he saw her. She felt oddly relieved too but still wanted to find out the reason for the howling at the back. The two friends decided to investigate. They went up to the three kids.

'Why are you so sad this morning?' Cuebee asked.

More tears.

'Are you hungry?'

Even more tears.

'Do you want to go for a potty?'

Tears and tears.

'Is there an insect inside your shirt?' BeeTee asked.

Deluge of tears.

'Oh, so you are crying for no reason at all. Does that feel good? BeeTee, let's try too.'

And then Cuebee and BeeTee joined in, though in a simulated fashion. That brought me, the classroom, down in a din of incessant and loud howling.

Soon, the teacher came rushing in. 'What just happened?' she asked in a concerned voice.

'Nothing really. These three like to cry, so we thought we would give them company.'

The three sobbing kids suddenly started giggling. They must have found this whole episode very funny. In fact, the whole class burst into laughter, and so did the teacher. She said an unspoken 'thank you' with her eyes to Cuebee and asked the kids to return to their seats.

Before going, Cuebee told the three kids, 'Whenever you feel sad, call me. I will try to make you laugh.' The three children and the teacher were perhaps not as dumbstruck as I was!

Cuebee was turning out to be quite an enigma and yet being noted with perfect distinction by our part of the school building. This evidently was not one of those years when I was going to watch the routine I was used to so far. We eight classrooms immediately got talking.

Frontal: Reducing it to its simplest terms, we seem to be once again experiencing magic!

Occipital: Magic? Once again?

Temporal: Don't you remember how Sarpanch Madam used to be lovingly addressed as Jaadugarni.

Frontal: Yes, it is magical indeed. Cuebee appears to be a confident child. She has been nurtured well, not controlled.

Hippocampus: Yes, a conducive and joyful environment always helps the child realize their unique potential. Look at Frontal, for instance.

Parietal: Fine. Looking at him. What now?

Frontal: Yeah. What have I done?

Hippocampus: We have created a joyful environment for you, and how well you have realized your potential to joke at others' expense and yet lead a blameless life!

Frontal: Oh, come on, stop fooling around, Hippocampus. Give you any lead, even if a trifle small, and you are the merrier for it.

Hippocampus: And look who's talking!

Cerebellum: Let's keep the elaboration on Frontal's abilities and potential for another day! Going back to our discussion, I would say that Cuebee is making me realize that every child is special and capable, and she needs utmost care and attention, particularly at key stages of development.

Amygdala: What key stages?

Occipital: Do you remember how our Head Teacher was training the *Anganwadi* workers the other day?

Amygdala: I do. It was in your classroom, if I recall correctly.

Occipital: Well, yes. He told them that even though the number of brain cells we are born with never changes, but just having them is not enough. It is the multiple connections between the cells that are crucial. And it seems that between the ages of zero and five or six, children develop almost one million new neural connections between the brain cells every second, provided they undergo myriad experiences, particularly the positive ones.

Brainstem: So, what it implies is that it is crucial that children are exposed to multiple stimulations and interactions of the right kind during this period.

Frontal: Occipital, I also remember you saying that the Head Teacher stressed upon imbibing reading skills early in children. For any child to be able to develop proficiency in any subject, be it mathematics, science or humanities, it all begins with mastery over this one non-negotiable skill.

Brainstem: But teaching children to read at such a tender age, is it even advisable?

Occipital: According to our erudite Head Teacher, research has established that the first attempt of a child at developing her language skills, and as a corollary, her reading skills, begins as soon as she starts responding to sounds, such as noise, cooing, words, etc., by crying or gurgling.

Hippocampus: That's right. I too have heard that the subsequent sounds that the child encounters, such as the sound of conversation, water, birds, music, etc., lays down the foundation for the child to acquire language, reading and writing skills.

Brainstem: The crucial role of *Anganwadi*s is now clear to me. If the child is exposed early to storytelling, rhymes, songs, conversations, etc., she shall be reading-ready by the time she comes to us.

Frontal: So it appears that Cuebee must have got very early exposure to multiple stimulations in her *Anganwadi*.

Occipital: That may not necessarily be entirely true. It could also be her family environment that provided her with these interactions. Did you not hear what her grandmother said? She is a storyteller. It's obvious that Cuebee has been brought up on a recipe of love, storytelling and humour in a democratic home environment.

Temporal: You mean to say parents have a role in the academic excellence of their children?

Occipital: I think it's time for a mathematical exercise.

Temporal: Nooo! I don't like maths. I have this vague impression that it is a cross between gibberish and magic being practised by an uninitiated person!

Parietal: That is because you have not heard the right teacher.

Brainstem: But tell me, where is the maths in all this?

Occipital: Fine. Calculate with me. For how many hours do the children come to school each day?

Brainstem: Five.

Occipital: How many days in a year do they come to school?

Cerebellum: About 230, give or take ten.

Occipital: Let's assume 240. So how many hours do they spend at school?

Frontal: 1,200.

Occipital: Impressive! Now how many hours are there in the 365 days of a year?

Amygdala: I know this one: 365 x 24 = 8,760.

Occipital: Bravo! Now comes the difficult bit. What percentage of her life in one year does a child spend at school?

Cerebellum: That's a trick question, right?

Amygdala: Not fair to ask us such difficult questions. We cannot do cerebral maths beyond a point.

Brainstem: But I know this one. It will be 13.6 per cent.

Cerebellum: You mean to say a child spends about 86 per cent of her time with her parents, family and in society! Bless the universe! This is a revelation!

Occipital: Exactly. So now tell me, do parents have a role or not in the cognitive and holistic development of their child?

Temporal: Not just the parents, the whole family and society have a huge role, without any shred of doubt!

Meanwhile, the teacher had begun to address the class, and I was keen to catch it. With common assent, we decided to adjourn our animated discussions to the quiet of the night.

'Children, today we will begin by first introducing ourselves. Since a certain someone was quizzing me on what I know about her, we shall play a game to introduce ourselves. First, I will say what I know about one student and then you all will guess who she is. If you can't, the student will stand up and introduce himself or herself.' The teacher looked at Cuebee and the two exchanged conspiratorial glances, as if they were partners in a fun crime. Cuebee seemed to be loving this!

'I love playing games, Teacher,' Crying Kid-1 said.

'Me too,' BeeTee added.

'Who will be the *sipaahi*, Teacher?' Crying Kid-2 asked.

'*Sipaahi?*' The teacher was flabbergasted. 'You mean you want to play *Chor–Sipaahi?* Interesting!'

'Yes, then we will have a *chor* in the class,' Ocean persisted.

'Why not play the Butterfly–Flower game?' Cuebee said thoughtfully.

'What's that?'

'A butterfly hops from one flower to another, sits on a variety of flowers, and kind of knows all of them. But the different flowers do not know each other. So, the teacher is the "butterfly" in the game who will hop from one of us to another and say something about each of us. We "flowers" will try to guess which flower she is talking about,' Cuebee informed her teacher.

'That's a wonderful game. Where did you learn that game?' the teacher was curious.

'Oh, I just made it up, because I don't want anyone to be labelled as *chor* in the "*Chor–Sipaahi*" game.'

'Yes, yes, we want to play Cuebee's game, please. Please!' the students said in chorus.

'Fine, fine,' said the teacher after a good ten seconds because she was tongue-tied!

And so started an astoundingly new game, designed by a six-year-old!

'A girl flower who loves to speak in rhymes, who is she?'

'That's Millie!' a few kids replied in unison.

'Millie, say something about yourself please.'

'My name is Millie. I love jelly and also *billies*.'

Chuckles in the room.

'A boy flower who thinks benches are meant for playing hopscotch on. Who is he?'

'That's Ocean!'

'That's right. Ocean, would you like to say something?'

'Benches are also for dancing on.'

Loads of giggling.

'A girl flower who loves helping others and is very curious.'

'Cuebee!'

'What would you like to add, Cuebee?'

"I am a box full of questions, a Question Box. That's why I am called Cuebee!'

Room resounding with tee-hees.

'A girl flower who wants to know more about how the car outside the school works, from the moment she saw it.'

'That is Techie!'

'Techie, how would you describe yourself?'

'Give me anything, and I will know how to take it apart. But I won't know how to put it back together!'

Snigger. Snigger.

'A girl flower who is the tallest of all.'

'Teacher, you!'

'Yes, that's me. And I love teaching, and I also love learning new things.'

'Me too,' agreed, many tiny but ardent voices.

And so it went on. Sky, Arty, Jadoo, Kancha, Buddy, Cookie, Yoga, Zouzou and about fifteen others were introduced. The three crying kids were Imli, Amla and Simla. Cuebee and four others—BeeTee, Millie, Techie and Yoga—became thick friends that day. Yoga, a very playful boy, was Techie's twin brother and after meeting him, Cuebee's repository of questions must have expanded to include the origin of twins.

I called an emergency meeting of the eight classrooms because there was something really bothersome happening here. So far, teachers had been entirely composed of brilliant rote-based educators or outstanding disciplinarians whose harshness was the stuff of legends. But that's how teachers were supposed to be, or were they not?

Frontal: I need to discuss my teacher!

Amygdala: Why disturb me in the middle of a perfectly quiet and disciplined classroom, especially when I am on the verge of nodding off?

Parietal: I am no longer the Patient Parietal. I have changed for the better, so this hijacking of my time better be for the greater good.

Temporal: Brick-and-cement time is precious. And we are not about to waste it.

Occipital: To attempt to classify this meeting as a waste of time would be fairly presumptuous. Now, about our object of interest right now, well, I do not think we have much to worry about this teacher. It's only her first day.

Frontal: Yes. But what if she manages to continue in this manner, say, beyond four weeks? Should we delay the debating on her virtues viz-à-viz other Teachers for that long? Any opinions?

Occipital: I sort of like her. The combination she presents—the audacity of sheer competency and ability, along with the astonishing courage of patience and love—it fascinates me!

Brainstem: Would you have preferred a complete separation of passion from intellect as we are often used to seeing in this school?

Amygdala: Certainly not!

Parietal: Then that decides it. We like her. But let's wait and watch. After all, sometimes people turn out differently from what they seem to be initially.

Frontal: Like who, Parietal? Who just changed for the 'better'?

Parietal: Ah my friend! You certainly have a great faculty for remembering the trivial and forgetting the crucial!

Meanwhile, the teacher was saying, 'Now, before we settle down for some lunch, I am going to take you on a tour of the school.'

I surmised that by now, the kids had already begun to adore this lady, whose hair had the sunlight playing in it, whose face was the kindest they had ever known, whose words had a sense of adventure about them and whose warmth was felt in the bones of the tiny bodies that day.

'These are the seven other classrooms. And this space outside is called the corridor. Do you know who got this school built?'

'*Jaadugarni* Sarpanch Madam,' the students shouted out in unison.

'That's right. And this is the hand-wash area. Every time you eat something or use the toilet, this area calls out, "use me, use me, before and after every meal; use me, use me, after every potty and pee"', the teacher said, gesticulating hand-washing with her two hands.

'Use me, use me, before and after every meal; use me, use me, after every potty and pee,' Millie and the others repeated after the teacher.

They were really enjoying this tour.

'This is the staff room. We Teachers work here when we are not in class. Whenever you come by here, do greet us with a namaste.'

Namaste, namaste,' they chorused.

'This is the girl's toilet. Boys may go ahead with the Sports Teacher. He will show you yours.'

All the girls peered at the water closet as the boys left.

'We have a water closet at our house too. But we keep a bucket and mug to pour water after use. Why is there no bucket here, Teacher?'

'Because here you can flush by just pressing this handle. This has been installed recently,' the teacher said and pressed the flush down.

And, at that moment, pandemonium struck. The children began running out of the toilet, helter-skelter and screaming loudly. A teacher from the nearby classroom came rushing out, grabbed Cuebee, and asked her what happened.

'There is a water monster in the toilet! It is trying to come out of the toilet and drench us. Run. Everybody, run, unless you want to get wet with pee water. Go save yourself!'

Meanwhile, Cuebee's teacher came out of the toilet with a helpless look on her face. Most of the school staff and even the Head Teacher had collected at the disaster site by now.

'No, no children, it's not a water monster,' the teacher entreated. 'I am so sorry! I did not know that you have never seen this before.'

'But we saw the toilet turn into a water gun,' one child exclaimed.

'It was trying to play *Holi* with us,' said another.

One of the Teachers who had rushed out of her classroom tried to explain. 'The flush is a machine. It is able to throw up water.'

'But why don't we have such machines at home then?'

The Head Teacher told the teacher in low tones. 'When a child is upset, logic does not work. We need to first respond to the child's emotions.'

He looked at Cuebee's teacher and said, 'Why don't we take them all back to the class and hear them all first. Then, we can address all their queries.'

So, the students were marched back to the classroom as they continued their animated discussions. They had questions, many of them from Cuebee.

'I have always seen water falling down. Here, it was going up!'

'Why did it make so much noise?'

'Was it just previously collected pee, or was it really water?'

'Where was the water hiding, before it decided to attack us?'

'Can we open up the water closet to check where the water is hiding?' This one was from Techie.

'Would you be able to handle them now?' the Head Teacher asked earnestly.

'There are only two credos that I follow, sir. Firstly, everything around us is a learning tool, and secondly, practising patience with children. I will take it from here.'

The Head Teacher, visibly impressed, wished the children well and left. We classrooms admired the way he facilitated autonomy for the teachers in their own space, their classrooms.

'Children, when you see, feel or use water, what feeling does it give you?' the teacher began as the class settled down.

'Cold.'

'I cannot catch it.'

'It cleans me.'

'Slippery.'

'I can see myself in it.'

'Thirsty.'

'Right. So many aspects of water. Water is a part of our nature, our environs, our surroundings. Can we live without water?' the teacher asked.

'Nooo!' responded the class in concert.

'Did you know that most of our body is also made up of water?'

'But why can't I see it on my body?'

'Will I flow away?'

'Teacher, is our body water like the juice in fruits like mangoes or lemon? Until we really squeeze them, we do not know they have watery juice,' Cuebee deliberated upon the question.

'Yes, Cuebee,' the teacher said and clapped simultaneously. 'So, tell me, something that is a part of us, which quenches our thirst and cleans us and is like a mirror—can it really be a monster?'

'It should not be, but why did it growl at us?' Cuebee asked.

'That is the sound water makes when a lot of it flows out with force.'

'Why did it jump towards us?' Cuebee was irrepressible.

'Yoga, come stand next to me,' the teacher called out.

Yoga came and happily stood next to his favourite human being of the day.

'Now walk, Yoga.'

Yoga walked five steps smoothly.

'Now Zouzou, you come here and help him walk by giving him a sudden push. That would mean you would apply force on him.'

Zouzou was in her element. She got up, went to Yoga, and without a warning and distinctly unapologetically pushed Yoga. Yoga literally jumped forward!

'I have understood. I have understood, Teacher. When you put force on something that otherwise keeps falling, it will jump towards the side in which you are forcing it to go,' piped in Cuebee after an almost imperceptible start.

'Like when I do not give my toys to my younger brother, he just snatches it away from me,' Zouzou added.

'Like a cup cannot move on its own, but whenever my cat wants, she just pushes it off the table.'

'Like when I did not want to get up today morning to come to school, my mother just picked me up and put me next to the basin to brush my teeth.'

The class was immersed in the excitement of their understanding of force, and it was getting difficult to contain their Eureka moment. The teacher allowed them a few minutes of heated discussions.

'Now, coming back to the toilet flush. Tell me, what goes into the toilet?'

'Poop and pee.'

'And what is poop and pee like?' the teacher asked.

'It is smelly.'

'It is dirty.'

'If it stays in my stomach, I also release a bad smell.'

'We release both smell and sound, Teacher. Like this.' Buddy made a sound using his mouth that had the whole class in fits. They were having so much fun. The teacher was also enjoying their little jokes.

'You kids know a lot about pooping and peeing. So, you are correct. They are waste, and if they remain at one place for long, whether inside us or inside the water closet, they give out smells that can make us sick.'

'But why was this toilet not smelling, Teacher?' Cuebee was so curious by now that she was literally falling off her desk with her questions.

'Exactly! Now you all agree that water cleans and waste smells. So, here is what the flush toilet does—it draws water from the overhead storage tank, which is the big black drum-like structure you see on the rooftop. When water comes out with force, it jumps up a little in the closet and forces the waste in it to move through a pipe, to an area much farther from our homes, where all waste is collected. That way, there is no smelly waste left in our toilets and our toilets remain clean and welcoming.' The teacher explained the process using appropriate hand actions.

On hearing the teacher give this fabulous piece of 'breaking' news, the children started clapping. It seemed like all was well with the world again. The class ended with yet another question by Cuebee.

'Teacher, does water have feelings? Do you think it was hurt because we called it a monster?'

'Interesting that you ask this question, Cuebee? Let us deal with this issue next time.'

'When is that?'

'Save all these questions, Cuebee. I shall surely take up each of them in time.'

The teacher then took them all down to the hand-wash area and demonstrated how to wash hands properly. She oversaw each child's cleaning operation. Then, they all sat in the eating area and were served a hearty meal of rice and *dalma*. While the children of all other grades appeared very subdued at lunch, the first graders were gregarious, talkative, happy and comfortable.

After lunch, the sun decided to take a nap. The weather had turned. It was storytelling time under the tree in the school playground. The teacher asked the children to sit in a circle while she narrated the story of the thirsty crow. The children sat in rapt attention.

'It was the middle of a very dry summer. A crow that was very thirsty was unable to find water to drink, until he came across a clay pitcher with a long narrow neck and a small amount of water in it. The crow tried very hard to insert his beak into the pitcher to drink. But the water was way down, and the pitcher's neck was too narrow for his beak. Nothing seemed to work. Then, suddenly, the thirsty crow had an idea. He flew around looking for pebbles. When he had gathered quite a few, he started dropping them into the pitcher, one after the other. As the number of pebbles inside the pitcher increased, the level of water began to rise, until finally it was high enough for the crow to reach. The delighted crow could finally quench his thirst.'

Butterfly Teacher then asked the children a question. 'Had there been no small pebbles, how would the thirsty crow have drunk water from a narrow-necked pot?'

'The crow can look for a straw and drink water using the straw.'

'The crow can put small lemons in the pot instead of pebbles.'

'He could break the pitcher.'

'He could tilt the pitcher.'

'I will start keeping water in a bowl outside my house for the thirsty crow. Teacher, can you please tell him to visit!'

'He could look for a toilet and flush it!'

Peals of laughter.

I have always found the story very interesting, but I was used to listening to it each time in the same style and manner. It was always a story with a fixed ending. I was amazed to hear the creative solutions provided by such young children.

As the first day of school ended, fathers, mothers and grandparents came to pick up their wards. Just as the children went running to them, all the adults dived straight to the point. They all seemed to be asking the same question, even if framed and delivered differently in accordance with individual capacity for patience: How was your first day at school? Did you learn anything?

The responses, however, were varied.

'I love school. I love my teacher.'

'We learnt about pooping and peeing.'

'We learnt about where poop and pee go.'

'My teacher is the best.'

'I made many friends.'

'Buddy showed the whole class how to take out the sound of poop.'

'Cuebee made me laugh today.'

'We talked and talked in class.'

'I want to place a bowl of water outside our house for birds to drink from. It is so hot, they need water.'

'Why does our toilet not have a flush?'

'Can you take me to the place where all the poop from school goes?'

'I have named my teacher, Butterfly Teacher.'

Naturally the guardians were perplexed. Why wouldn't they be? After all, they were not sending their children to school to chit-chat in class and learn about toilets, excreta and sludge!

Since Cuebee's three-month-old brother, Joy, was giving their mother a hard time, her grandmother had come to pick her up from school. Cuebee skipped around her grandmother and informed her of the highlights of the day. Then, on a serious note, she asked her, 'Grandma, where is your school?'

'Oh, it's in another village. I could not study much anyway because I had to get married. And that was a perfect tragedy because I can barely read and only do some basic maths.'

'Married? Oh, will I also have to stop studying like you?'

'Over my dead body!'

'What?'

'Nothing. You will do no such thing as get married early. Those days are gone. You will study till college and make something of yourself. If anyone comes in the way of your studies, they shall have me and my karate chops to contend with!'

'Thank you, Grandma. You are the best.' Cuebee hugged Grandma.

'Dream big Cuebee, and I will always be there to help you achieve your dreams.'

'I want to grow up and become a teacher, like Butterfly Teacher.'

'Of course. Whatever you choose to be, I will support you. Butterfly, hmm!'

As was our tradition, we *Ashtadal* would chat at the end of every day under the influence of a moonlit or moonless, starry or cloudy, but peaceful night. The meeting of classrooms that night was just waiting to get started.

Cerebellum: The rooftop informs us that it is glad to be the keeper of good clean water, while we have filth flowing in pipes somewhere beneath us.

Temporal: Point taken. So, what have we learnt today about the world in general and our school in depth?

Frontal: I love the fact that the kids have given a name to their teacher—Butterfly Teacher.

Brainstem: This Butterfly Teacher, though a fresh appointee, is enthusiastic, motivated and patient. She believes in the innate qualities of children and has an activity-based approach that includes games, tours, experiments and stories. Who knows, maybe art, music, rhymes, toys, clay is in store.

Cerebellum: Now that we have established that the family and the community have a huge role to play in a child's holistic development, I, for one, am curious about how Butterfly Teacher plans to engage with them.

Temporal: I appreciated the way the Head Teacher trusted Butterfly Teacher to explain the new concept of toilet flush, instead of jumping into it himself.

Parietal: Our Butterfly Teacher appears to be a voracious reader, and so connected to real-life. The Head Teacher probably sensed her innate abilities.

Occipital: I loved the storytelling bit. The Head Teacher always says that these small but different ways of telling a simple story sow the seeds of critical thinking in kids in years to come.

Frontal: I, for one, admired the way the toilet flush simply crept into the learning process, totally unannounced.

Hippocampus: O ye comedian at one point of time and genius at another, I never really know if you, Frontal, are serious or otherwise!

Parietal: Nor do any of us for that matter. And I, for one, have stopped trying to decipher it.

Frontal: Who would have thought that you, Parietal, are the type to run away from danger. There is so little danger in our lives. Enjoy the confusion of my words and the danger of misinterpreting it, while it lasts.

Parietal: Ha ha … Frontal, you always make me laugh. You and Cuebee are so alike.

Frontal: I take that as the best compliment I have received ever since the dinosaurs disappeared from the earth!

Temporal: Exaggerator of the highest order! You never existed then!

Frontal: Oh yes, I did! As mud, soily, weedy and innocuous!

Brainstem: Bringing back order to this discussion, I tend to agree with Frontal. Butterfly Teacher did not go by the book. In fact, by any book. She simply ensured that the children are comfortable in the class by answering all their questions.

Amygdala: Do you think she was playing to the gallery?

Frontal: Impossible! Nothing was orchestrated!

Occipital: Yes, all the learning that happened today was experience and real-life based, even if rather haphazard. Even then, I could not help noticing Butterfly Teacher's prowess in navigating the class through all the randomness and chaos to bring order in such a creative fashion.

Cerebellum: Yes, today is a momentous occasion, for we have been witnesses for the first time in our brief but bustling history, to several random acts of learning!

Frontal: So much of theatrics are certainly not becoming of you, but you summarized well, Cerebellum!

2

Lion, whale and teddy bear

THIS NARRATION CAN GET JUICIER BY SIMPLY FOCUSING on the histrionics of the neighbourhood, homes and kitchens, or the conflicts between friends and neighbours, in-laws and spouses, grown-ups and youngsters, teenagers and parents, and so on. But that is exactly what I will not do! Instead, I intend to further the concept that we have been developing in the previous chapter, that is, the need to appreciate the value of random learning. For the present you may not be able to distinguish between what is being randomly picked up by children and what is being deliberately taught to them, but I assure you, we shall get there.

Three weeks into school and the First Graders had already settled in comfortably. Their boisterousness showed no signs of dissipating yet. I, for one, was really pleased with that, for over the years I have found the calmness that overtakes classrooms post the 'disciplining', very aggravating. Over the past two weeks, the children had learnt a great deal. They now knew their classmates' names, with whom they formed friendships; they attended morning assembly together and had even been eagerly introducing themselves to several of their seniors, much to the surprise of the seniors! They bonded with the gardener, the cook and her helper, heard many stories, sung songs and played several games in the classroom. Their teacher was trying to make them feel at home in school and was obviously succeeding at it.

The children were by now in love with school and somehow felt it their moral right to discover every corner of its premises. The toilet flush had been tried and tested by each one of them, and they had jointly arrived at the conclusion that its chief characteristics were noise and foam, and the gushing water was definitely not drinkable. Techie had opened up the switchboard in the classroom to double-check if it was similar to the one at home. Yoga had discovered the joys of climbing the large peepal tree in the courtyard. Millie would greet everyone with a silly poem made up on the spot. Here's one: 'Dooby-cooby-hooby-choo, Hello Didi, how are you!' BeeTee had decided to get chummy with the stray dog that sat expectantly at the school gate every day, looking for food, while Cuebee had befriended the Head Teacher and would have a set of questions ready for him every morning.

'When we cycle at night, how is it that the moon moves with us?'

'Why do plants grow so fast, while we grow so slowly?'

'Why do we join hands when we say namaste?'

'Why does the ceiling fan move in only one direction?'

'Why does the stray dog outside the gate have no family?'

'Do plants and trees have families?'

'Why is my hair curly and BeeTee's not curly?'

'Why are adults all of different height?'

'Why are fruits from a green-leafed plant not green?'

'Is our head to be used only for donning ornaments, like earrings, bindi, hairstyle, or does it have any other use?'

'Why are mountains colder if they are closer to the sun?'

'Why is the egg harder after boiling?'

Anyone with a weak heart and fleeting patience would have shooed her away, but not the Head Teacher. In fact, he began to eagerly look forward to Cuebee's questions every morning. He would disentangle himself from whatever he was doing and almost like Shackleton and his men on a voyage, the two would embark upon a journey of exploration right until the bell would ring for the assembly.

On the third weekend, Butterfly Teacher handed over the new uniforms to the parents. From the fourth week onwards, the girls were sporting light blue shirts and navy-blue pinafores, and the boys, light blue shirts and navy-blue shorts. On the first day of sporting new uniforms, Cuebee and Millie were skipping into school, Yoga in tow, all in neat uniforms, when they noticed the Head Teacher beckoning them. Cuebee was armed with her questions for the day. They raced towards him. His hand was tightly clutched by a boy with the most beatific smile and the curliest crop of hair on his head.

'Cuebee and Millie, meet Geekay, your new classmate. Can you show him your classroom?' said the Head Teacher, unclasping the boy's tight grip.

'Hello, Geekay. Come, I will take you there,' Cuebee said with a smile.

Geekay's defining physical trait was not his crop of thick black and curly hair, but that he wore it a little longer than most boys of his age group. He was tall for his age with clear, light-brown eyes and a strong bone structure. He seemed like a pleasant person. Geekay looked at Cuebee intently, particularly at the way her lips were forming words.

'Fine,' he replied with a joyful smile.

'Where have you come from? What language do you speak at home? Do you like to play *stapoo*,' Cuebee asked half quizzically and half in zest.

Suddenly Geekay went quiet and stopped smiling.

'Cuebee, Geekay is very shy. You must help him catch up in class. He will make a marvellous friend. Isn't that so, Geekay?'

Geekay did not respond. He was still looking intently at Cuebee, as if awaiting the formation of the next few words on her lips.

'Geekay, now you are in our care.' Cuebee, always quick to welcome friends in her fold, beamed with genuine affection.

The Head Teacher seemed very pleased and urged Geekay to go on. Geekay smiled again and appeared to be more confident as he proceeded with her. Cuebee took his hand in hers and pointed towards me, her classroom.

'My mother says, all children are brought into this world by God. Geekay is also a baby of God, so it is God who decided that he should be a shy person,' said Millie.

'No, that is not correct. I have been given birth by my mother. Geekay came out of his mother too,'

'No. It has to be God.'

'Then tell me, where does God live?'

'In space.'

'How does God get oxygen to breathe in space? And if God gave birth to you in space, how did you get here?'

Geekay did not participate in the conversation, but each time something was said, he would stare hard at the instrument of speech, the lips.

Butterfly Teacher was passing by them and must have overheard this interesting conversation. 'Now all of you come to class. Bring Geekay along,' she said, urging the children to move along.

Cuebee entered the classroom and suddenly felt a haze of blue uniforms all around her. She gave an involuntary tug at Geekay's hand. He looked at her and said, 'What happened?'

'I don't think I was prepared for this. It feels like the blue sky and blue streams have suddenly flowed into this room.'

Geekay was watching her as she spoke and then he laughed and said, 'With blue flowers popping out from behind classroom benches!'

Millie, Cuebee and Geekay were giggling when the teacher good-humouredly asked them to settle down.

'Children, today I, the butterfly, will introduce you to a new boy flower in the class. This flower is quietly curious and loves to discover more and more about everything around him.'

'He is Geekay,' Cuebee, Millie and Yoga said in unison.

The teacher then asked Geekay to share something about himself with the class. He immediately got up, faced the class and said, 'I love nature.'

As if Geekay had an instinct of self-preservation, he abruptly turned around, back towards the teacher and sat down next to Cuebee with an expressionless face. Cuebee was surprised that he did not even wait for a response from the rest of the class. The Head Teacher had given her the responsibility to help him catch up in class. For Cuebee, catching up also meant making friends with her classmates. A moment later, she appeared as if she had arrived at a crucial decision and in dramatic suddenness got up and said, 'I love nature too!'

'And I love to climb trees,' Yoga added.

'I love dogs!' BeeTee spoke up.

'I love making silly poems on everything around me,' Millie said.

Butterfly Teacher realized what was happening. The five friends were trying to assimilate Geekay in the class. 'Cuebee, Millie, Yoga and BeeTee, I also love the outdoors,' she said, as the intent of the conversations stole upon her.

There was stunned silence for all of five seconds in my classroom, before the commotion started again.

'Teacher, I love roses.'

'I have a pet parrot. I love to talk to her.'

'I love the riverside.'

It went on and on, until Zouzou walked up to Geekay and said, 'I like you, Geekay.' Geekay smiled and giggled and showed his happiness by climbing on top of the bench and clapping. As if on cue, everybody began clapping, and there was a general atmosphere of celebration on Geekay's admission to the class.

Cuebee, you are a godsend!

Of the methods of teaching alphabets to eager-eyed fresh entrants of Grade 1, I had working knowledge. But of innovative pedagogies, I was completely ignorant. After depositing Geekay back at his seat from his high position on the bench, Butterfly Teacher informed the class of the day's lesson. 'Today we will learn about alphabets, the "*Akshar Gyan*".

'I am going to tell you the story of a brother–sister duo, their Mummy and Papa and their Dada and Dadi,' she said.

'Teacher please add Nana and Nani.'

'And also, my doggie at the gate.'

'And the toilet flush too.'

'Sure,' she said and began to spin a tale around the originally planned and the subsequently requested characters. The story revolved around how each of the characters tried their best to teach the doggie to use the toilet and then flush it. It was hilarious. But during this storytelling session, the teacher began stressing on the first syllables of the words familiar to the children. [Readers may note that these conversations take place in an Indian language/dialect that can be learnt phonetically.]

'Da-dadi.'

'Na-nana.'

'Da-doggie.'

'Ma-mummy.'

'Fa-flush.'

The students began to involuntarily repeat the familiar words and their first syllable after her, until Geekay abruptly said, 'Ta-toilet'. The fun had just started. Catching on to this moment of realization, Butterfly Teacher fished out a set of paintings of fruits and vegetables that she had prepared. She continued the word–syllable session while displaying the sheet.

'Ma-mango.'

'Ca-cauliflower.'

'Ba-banana.'

There was so much excitement and commotion in the class that the teacher from the neighbouring classroom suspended her chalk-and-board operations to check on my class. She stood there at the door, hands on her hips, stern-faced and irritated. She stared at Butterfly Teacher with a look that seemed to communicate 'you-just-committed-a-crime-by-making-these-children-joyous-and-noisy'! Butterfly Teacher smiled back at her and said, 'They are learning the alphabet.'

'But I am not hearing them speak the alphabet in sequence—A, B, C, D, and so on. They are just repeating some random words! Your kind of new-breed teachers are spoiling the whole atmosphere of the school.'

She followed up her outburst with a solid glare at the kids, and an oft-repeated phrase was thrown in their direction, 'Finger on your lips!'

Before Butterfly Teacher could respond, Cuebee got up, locked eye to eye with the neighbouring Teacher, and said, 'Fa-finger'.

'O-on,' added Imli.

'Ya-your,' said BeeTee.

'La-lips,' said a very excited Zouzou.

And that was the beginning of several syllables spoken by the First Graders that day, much to the amazement of the other teacher. She stared open-mouth, dropped-jaw at the children as they continued. Ta-table. Ba-bench. Ta-tap. Ta-tree. La-leaf. Ma-milk, and so on. It was as if their tongue had run away with them to a jolly place and had no intention of ever coming back to where it belonged.

The stunned neighbouring teacher muttered something to the effect 'these youngsters will never learn', and left in a huff followed by a puff. Cuebee turned secretly to Millie, Yoga, Techie, BeeTee and Geekay, all of whom sat close by, and said, 'Let us name the next-door teacher Alphabet teacher.' Soft giggles followed in a spirit of secrecy.

The classes continued. Butterfly Teacher then asked the children to name other things from their surroundings that started with specific syllables.

'Ka—'

'Key.'

'Fa—'

'Furniture.'

'Ch—'

'*Choti*—'

'Aa—'

'*Anda*.'

'Ba—'

'Bag.'

'La—'

'Lunch—'

And so it went on. The children were not always right, but they had caught the flow. In the later days, they were also introduced to the sound of the last alphabet in a word. Fa-furniture-ra, Da-door-ra, ta-toilet-ta, Na-nani-ee, and so on. Geekay was often found contemplating hard on the lip movements of the teacher and kids as they would speak the words and lay emphasis upon the sounds. Cuebee was keenly noticing this tendency of his and her perplexity was growing to bothersome levels.

Soon, whether this fun-and-frolic format of learning introduced by Butterfly Teacher was intentional or accidental of monumental proportions became the subject of our nightly discussions for the next many days.

Brainstem: There appears to be plenty going on in your classroom, Frontal, that we are just not familiar with.

Occipital: It all appears unplanned. Butterfly Teacher does not seem to be getting anywhere.

Amygdala: I am convinced that there should be no experiments in teaching and learning the alphabet. After all, this is the primary objective of going to a school.

Hippocampus: I agree. The problem here is the manner of learning of the alphabet. And trying to solve it by amusing the children, appears to me as a far-fetched, lazy and too random a system.

Frontal: It does appear random to the unpractised eye, but hear me out. She did not start with the first alphabet and go on routinely till the last. Instead, she started with the words that the kids use in their day-to-day conversation and stressed upon their first syllable. They grasped the concept so fast.

Cerebellum: Gosh! This is an eye-opener. I have got so used to the A for apple routine or *Tha se Thathera* drill …

Frontal: Where most kids don't understand the meaning of *Thathera*. In fact, I doubt any of them would have ever met or seen one.

Temporal: By the way, what is *Thathera*?

Frontal: There you are! If in so many years, our very serious intellect and linguist Temporal does not know what is *Thathera*, the rest of us need not even hazard a guess!

Parietal: I also heard the Head Teacher questioning the teachers' tendency to condition the minds of the children. He said that when somebody says the letter A, the first image that comes to their mind is of an apple, and they are unable to think beyond it. Children's minds must not be conditioned.

Cerebellum: Whereas in Butterfly Teacher's class none of the children said A for apple. Instead, they used so many other words like air, animal, *anda*, *atta*, *Anganwadi*, etc.

Frontal: I have watched Butterfly Teacher teaching the kids how to write these letters too. Kids are encouraged to draw pictures of things starting with certain syllables. The children are already in critical thinking mode.

Occipital: After hearing you all out, I have come to a very important conclusion.

Frontal: Do tell. I am all floor and plinth!

Occipital: I am going to give up my so far well-preserved no-need-for-reforms-and-experiments-in-teaching idea.

Frontal: Well ... if you had not given up, we would have probably appointed a board of directors with an able secretary to help you make that decision!

Occipital: I am giving up my idea only because I see a great deal of sense in the randomness, which strangely has an underlying consistency too. Sounds oxymoronic but I am convinced that a good teacher must adapt her pedagogy in accordance with the requirements of the class. She cannot follow a set system just because everyone else does so.

Frontal: Point of order, classrooms! So, what now, in our esteemed view, is a bad teacher?

Hippocampus: The sort of teacher who does not innovate!

Frontal: And what does a good teacher do?

Occipital: She never tires of innovation in her classroom transactions!

Frontal: Friends, classrooms and alter egos, I bow before thee and thy diagnosis!

Cerebellum: *Nautanki*!

The manner in which Butterfly Teacher introduced numeracy was equally interesting. It afforded a great opportunity to learn new words too. Though the grade-appropriate learning outcome was to recognize, count and write numerals from 1–10, the teacher's methodology was such that children learnt numbers up to twenty. She taught numbers to them through their own bodies. She started with things that were singular, such as one nose, one chin, one stomach, then went on to two ears, eyes, hands, etc. Finally, she moved to counting fingers and toes. The game she used in class was a winner.

'Show me two eyebrows.'

All kids would put their fingers on their two eyebrows.

'Show me three hands.'

Loud protests from all children. 'We have only two.'

'Prove it,' she would say.

Children would thrust their hands above their heads and say 'See, only two hands!'

'Show me six fingers.'

Children would start counting loudly and then thrust five fingers of one hand and one finger of the other in the air.

'Count all your fingers and toes.'

And that is how they learnt to count up to twenty.

'Show me through your body how old you are?'

Zouzou poked her two ears, two eyes and two eyebrows with her fingers. Yoga touched five toes in one foot and one in the other. Cuebee actually counted six of her hair strands and asked the teacher how she could count the rest of it!

The children understood the concept of less than, more than, equal to, and so much more. Butterfly Teacher introduced language and numeracy in every aspect of their day at school—from counting the children standing in one line in the morning assembly, to counting the number of children taller than a given child, the number of doors or windows in a classroom, number of girls in class, describing something in the child's own words, etc. Consequently, Grade 1 students were often found all over the school counting something or the other. Sometimes, she would make them sit in groups of 5-6 and give them simple mathematical problems to solve. For example, if the other group was invited to this group's table for lunch, how many extra *rotis* would be needed. At other times, she would bring different toys to the class and ask a group of kids to pick up one toy each and converse with each other as if the toys were talking. Sometimes, she would herself join a group and act out as a toy and the children would end up learning something new and entirely unconnected to the syllabus at hand.

Cuebee, BeeTee and Butterfly Teacher once had a very interesting conversation while role-playing as a lion, whale and teddy bear, respectively.

Lion: I love chocolates and biscuits. Whale, what do you like?

Whale: I love chips. And you, Teddy?

Teddy Bear: Eating home-cooked food, green vegetables and fruits is healthy. Chips, chocolate and biscuits will spoil our health, and we may not grow up to be fit.

Lion: What if I eat you up? Is that healthy?

Teddy Bear: You are a lion cub and I am a big bear. You cannot eat me up.

Lion: Then I will continue to eat lots of chocolates. All parents let their kids eat chocolates and biscuits, so how can these be unhealthy?

Teddy Bear: Maybe because parents do not know that chocolate and biscuits are junk food and contain a lot of sugar which can create cavities in your teeth.

Whale: What is the meaning of junk?

Teddy Bear: It means something that is not of any use or has no value for your body. So, tell me Lion, how will you remain king of the jungle if your teeth are spoilt? And Whale, how will you become so big if you are not healthy?

Lion: Can the king of the jungle eat them occasionally?

Whale: Every Sunday?

Teddy Bear: Well, both of you could decide not to have it too often. Then all the other animals can learn from you. The king of the jungle and king of the ocean must never fall sick due to junk food.

Lion: The jungle king promises to have junk food only once a month!

Whale: Me too!

Butterfly Teacher had come up with many interesting games, such as looking within the school premises for objects whose names began with a particular letter; role-playing as a TV news anchor or as an interviewer; playing games related to sorting, seriation, pattern-making, model-making; and showing them interesting YouTube videos on her cell phone. Once when she told them about volcanoes, Cuebee decided to make her own volcano. She made a little sand mound while playing with her friends in the sandpit at the playground. Then, she and Millie created a small hole on top of it and placed some grass and wood sticks in the hole. They ran to Butterfly Teacher and asked her for a match box, so they could light the 'volcano' and watch the 'lava' and 'hot gases' erupt from it. But Cuebee and her friends were only six! Butterfly Teacher must have made a mental note of this incident. No match boxes for them. Kids this age are extremely impressionable, so she needed to bear this in mind while introducing new subjects. Roof overheard her discussing this with the Head Teacher. Safety first, always!

One of the games the children seemed to love to play was the storytelling game. To play this game, Butterfly Teacher would begin a story by saying one sentence, and each child would continue building the story by adding one more sentence each. One day, she started with this sentence: 'Once upon a time, there stood a blue car outside the gate of the village school …'

'Though it was not in working condition, children in Grade 1 longed to open it up to know more about it.' Techie continued the story in this way.

'The car was a sedan,' added Cuebee.

Simla could not wait for her turn and hastily added, 'Though some children in class knew the meaning of a sedan, but most did not, so their friend explained it to them.'

Cuebee got the hint, and somewhat glowing with energy, continued the story. 'Cars can broadly be categorized into three kinds—sedan, sports utility vehicle, that is, SUV, and sports car. A sedan is for comfort driving, an SUV for off-roading on rough roads and a sports car is identified with high-speed driving.'

'Then children became very curious. They wanted to know more,' Imli continued the story.

BeeTee butted in with, 'They wanted to know how one car can go on rough terrain but another cannot.'

'A girl in the class replied that an SUV can be used to drive on rough terrain because it has a four-wheel drive and has a "differential" that sends power to the rear wheels for doing this,' added Cuebee to the story.

Butterfly Teacher was completely taken aback at the turn of events in her story. It was a rare moment when she allowed herself to be stumped thus. Unable to handle the surge of disbelief within, she rushed out of the classroom and ran straight to the Head Teacher's office. She replayed the whole storyline before him, to his utter stupefaction too. He took a few minutes to settle his mind and then arrived at a decision.

Together, they made their way back to me, the classroom, and the Head Teacher said, 'I am told that you all weaved an instant story on a car and are really interested in learning about the car parked outside.'

'Yes! Yes! we are.'

'Fine, then. Tomorrow I will start the work of getting the car shifted inside the school compound so that we can start learning more about it. But before we do that, Cuebee, tell me, how do you know so much about cars?'

'My father is a car mechanic, and he often takes me to his garage. He has taught me many things about how a car works.'

I mulled over two things. Firstly, that the method adopted by Cuebee's father to generate interest in such matters must be the product of a scientific temper and disposition. And secondly, that in my entire existence of twenty years, my understanding of 'true and qualitative education' was finally showing signs of evolving further and with a great deal of creativity sprinkled on it. Meanwhile, the glad-looking Head Teacher turned and left my space to direct his batteries towards the task of shifting the car. The children were brimming with excitement and imagination, though their imagination was quite unequal to the learnings that they were about to be flushed with.

It took almost two weeks to shift the car. Butterfly Teacher continued to jog the minds of the children by letting loose pieces of random learning, now and then. To keep the interest in the car alive, the teacher would often refer to the car while taking her class. To teach the children about living and non-living things, for example, she took them to the kitchen garden in the backyard of the school.

'The plants grow through a process of germination,' she said and added, 'living things are those who develop by growing and require water and food for their growth. Now tell me children, is the car a living thing or a non-living thing?'

'This is confusing me, Teacher. A car moves, so it could be a living thing?' asked Cuebee.

'No, Cuebee. The car moves because it is a machine. The car does not drink water and does not grow, so it is a non-living thing.'

After the class, Cuebee was still a little puzzled. When Millie, Techie and Yoga asked her what was wrong, she told them, 'We need to test if our parents are machines or living things, because we have never seen them growing. Their height has remained the same since the beginning.'

They were in complete agreement though fairly perturbed at the thought of being brought up by machines.

'What is the best way to test this?' Millie said.

'We will ask them to drink water in front of us.' Cuebee said with the confidence of a person who knows she is working for a good cause.

'But I have seen them sip water before,' Millie said.

'So have I. But I don't think anyone of us have observed them guzzling down water. So, if they are able to drink one full glass of water at one go, then they cannot be machines. Remember, Teacher told us that a machine does not drink water.'

The kids must have surely conducted the experiment with their parents because the permanent suspension of any doubt in this regard was evident on their much-relieved faces the next day.

The car was placed in the school campus after two weeks, and in such a manner that it was clearly visible to children from their classrooms. Obviously, there was a design to this. This was the beginning of the First Graders' omnipresence, for they were found simultaneously inside their classroom as well as outside! On the bonnet of the car, hugging the car, talking to it, noisily singing rhymes and skipping around it, or simply claiming their rightful place next to it—they were everywhere. Though Alphabet Teacher continued to remain unimpressed, the Grade 3 teacher, who had joined the school three years ago, began to feel a rush of interest charge through her veins for this style of teaching. She too would often bring her students out to check the car. She was promptly named Buddy Teacher by Cuebee and her friends.

Many nights were spent by us eight classrooms, in conjecturing, in a juvenile manner, the next move by the Head Teacher and Butterfly Teacher, or simply in deep thought over the way Cuebee-led events were unfolding in the school.

Amygdala: We are the proud recipients of a non-functioning, rusted and curious invertebrate car that stares at us every day from the compound abetting us.

Occipital: The Head Teacher appears to be a case of confirmed addiction to experiential learning.

Amygdala: And this Butterfly Teacher's exuberance and devotion to randomness appears incurable!

Hippocampus: The logic and sense with which Cuebee extolled her knowledge of cars simply defies me. She is a six-year-old for heaven's sake!

Parietal: Did you not hear Cuebee? Her father is a car mechanic, and that is why she has developed immense interest in automobiles, simply by watching him, questioning him and learning from him.

Brainstem: You know, outwardly I give the appearance of being unmoved by all these developments, but inwardly I am performing jumping jacks in sheer gladness.

Frontal: That in any case is your chief means of recreation. But do tell why this dichotomy between your inside and outside?

Brainstem: I overheard that Cuebee's father is not educated beyond Grade 8, but he has a technical mind and augments his knowledge through experience and watching videos about newly launched cars and their features on his smartphone.

Occipital: I observed a strange game this morning that Cuebee was playing with Millie, Geekay and Yoga. Apparently, Cuebee's father told her how roads are constructed with the help of machines, that is, concrete mixers, road rollers, excavators and dump trucks. So, Cuebee devised a road construction game today on the strength of that exposure. She used clay to make machines and wet sand for building a road and her friends also learnt so much.

Temporal: Rooms, do you notice that whatever topic we may begin to converse about, how we always zigzag our way back to Cuebee?

Frontal: As a central player in this group, I must point out that presently our duties as well as happiness lie in Cuebee's direction. Hence, I am glad all our views coincide and not collide.

Parietal: What do you think the Head Teacher will do next?

Frontal: If you are attempting to complete the character and intention study of our favourite people in one night, abandon the thought. We are going to be here for a long, long time. We need food for thought for many, many nights. All I can say is that the Head Teacher believes in joyful learning, but is not one to use force to reform the members of his ecosystem.

Occipital: Yes, force is definitely not the first characteristic that I would use to describe him.

Frontal: Or the tenth for that matter!

The Head Teacher appeared somewhat tense after shifting the car, though briefly so. My reading is that his thoughts of experiential learning through the medium of the car, must have begun to compete with his own graver reflections on the textbooks to be completed, and answers to be given to the Education Inspector, as and when he deemed it fit to visit the school. This conflict within turned out to be brief as I mentioned earlier, limited to a period of temporary uncertainty that lasted all of half an hour. I am certain of this, for he soon announced that he had arrived at the delightfully ingenuous decision that the exposure to the car for learners of all eight grades would lead to far greater competencies than what could be gained by only ticking the boxes related to textbooks. Before any extraneous factor could goad him to change his mind, he called for a staff meeting.

We classrooms had seen over the last three years that for the teachers of senior classes, each staff meeting was perceived as a fresh danger to their age-old beliefs. Their lack of enthusiasm in receiving new suggestions during staff meetings would always be accompanied by their ill-concealed anxiety. It seemed as if it was quite an effort for them to sulkily, unwillingly and abashedly, comply with directions from their superior. Perhaps, they had realized that they had only two courses available to them in this school and with this Head Teacher. They could either shut themselves away from the new ideas and earn the mistrust of the Head Teacher and a general reputation in the village of being a below-average Teacher, or they could participate in the new initiatives, even if they had to summarily put down the flames of protest rising in their chests. On the other hand, the teachers of junior classes were quick to see reason in the ways of this maverick Head Teacher.

The Head Teacher started the meeting with a short speech.

'We must connect the children to certain things that they see in real-life, like the car in this case, and grade-appropriately build their competencies through these connections throughout the eight years. Let this car become a learning ecosystem. Please integrate aspects of the car in the teaching of all subjects. There can be nothing better than teaching through a multidisciplinary approach.'

The Science Teacher who taught Grade 5 onwards was waiting to work off his indignation. He said, 'Though the idea is appreciable, the prescribed textbooks and timetable are my master and they are not designed to offer any so-called real-life activities. So, do guide on how to find time in our busy schedule to explain so many concepts related to the working of a car?'

The Social Science Teacher was known to sport a festive look every time he completed teaching a chapter of a prescribed textbook! It was the only time when he would temporarily suspend hostilities against the drabness of timetables and timelines. He was rather rattled.

'Sir, the car is a piece of technology. How are children expected to understand history, geography or civics with the help of a car? It's a different matter that at a personal level, I am fascinated by all machines on four wheels. It is indeed a marvel.'

Before the Social Science Teacher could lapse into a detailed description of why he was mesmerized by cars, the Language Teacher added her bit. 'I could understand if you meant writing about their experiences of being inside a car, or a bus, etc. That is one way that children can learn some nuances of the language associated with automobiles, but beyond that, this is just an ordinary platitude. I feel the kids need to interest themselves in something less distracting yet more creative for their studies. What's special about the car, sir?'

The primary grade teachers were silent in the face of such disconcerting discussion. But inside their heads, they were pretty clear that they were looking at very exciting times ahead.

But the Head Teacher was quite the expert in dissolving and resolving militant ideas amongst the Teachers.

'I do not know of any better experts than you to find out the methodology for this new approach to teaching. Each time we have stood at the edge of an abyss, you have shown the way. So, whatever your doubts maybe, I, for one, am confident that you are my Archimedes and you will soon share your Eureka moment on this idea.'

So much glory to their names certainly did not go unnoticed or unfelt. But before they could recover from such an onslaught of naked praise about virtues they did not even know they possessed, the Head Teacher expanded the scope of their venerability.

'I am thinking that once you have prepared your grade-appropriate lesson plans by incorporating the car as the central idea and started implementing it, I will request the education inspectors to designate you as teacher trainers for other schools. No better way to spread your expertise far and wide than to disseminate your priceless ideas.'

All may not have been well with their indifferent worlds, but the compliments, though of a rustic order, did ensure that the teachers grudgingly agreed to implement the idea of the car as a learning ecosystem, and thereby reform the education system, even if by the application of force. In the course of human history, at least that of the humans I came in contact with, this was a turning event. The school might have been celebrated earlier for giving the village students access to education but now it seemed like Cuebee and the car, as well as the Head Teacher and Butterfly Teacher, and perhaps all other teachers, were becoming the protagonists in a saga of educational transformation.

Like all other classrooms, I too had an uninterrupted view of the car. Word had trickled about the Head Teacher's latest venture, and as soon as the school gates opened every morning, children from all grades would find themselves around the car. They would scream with unfettered joy, playing with the steering, trying to open the bonnet, and some would even climb on the roof of the car! The senior teachers observed them dispassionately by commanding a generous dose of patience.

'Hmm. It may well be an idea to work upon, but I have this creeping discomfort about all the questions that the children will ask. I might not even know the answers! They will label me as a fool,' the Language Teacher said worriedly.

The Maths Teacher smiled broadly and said, 'Now that will be interesting, seeing you open your mouth with nothing to say!'

They both chuckled.

'I am still wondering what I have let myself into. I must have been decidedly dissipated to even agreeing to this.'

'Well, we can actually become students once again. Let us call on the Science Teacher to teach us about cars.'

'This is what happens when you accept praise heaped upon you for qualities you know you neither have, nor will ever have!' Alphabet Teacher was indeed sharp.

On the other hand, Teachers of Grades 1, 2 and 3 were not in the least bit timorous. Butterfly Teacher knew as she entered class that day that a storm had arrived, bringing in winds of change. There was overpowering noise in the class; the car was, of course, the only topic of excited conversations.

'Settle down, children. Hmm. Looks like you don't want to.'

'Teacher, we want to see the car.'

'Fine. We will go out to see the car. But we will not just see it today, we will observe. Is that fine by all of you?'

'Teacher, what is observe?'

'Good question, Cuebee. Well, you should look at the whole car and all its parts very closely. Try to name the parts, try to make out what the function of each part could possibly be, find out why it is there and be armed with all your questions when you return to class.'

'Teacher, like I "observe" all the parts inside all the equipment that I open up?' asked Techie.

'Yes, somewhat like that,' Butterfly Teacher said with a laugh.

'Can Techie and I open up the insides of the car to observe?' Cuebee said.

'No, you cannot. First, we will observe all that is outside and visible. We will try to learn new words related to the car with their meanings. Once you have understood that, we will slowly start looking inside. Is that understood?'

The class reverberated with 'yes, Teacher' as the kids in their typical mode of progression, ran out helter-skelter towards the object that was gripping their imagination and curiosity.

The car was a grand old model of Ambassador, the Indian version of Oxford Morris. It had five gears, not a very modern system, but had most of the equipment found in cars these days. Children's behaviour is hard to forecast, and Butterfly Teacher may have been right in marvelling at her own decision to let them lose, over the car. However, over the next two hours, the kids began identifying parts of the car in right earnest to her very own amazement.

'This is the wheel.'

'And this is the door.'

'I will call this the front part.'

'Look, here is a cap,' said Techie when she noticed the knob that appeared to open into something.

'Light, light and light,' they said on spotting the front light, back light and other small lights.

'I can see myself in this mirror.'

'All the windows are made of glass, even the front and rear ones.'

'The benches in the car are so big. Many people can sit on it.'

'Hey, there is a place to put a key in. Look, look, right here on the door.'

'There is a stick on the floor near the bench in the front,' they said on discovering the gear.

'And my cycle's pedals are here too.'

'What do you think this stick on the outside does?' they said on finding the exhaust sticking out of the rear of the car.

'Wait, do you see that box on the rod that is connecting the wheels in the back? What could that be?'

'The numbers and letters at the rear are the same as those in the front!'

I noticed that Cuebee was 'observing' and helping her classmates understand.

'These are not windows. They are called the windscreens.'

'These are called seats and not benches.'

'That is the gear.'

'That is called the exhaust.'

When the children came back to the class, a look of eagerness combined with strange satisfaction seemed to rest on their faces. The Head Teacher was waiting along with Butterfly Teacher to listen to the kids and their questions.

'So, children, I could sense your excitement and fun. Did you like the car? Do you have any questions?'

All of them started together, but the Head Teacher let them be. He did not restrain their enthusiasm or the noise that accompanied it. It was, after all, their first close exposure to technology, its complexity, and yet its simplicity if 'observed' closely and understood.

'Why is the wheel black?'

'How will the car move, who pushes it?'

'Who turns the car?'

'Why does it have so many lights?'

'Does it have two lights because we have two eyes?'

'Cuebee showed us the exhaust and the differential.'

'Cuebee, do you know any of the answers?' the Head Teacher asked, delighted by the dual development—such good observations and Cuebee's prior knowledge of cars extending to exhaust and differential.

'I know a few of the answers. The wheel is black because something is added to the rubber tyre to give it more stability. The car moves when petrol is filled in it, and the exhaust pipe at the back gives out smoke as if giving force. The lights are to see in the dark.'

'Excellent answers, Cuebee. Now, your teacher and I will take questions from each one of you—but one by one by show of hands—and we will try to answer them.'

The class went on as noisily as earlier. The fire in the children's belly was unstoppable!

'Why do you think the car attracts them so much, when it's such a common sight in their everyday lives?' Butterfly Teacher asked the Head Teacher next morning after the assembly.

'Yes I know, but have they had the opportunity to climb on it, go under it, observe it, understand its functioning and most importantly do all this as a part of their school education? I don't think any car has ever equalled this role in their lives.'

Over the next few weeks, the First Graders became adept at reeling out the technical nomenclature of car parts. They knew the sounds of the syllables that composed the words related to cars. They could draw the car and its parts in their own tottering styles, just from observation, and had even begun to understand how each part had to function in a synchronized manner for the whole car to move.

'Synchronization and harmony are important for all of us too. We have to see that all the children in the class understand everything; only then will the class progress.' Butterfly Teacher never let an opportunity to explain inclusion values, slip from her hands.

Though textbooks had been introduced in Grade 1, rather than learning words from it, by now the children had learnt the alphabet and several words related to a car. One day, Butterfly Teacher made a rough sketch of an SUV on the blackboard and showed them the 'differential' that connects the rear wheels. She explained through the drawing how the differential obtains power from the engine through a shaft and transmits it to the rear wheels.

'And that is why, SUVs are able to drive on rough terrain whereas the other cars cannot.'

'Teacher, how will we know if a car is an SUV or a sedan?'

'The car will be higher from the ground, as compared to a sedan. It is called having a "higher ground clearance".'

'Our blue car is not an SUV!'

'That's right. Today onwards, whenever you are on the road, start observing which car is a sedan, which is SUV and which is a sports car.'

'Isn't an SUV the same as a sports car?'

'No. A sports car is one that can run at a very fast speed.'

At school closing time in the afternoon, when parents would come to pick up their children, the energy of the children would be difficult to contain. On being prodded to tell how their day had been, the joyous responses had invariably nothing to do with studying, but everything to do with their adventures of the car-kind. Many of the parents had resigned themselves to the 'bad schooling' that their wards were receiving, but not Cuebee's grandma.

'Tell me everything that you learnt about the car today,' she would urge as soon as Cuebee would run to my door to meet her.

In exacting detail, Cuebee would unleash her learnings to her enraptured grandmother, who would absorb it all, as if making up for all the lost time in her own education.

We would be raring to go at our wordplay every night. It was as if we were in a state of delirium as we watched the school undertake activities that in our wildest imagination had nothing to do with school education.

Frontal: The historical era noted as BC stands for 'Before Cuebee' for my life, hereon.

Occipital: I think you have said it for all of us!

Amygdala: I hope we are not making a mistake in our judgement in all our cleverness. Let us decide not to get carried away as yet.

Hippocampus: So far, I had held on to the view that there is nothing special about a car besides being a means of modern transport. But becoming the means of a learning trajectory in geometrical progression for Cuebee and her classmates is baffling me. It was too random a decision to use the car for learning. Was it not?

Occipital: My working theory is that the Head Teacher has discerned that most children, including young children, do not like every interaction or every stimulation for learning to be structured or as per schedule. They love to be given time to do things independently.

Parietal: You are right. The discovery of these hands-on methods of learning have rekindled my curiosity in the art of learning. The Head Teacher's endeavour to facilitate learning for children of all grades through some activity is now acquiring a method in the whole madness.

Temporal: This unstructured time that the children get every day has indeed caught my fancy!

Brainstem: Mine too! When I see children on their own devising and playing many interesting games during this unstructured time, it bewilders and delights me no end.

Occipital: I was witness to their "*Jungle ka Judge*" game.

Brainstem: Sounds interesting! What were they up to?

Occipital: So Cuebee became a lion and as the king of the jungle, also the judge. Her friends assumed the roles of different animals—elephant, monkey, rabbit, deer, etc. They would come to her with their contentious issues, and Cuebee would resolve their disputes amicably.

Amygdala: I too regard these developments with adequate admiration; however, I still believe that we have not given this matter of the car—and all its randomness—enough consideration to enable us to arrive at a logical conclusion.

Temporal: Well, for me, the emergence of this Head Teacher in the school is a good omen. Have you noticed how he treats young children at par with adults and explains the most convoluted and complicated concepts with ease to the satisfaction of their inquisitive minds? My earlier experiences had embedded the belief in me that younger children do not have the ability to understand complex scientific concepts. But now I revel in the knowledge that this notion is downright incorrect.

Frontal: Still awaiting your conclusion, Temporal, after that impassioned speech.

Temporal: Inspired by the Head Teacher, I therefore and hereby declare that children of all ages are inherently and immensely curious and possess age-appropriate scientific temper. We must stop underestimating their abilities forthwith!

Frontal: I can see that most of you are still reeling from the impact of a human tidal wave in the form of the Head Teacher! He sure is contagious!

Hippocampus: I am still weighing all your opinions. I have many unanswered questions, as yet.

Frontal: Well, as the Head Teacher loves to say, questions must be asked at every age, even if you are bent and old and beyond repair!

Hippocampus: Talk about yourself, Frontal. I am not even twenty-one!

The unstructured and random—but definitely not aimless—learning had become a thing in the school. The Head Teacher and Butterfly Teacher were very clear in their approach. Children must be exposed to newer and newer stimulations in their growing years, from simple to complex, from concrete to abstract, and from known text and matter to unknown text and matter, beyond the prescribed textbooks. They must be empowered to not accept things as they are and never stop asking questions. Imagine if Galileo had not challenged the theory that the earth is the centre of the universe. Though the vast supplies of related theories would have surely ensured a sturdy reverence of the earth, but then, there would have been no walk on the moon, no exploration of Mars, and worst of all, no connectivity!

But this had not become a thing with all the senior-grade teachers as yet. Under ordinary circumstances, it would have taken a great deal to daunt them, but this invasion of outlandish ideas by the Head Teacher, supported by the teachers of Grades 1, 2 and 3, had completely shaken them. The vicissitudes faced by them grew in proportion to their impatience at the additional work they were having to do to integrate the idea of the car into their teaching.

'Every few years, along comes a Head Teacher, propelling new ideas at the rate of a dozen a day and we are expected to dance to his tunes.'

'My mental health has been impacted with all this. The Head Teacher wants children to be free to ask questions. You give them one chance and they will question away your sanity! I don't even have half the answers. What do you think it does to my self-esteem?'

'I am tired of imagining new lesson plans. The only notable event in my life these days is when the school bell rings announcing that we are done for the day.'

Gloom was spreading rapidly over this section of teachers in the face of the new 'burdens' that they were being asked to carry. Some of them were even looking for ways to discipline the children who would be found playing near the car. One day, Cuebee and her friends were happily running around on the school playground for no cogent reason other than that they had ample energy and they were using it to run for now. In the midst of this, they ran to the main entrance of the school, and Millie attempted to jump up to look over the school gate. And, at that moment, Alphabet Teacher saw them and came rushing forward.

'Has your teacher not taught you anything? Are you trying to run away from school? You must not even try to go outside alone,' she shouted, rallying in all her forces.

'Why can we not go out alone?' said the ever-curious Cuebee.

'If you go out alone, then bad people, who are always lurking around corners, may kidnap you and turn you into a beggar! You will then end up selling balloons to passers-by on the roads.'

'Oh, is that how it happens? Which colour balloons do you think I will sell?' asked Millie in sheer innocence and then sang, 'Ting-a-ling-ling, I will sell only pink'.

'Cuebee, looks like you too want to become a balloon-seller when you grow up?' the angry teacher said, drawing upon all the sarcasm at her command.

'No, I don't.'

'Then what do you want to become when you grow up?'

'*Badi* Cuebee,' she replied guilelessly.

The teacher must have been burning in copious wrath as she muttered something to the effect 'this much, and no more', and stormed off.

3

The chalk, green board and textbooks

I COULD NOT POSSIBLY SAIL THROUGH TO THE NEXT chapter without a small parenthesis. I have spent almost two decades waiting for the familiar footsteps and ceremonious start of schooling of First Graders, and have got accustomed to a quiet life thereafter. But as you must have deduced by now, this year everything was different and our—we eight classrooms—erstwhile contemplations on the wreckage of education were instead now rallying around the humongous possibilities that school education presents. I cannot but proceed without taking you through the thrill experienced by Cuebee and her classmates on encountering the green chalkboard and being gifted textbooks. Why in the world had we not seen, or thought of, the huge impact that the combination of these two conventional tools of learning could have on young impressionable minds! Though this would imply going back in time, I have come to believe that it is always worthwhile to spend more time on great ideas, thoughts and expressions.

Most children in my class, including Cuebee, had come across a handheld slate with a wooden frame, used to write or draw. They would have had them in their homes. What they were not prepared for was the huge green-coloured chalkboard fixed at the centre of one wall in their classroom. For the first 2-3 weeks, there was a cloth carefully draped over the board. It had been newly fixed in the classroom. Eventually, one day, Butterfly Teacher removed the cloth, to reveal the smooth, flat, green board. There were four distinct stages in the progression and evolution of the kids' appreciation of what the chalkboard was about to do for their lives.

First was the deluge. When you are barely 3 feet tall, you are so conscious of things that appear larger than life, that being overwhelmed with the hugeness in green hanging over your heads must be a natural corollary. I would not be wrong in surmising that the kids were stunned to the extent that when they saw it for the first time, they perhaps felt a sense of being deprived of their human powers of locomotion and breathing for several moments! Next came the stage of curiosity and questioning. In the third stage, there was a general acceptance of its omnipresence. Finally, the thrill and excitement of the knowledge that their tiny hands could reach the board and chalk was available in joyous abundance. Thereafter, they seemed to be drawn to the board and were clear that it was sheer provocation at sight that compelled them to scribble their way into the very heart of the board.

The questions were interesting and came in droves.

'Why is it so big?'

'Will it fall if I touch it?'

'Why does it make that bad sound sometimes when you write?'

'Why does that sound make me uncomfortable?'

'Can you break the chalkboard into pieces to make slates for us?' This one from Millie.

'I saw a white-coloured board in the Grade 8 classroom. Will ours also turn white?'

'What will you do with the board?'

'Why is my slate at home black, this board green and the chalk white?' This last question was from Cuebee.

Butterfly Teacher surveyed her class without losing her composure. She had a look of unqualified admiration for the students' varying and intelligent questions as she began to address them one by one.

'It is big so that the whole class can see it, and it is fixed to the wall—so, no, it will not fall down. That screeching sound is due to Mr Friction. Now, how do I explain Mr Friction to you? Let me see. Friction is a force that does not want to allow movement of one solid thing over another. Did that help?'

'So, if I slip on a wet floor, does it mean that Mr Friction has gone missing?' asked an intrigued Cuebee.

'Well, yes, Cuebee, a wet and smooth floor has less friction as compared to a rough floor. Mr Friction actually slows down or sometimes even prevents movement.'

'Mr Friction is not nice?'

'Cuebee, without Mr Friction, you will not even be able to walk without slipping. Mr Friction is good for us.

'Maybe ...,' Cuebee conceded a bit, 'but all that screeching is really bad, Mr Friction. Are you listening!' Cuebee said raising her head as if to address the fictitious Mr Friction.

'I will try my best to not let Mr Friction make any sound. And Millie, you can work on your writing slates at home. If we break this board into pieces, how will all of you know what I am writing on my piece of slate? I am your teacher. All of you should be able to see at the same time what I am teaching on the board.'

'Hmm. That makes sense, Teacher,' Millie respectfully agreed.

The class was giggling and seemed to be enjoying the discussions. Statistically, we classrooms have estimated that at any point of time on the globe, there will be at least a few million teachers who would insist on giving an answer to a student's query, irrespective of their own limited knowledge or the correctness of their answer. But not so, in the case of Butterfly Teacher.

'Now about the colour of the slate, chalk and chalkboard ...,' the teacher turned towards Cuebee, shook her head with a grin and continued as if she was addressing adults and not a bunch of six-year-olds. 'Since I have never really thought or checked it out, I don't want to hazard a guess. Cuebee, I shall answer your question tomorrow. May I take it as my homework for today?'

'Yes Teacher, but please do not allow Mr Friction to stop you from looking for answers,' said Cuebee with a smirk.

The teacher who loved this kid and her attitude, broke into giggles herself.

Butterfly Teacher, as you might have already inferred, believed in turning every classroom situation into a random act of learning. The next day, armed with information and a thermos with hot tea, she decided to introduce a bit of chemistry laced with a dose of physics into the lives of these eager-beaver six-year-olds.

'I have done my homework. But before I tell you why the colours are different, I am going to tell you about the substance that all things are made of. By all things I mean everything that you see around you and everything else that you do not see too. It is called matter. Everything is made up of matter.'

'Are you and I made up of matter too, Teacher?' asked Cuebee.

'Yes, we are made up of matter too. Matter exists in three states, or you can say that it can be found only in three forms—solid, liquid and gas. This blackboard and chalk, us, the furniture here, all this is in solid state. They each have a shape of their own. You can hold them in your hands, if not too large.'

Then the teacher moved over to Millie's desk, took her water bottle, and said, 'The water inside this is in liquid state, and water can take the shape of the container it is poured into. You will not be able to hold liquid in your hands.'

'So, the rice that we have at lunch is solid, while the dal that is poured over it is liquid? Does that mean that anything you can pour is liquid?' Cuebee was just getting started.

'Yes, Cuebee. That's right.'

'Are my feelings liquid?' she asked.

'Why would you ask that?'

'Because my grandmother keeps telling me not to keep my feelings bottled up, but to always pour them out,' replied Cuebee.

'Well, that is a metaphoric way of speaking, Cuebee,' said the smart teacher.

'What is a metaphoric way?' Cuebee asked.

'Metaphoric comes from the word "metaphor". A metaphor is when you compare one thing with another, even if they have no similarity. For example, even though you are a human being and not a box, you are called Cuebee, a "Question Box".'

'Because I ask too many questions?'

'That's right. Another example of a metaphor is when we say that someone has solid ideas, which means good ideas. We also say that a dancer's body flows like a river, which means she has very graceful movements.'

'My father says that some people are full of gas,' interjected Zouzou.

Peals of laughter filled the air.

'Well, in a manner of speaking, it indicates that some people do empty talking, without having much knowledge.'

'Will I turn into liquid, Teacher?' Cuebee was perplexed.

'Cuebee, why did you ask that?'

'Because I have seen solid ice turn into liquid water,' replied Cuebee thoughtfully.

'No Cuebee, you will not. Water exists in all three states. But all matter does not exist in all three states.'

'So, will I always remain solid?'

'Yes Cuebee, always,' replied the teacher, much to the relief of the whole class. 'Now for the last state of matter,' continued the teacher as she opened her thermos. Hot vapour immediately floated out of the thermos. 'This is gas. It occupies the entire space available to it.'

The children clapped.

'So, what comes out of the pressure cooker while cooking is gas?'

'That's right, Cuebee.'

'And what about when we release the smell from our tummies?' asked Yoga.

'That is gas too,' said the teacher, suppressing a giggle.

'So poop is solid, pee is liquid, and the rest is gas!' said Yoga triumphantly as if he had won a race.

The class was by now making sounds of releasing gas from tummies with their mouths and was generally feeling on top of the charts of the happiness index. The teacher let them have their moment.

'Teacher, what does all this have to do with your homework?' Cuebee was uncontainable.

'I am getting there.' This was her cue to bring the class back from its state of complete distraction. 'Now the states of matter have certain observable properties, such as colour, shape, temperature like hot or cold, weight, texture, taste, etc. By observable, I mean, what you can see, feel, smell and taste.'

'Now I get it. Every solid has a colour. But water is colourless. Are all liquids colourless?' Cuebee was exploding with curiosity.

'And my tummy gas also has no colour. So, are all gases colourless?' asked Yoga.

'Water is colourless because it reflects light.'

'Reflects?'

'Yes, Cuebee. Now tell me, can you see anything in a dark room at night?'

'No.'

'But if there is light in a room at night, you can see. Right?'

'Yes, with light I can see everything.'

'Exactly. We can see objects only because of light. Light is made up of several colours. When the light falls on an object and the object reflects some of the colours of the light back or bounces it back into your eyes, you see that the object is made of those colours. In case of water, it bounces or reflects back all the colours of the light, and together these colours look white or colourless. But let's get back to the board and the chalk.'

'So, the chalk reflects back all colours of light, and does not keep back any—that is why it is white?' said, Cuebee with utter and sudden realization streaking across her face.

'And when an object keeps back all the light, or absorbs all the light, and reflects nothing back, you will see black colour,' the teacher added.

'That is why the slate is black!'

'Yes, and the green board is green because the porcelain enamel that it is made up of reflects the colour green.'

There was commotion in the class again.

'So, our uniform is blue, because it reflects blue light?'

'That's right.'

'And the leaves are green because they reflect green light?'

'Right again.'

'Teacher, I want to see the colours of light,' Cuebee requested and the whole class joined in to reinforce her request.

'Fine, let us do an experiment. Cuebee, please pour some water in the glass lying on my table. Millie, please get a sheet of white paper from the cupboard. And class, all of you come out in the corridor.'

Outside the classroom, Butterfly Teacher held the glass of water against the white sheet in such a manner that a direct beam of sunlight hit the glass. A rainbow of colours suddenly projected itself on the sheet of paper.

'I can see a rainbow.'

'Me too.'

'So many colours!'

'Yes, light is made up of seven colours—violet, indigo, blue, green, yellow, orange and red.'

All this excitement and noise, however, did not go unnoticed. Buddy Teacher came out of her classroom followed by her children, and then many others, including the Head Teacher, joined in. Butterfly Teacher showed the light to one excited kid after another from other grades too, while Cuebee and her classmates took over the job of explaining the business of colours and states of matter. Even the senior graders keenly listened to the tiny kids explain science to them as they peered at the sheet of paper. Some of them carried such awestruck expressions that I felt like they actually understood these concepts for the first time in their school journey!

Meanwhile, Alphabet Teacher, of the 'uncertain temper fame', watched the scene unfold through her sideways glance—a tactic she had perfected over years of practice. She did not, of course, participate, choosing instead to follow the activity through her classroom's window. Nor did she relent when her Grade 4 students requested for one look at the colours of light.

'Don't strain every nerve of yours for something you have already read in your books. All of you need to learn to discriminate between studies and distraction,' she demanded of the dejected students.

The next morning, Butterfly Teacher decided to introduce the tenets of 'democracy' when she began the use of the green chalkboard.

'Can all of you see the board clearly?' she asked.

'No,' said a few pained voices from the back rows.

'So, class, tell me, do you all have the right to see the board equally clearly?'

'Yes,' in unison.

'How do you think we can make it possible?'

'I can stand on my bench to see what you write,' BeeTee replied.

'Those of us who are taller can go sit in the back row,' Techie said.

'Can we rearrange the furniture to see what arrangement works best to view the board?' asked Cuebee.

And then, without waiting for a response, there was pandemonium! The screeching sound of furniture being moved combined with the ideas in the form of directions emanating in multiple voices felt like war cries in a battlefield. Unfazed by this testing experience, Butterfly Teacher raised her voice. The class and noise, both subsided.

'Please sit down and hear me out first. Let me help you with a better way of doing this. I will call out one name after the other, and each of you will stand up and share your idea on the seating arrangement. Then, we will decide on one, by putting all the ideas to vote.'

She went on to explain what she meant by vote and how voting could be done. She also introduced them to the concept of majority vote. Thereon, it went off very smoothly. Amongst several ideas, such as sitting in a circle, sitting in a square, shifting all furniture outside near the car, sitting on the floor, etc., Cuebee's and Geekay's idea of sitting in groups was voted as the best idea by a show of hands. After that, a systematic shifting of furniture was achieved within minutes by rallying off the quiet strength of the teacher's personality and her starry-eyed followers.

The new arrangement was different and certainly emboldening. The classroom furniture was grouped at five places for six children each to sit on, facing each other. There were two groups each along opposing walls and one against the wall connecting the two opposing walls at the far end of the class. Basically, the groups sat in a rectangular arrangement with one of the widths of the rectangle being occupied by the teacher's desk. It was only when the teacher began using the green chalkboard that I realized how strikingly convenient it was for all the students. There was a sort of flexi seating arrangement now—they could work together as a group and as soon as the teacher would use the board, they could simply turn and face the teacher. The chalkboard was now 'equally' visible to all. Why had no one thought of this before?

The introduction of the green chalkboard to the students in such a manner was a first for me. I was longing to share this experience with my classroom friends, but the day felt like it had forty-eight hours squeezed into it. As soon as we assembled that night, without waiting for any courtesies, I exploded with all the happenings of the day. Unsurprisingly, the classrooms heard me out with brick-drop silence, stupefied, but mostly admiringly.

Temporal: When you started out being so sunny and cheerful about a green board and chalk piece, I was ready to choke the cement out of you for disturbing my peace and quiet with trivialities. But this narration, my walled friend, makes you my universal favourite!

Frontal: And what does your universe consist of aside from us, the 300 children, eight teachers, the gardener, the Sports Teacher, the cook and the helper?

Temporal: My universe and favourites expand and constrict at will. *My* will. Presently, my universe is restricted to us eight classrooms and Cuebee, her teacher and her class.

Frontal: Oh well, then I am indeed honoured to be chosen as a favourite amidst such stalwarts, even if temporarily!

Parietal: They are stalwarts for sure! I am never much of a classroom anymore, until I have learnt a thing or two from Cuebee or Butterfly Teacher!

Occipital: Me too. I started out innocent and unversed in the possibilities in school education, and here I am, everyday pipped about hearing, seeing, experiencing and eagerly embracing this engaging form of learning.

Brainstem: It is all so intriguing. The teacher started with friction, went on to states of matter, took a digression for metaphors, and then proceeded to light, its colours and quality, and rounded off with an experiment, democratic values and sitting arrangements. When the class started, I felt that inducing learning on the colour of a board was too far-fetched! But now, it has rather endeared me towards learning!

Frontal: I am open to being corrected, but isn't that the first time you have ever acknowledged your lack of intellectual pursuits?

Brainstem: Being slow on the uptake is only an impression I like to give, so that it does not impact the self-esteem of the rest of us.

Frontal: Honoured to be the proud recipient of your impressions, but the truth in this case is surely stranger than 'friction'!

It was one of those bright and pleasant mornings, well into the fifth week of school, when a classroom wishes there was a cool breeze to gently touch it, and even sway the trees around in perfect unison with its thoughts, when I spotted Butterfly Teacher enter the school much earlier than the morning bell. She was trying to precariously balance two seemingly heavy cardboard boxes. She aimed straight for me and on reaching my space, landed the two boxes at her desk with a thump and a sigh of relief. Soon, the children began to pour into the room as the school started for the day. All eyes rested on the boxes and there were questions thrown around in all directions. The teacher and the taught were in perfect harmony, for the teacher wanted to evoke the classroom's inquisitive antennas and the students loved a good mystery. The teacher motioned the class to be seated and then carefully began removing the sticking tape from the mouth of the boxes. She removed several smaller packets from the box. She went from group table to group table and left six packets at each.

'Teacher, what is inside the packet?' asked Amla.

'Please pick one packet each and open it and see for yourself.'

'I think my packet has toys,' conjectured Jadoo, feeling the packet.

'Is it a box of crayons, Teacher?' asked Arty.

'Mine has three books!' declared Cuebee, who had by now unravelled the packet and thereby the mystery.

'Books! What will we do with these books?' Sky asked.

'These are called textbooks and we will read and learn from them. Children, how do you like your textbooks?'

A series of sideways head nods and a peculiar expression verging on cold reception on Cuebee's face diminished the enthusiasm of the teacher to a degree. However, she recovered herself with a question.

'What happened, Cuebee? Are you not excited to see textbooks? This is going to take you to an entire new world where you will learn about so many new things?'

'But Teacher, these books do not have many pictures. Does it have stories inside like the ones that my grandmother narrates to me every night?'

'Hmm. It does not exactly have stories, but then it has many other interesting things. Don't you want to explore?'

'I do. What can I explore here, Teacher?'

'These books will firstly help you to read, write and understand language and numbers, and thereafter, you can read many storybooks all on your own.'

'But without pictures, will I enjoy learning from them?'

'Well, not all books have pictures but most books are interesting because you get to learn from them.'

'Who writes these books, Teacher?' asked Cuebee, a small smile tugging at the corners of her mouth.

'Well, people who can read and write well are the ones that end up writing books.'

'If I explore these books, will I be able to write books too?' asked Cuebee anxiously, her mind occupied with the future operation of storybook writing.

'Of course, Cuebee. You will be able to do several different things if you are able to read and write. For example, read all the good storybooks under the sun, read about science, history, our village, our country, write in newspapers, teach, and so much more.'

'Teacher, I think I am going to write interesting books with lots of pictures once I learn how to read and write.'

'Oh, that would be wonderful,' exclaimed the teacher with a dewy look. The world would certainly be a better place because the likes of Cuebee would be in-charge.

While the teacher had proceeded to establish the foundations of literacy with such extraordinary delight, she had clearly sensed the less than enthusiastic response of the class. She adjourned for a bit and ran to meet the Head Teacher for advice.

'Perish the thought that every incident or event in your classroom is going to end up as a stirring adventure for your students,' said the Head Teacher thoughtfully.

Butterfly Teacher paused for a moment and said, 'But if I am not able to generate enough interest in textbooks, then I consider it my shortcoming.'

'As long as you continue to do teaching and learning differently, it will not be futile. You shall see for yourself.'

Of the aforesaid pronouncement by the Head Teacher, what rekindled Butterfly Teacher's faith in herself were his words: 'continue to do teaching and learning differently'. She returned jubilant to the classroom and announced that the children deserved a trip to the school library, so they could learn about the several kinds of books that existed, which were only waiting to be read by them. She marched the children into the staff room where six tall steel cupboards alongside one wall held all the school's library books.

In the library, Butterfly Teacher took out several picture books and gave one each to each child. Her efforts to correct the effects of the new textbooks bore fruit. The students were wondrously flipping through the books. She had got back the undivided and curious attention of her class!

'Be kind to books. Make them worthy of your affections. Let us all be careful not to tear or spoil the books by scribbling on them. That is how class after class gets a chance to read all the books.'

'Can I keep this book, Teacher?' asked Cuebee.

'You cannot keep it, but you can borrow it.'

'Borrow it?'

'Yes, you can take the book for some time, but not keep it for always.'

'So, can I take it home?'

'Yes, you can. In fact, all of you can take one book home at a time. The library is meant for lending books that you can borrow.'

'Like I lend my crayons to Sky?' Arty asked.

'Like you borrowed my grandma the other day to tell a story in the class?' asked Cuebee.

'Oh yes. Both of you have understood it perfectly,' said the teacher clapping her hands in sheer joy.

That day, when Grandma came to pick up Cuebee after school, Cuebee was skipping around her and narrating the events of the day.

'I am going to write books, Grandma!'

'What kind of books? In what language? You will have to help me brush up my reading skills once you learn yourself, so that I can read books authored by you.' The ripening years had neither mellowed Grandma nor robbed her of her taste for newness.

'I will write storybooks with lots of colourful pictures, but I don't know in which language. Are there other languages too, Grandma?'

'Yes, my darling, there are many, many languages.'

'So, everyone does not speak as we do?'

'No, they don't.'

'Does that mean most people will not read the books I write?' Cuebee felt as if the fire that had erupted in her belly was about to be doused.

'No, that is certainly not the case. If your book is very interesting, then it can be translated into several different languages.'

Cuebee clapped. The flame within her had sparked again and attained heights.

Frontal: Today, the teacher distributed textbooks to the class, but Cuebee was not very happy with them initially.

Temporal: I thought the advent of any new thing alleviates the mood of children like nothing else.

Frontal: I thought so too, but she said the textbooks were not appealing as they were not splashed with pictures and did not have stories in them.

Brainstem: And why not? What meets the eye when you open one? Alphabets, words, sentences, questions and a few pictures, repeatedly, page after page. I have always wondered how children relieve the tedium of a textbook.

Hippocampus: Exactly! Why only academic stuff? How about DIYs, interesting knick-knacks, humour, jokes, riddles, anecdotes, stories, cartoons, projects, experiments, connections with other topics and subjects?

Occipital: But can everything to be taught be converted into a story or a joke or a project for that matter?

Temporal: Textbooks are essential. Fanned by their systematic layout, topic by topic, they have a soothing effect on the nerves of Teachers. It's because of textbooks that our Teachers know exactly what to do to earn their job satisfaction. How else does a teacher estimate what to teach students in a given year?

Frontal: The cooperation between textbook and teacher is notable, but it does not necessarily draw engagement of the student. Have you not noticed in so many years that happiness does not reign supreme in a class that is attempting to finish a textbook from the beginning to the end!

Parietal: Well, let us not be in a hurry to write away textbooks. Whatever else they may be, textbooks cannot be considered negligible in terms of value addition to the teaching–learning process.

Frontal: For some unexplained reason, I get the feeling that Butterfly Teacher is about to teach us a lesson or two in combining Cerebellum's knick-knacks and Amygdala's essentialism in a manner not achieved so far in the history of our school. And I am sure Cuebee shall have a role to play in it.

Parietal: You, my friend, are in love!

I have already taken you on a journey of how my favourite class learnt the alphabet and words through phonics. It all seemed so natural, and the whole system seemed to have a positive impact. When it came to sentences, Butterfly Teacher introduced the textbook. The less-than-amicable visuals of the textbooks were no deterrence to the determined teacher. In fact, she mitigated this absence with the help of music and dance. Inspired by a popular Bollywood song, she put to music the first set of six sentences made up of two syllables each in the textbook and got the whole class on their feet to follow her choreography. This was regarded with highly mixed feelings by the class though, and more so by Cuebee and her band of friends.

'My father told me that school is for studying. Why should we learn dance and music?' Techie's outburst represented the sum total of the aforementioned mixed feelings.

'Good question,' said the teacher without batting an eyelid. 'These things are necessary for growing children as they increase our fine and gross motor skills. Concentration, self-expression and, sounds and movement together help in establishing connections between our body and mind.'

'What are fine and gross motor skills, Teacher?' Cuebee detached herself from the group dance to pose this question.

'When you use the larger parts of your body, to, say, jump, run, exercise, walk, then you are using your gross motor skills.

When you use the finer aspects of your body to perform very focused tasks, such as stitching, eating, drawing, tying shoe laces, pushing buttons through button holes, then you are using your fine motor skills.'

'So, when I twirl, I am using my gross motor skills, but when I make gestures with my fingers, I am using fine motor skills?'

'That's right.'

'And why do I need to establish a connection between my body and mind?' Cuebee pursued.

By now, the whole class was in rapt attention, soaking up the conversation between Butterfly Teacher and Cuebee, interspersing it with wondrous sighs.

'How you feel, think and sense through your mind is connected to how your body functions or feels. All of us need to be aware of it. It helps us have a good balance in our health and outlook.'

'What if the mind is not liking what the body is doing?' Cuebee asked.

'That will create an imbalance and may stress you out.'

'Teacher, my mind is not liking this song and dance that we are doing.' Cuebee could hold back no longer.

'I too find it a little boring,' Techie chimed in.

'Tell me, what can we do to correct that feeling,' Butterfly Teacher asked in her singularly democratic fashion.

'Teacher, why can't we kids decide the dancing steps on the words that you are teaching?' Cuebee's question took her teacher by complete surprise.

'Oh, would you like to choreograph your own dance? That would be lovely!'

'Yes, Teacher!' Everybody joined in with gusto to add force to this affirmation.

The kids ploughed their way through a series of words and sentences and choreographed their own dances that would explain the sentence through gestures and expressions. The fun quotient of this exercise was sky-high, and Butterfly Teacher could not help but feel relieved that she was able to channel their incessant energies in a constructive manner.

But this was not the high that you might suppose it was. The high point was when the children began devising their own poems too, egged on by Millie. Her first instant poem was an instant hit!

Cuebee, Techie, kahan chali,
Jhund banakar kahan chali.
Merey ghar bhi aao na,
Pani puri khao na.
Chalo baithe hum chatai par,
Aur gup karein hum patar patar.

The kids soon discovered that the world could be full of poetry, and they are meant to be put to tune, and the only task of all rhyming verses is to be unobtrusively danceable.

For several days thereafter, every parent's question about the learnings at school that day was met with an enthusiastic 'oh, we danced today!' The whole world of learning seemed to have changed for them. It was as if their bodies were experiencing happiness in sync with their minds. Life may be complicated and perfection may be difficult to attain for many, but that was not so for this tiny school of ours tucked away in an ordinary village. We, classrooms, were witnesses for the first time in two decades, to true happiness and the ultimate balance between mind and body!

4

Clay, three legs and storytelling

THE SCHOOL WAS BUZZING WITH ACTIVITY THE PAST FEW months and had but one subject of conversation, or conflict, curiosity, argument, protest, criticism, distraction or delight—the car. The senior grade teachers had become adept at faking classroom discussions on the car, without really meaning to achieve any learning goals, to the utter confusion of their students. The students were going along for the sake of going along, nothing more. The option of not doing so was not really something these students were conditioned to explore. The junior-grade teachers on the other hand had combined forces to dissect the car—literally and enthusiastically—and integrate it in their teaching of language as well as mathematics and science. The Head Teacher was acutely aware of the machinations at every level. He, however, displayed neither animosity nor affection towards any of the teachers. The equitability of his interactions with all teachers in fact led each one of them to believe that they were for sure in his good books, if not his good library.

Dissent always finds a way of brewing itself, for it probably belongs to the category of emotions that can overwhelm all others simply by falling in the company of co-dissenters. The senior grade teachers were often found huddled together in some less-visited corner of the school, expressing their defiance in hushed undertones. Classrooms would enact their caustic conversations verbatim in our nocturnal meetings.

'Did you see the noticeboard?'

'If I see one more notice for a staff meeting, I may have to let loose the monster in me!'

'Well then, it's time.'

'For what?'

'To let loose the monster in you. The Head Teacher has called for a staff meeting next week.'

'I wonder what degenerate idea he will come up with this time?'

'He thinks he is rendering a service to mankind, by swaying from the well-established methods of teaching and learning.'

'Yeah, we were taught exactly in this way in school, and who can doubt our capabilities.'

'He too must have been taught like we teach, and it made him the Head Teacher, didn't it?'

'Something serious is amiss in his world. Either he and his spouse spar with each other every morning before school or he is just a chronic grouch.'

If the senior grade teachers had their way, they would have probably straightened up the junior-grade teachers, ensured discipline of the pin-drop-silence kind in the school, and banished the car along with Head Teacher from the school campus for all time to come!

Butterfly Teacher, Buddy the Teacher and the Grade 2 teacher, aptly named Rainbow Teacher by Grade 1 students, had realized that there was common ground among them and that their hides were yet to be hardened with cynicism. They were keen to entertain all of the Head Teacher's bright ideas with an open-minded and indulgent approach embellished with warm regards. Seeing the success of engaging the children in learning through different stimulations, such as the car, the three had decided to have at least one unstructured hour in each of their classrooms every day to the sheer delight of the children.

Butterfly Teacher would have storytelling sessions from volunteer parents and grandparents, role plays by children around situations devised by her, oratory by children on any topic of their liking, learning gardening from the school gardener, and so on. Even the Sports Teacher was cajoled by the kids one day to give the outdoors a miss and tell a story around the characters chosen impromptu by them—a *kaan khajura*, a snake, a buffalo and a monkey—with the Sports Teacher himself as the central character. The kids, and to his own utter surprise, the Sports Teacher, discovered his brilliant storytelling or rather story-weaving skills, with the active contribution of the audience. His story went somewhat this way:

'The Sports Teacher of the animal school was issuing sports shoes to all the animals. He had only four pairs. First, the monkey came and left with one pair of shoes. Next, the buffalo arrived and was issued two pairs. Finally, when the centipede came, the Sports Teacher told him that he was lucky as the snake did not need shoes and therefore, he had one pair left.

But the centipede argued.

'I need more than one pair or I will have to run barefoot.'

'Well, I have only one pair left. Why don't you wear shoes only on your front feet, so that the rest of the feet can then get pulled along?"

The centipede was very sporty. He loved the idea and was willing to try it.'

The Sports Teacher stopped narrating at this point and asked the children a couple of questions.

'What games or activities do you think these four animals can play or do together? And what is it that they can't do together?'

'They cannot do a three-legged race for sure,' Cuebee said.

'And they cannot climb trees.'

'Perhaps they can play hide-and-seek.'

'Yes, but they definitely cannot swim together.'

'And they can play catch-catch.'

'So, even though each animal is differently enabled, there are some common activities that they can do. Right?' asked the Sports Teacher.

'Yes Teacher!'

'Do you think a team like this, with different abilities, would be useful in a crisis?'

'We don't know, Teacher.'

'Fine, then let's contemplate on a problem and let's find out if there is a solution that these four animals can bring about together. What if a woodcutter decided to cut down the trees in the forest where these animals lived, where the forest was already thinning down?'

'Teacher, the snake will keep the woodcutter away.'

'Amazing answer! And the monkey will spread the seeds that stick to its limbs by jumping from place to place; the buffalo's poop is a nutrient for the soil; and the centipede will eat up all the locusts that destroy trees. This way the forest gets a chance to regenerate. So, what does this story tell you?'

'Every animal has different abilities.'

'All animals are useful.'

'I like this team. I also want a team of different classmates when we try to solve a problem.'

'It must be like this in humans too. We all must have different abilities.'

There couldn't have been a better way of getting across the idea of inclusion at such an early stage for these children!

Meanwhile, Butterfly Teacher insisted that interacting with new people, and group and individual presentations before the whole class, were essential for developing listening and communication skills. Cuebee discovered the joyous moments of plant germination from a seed and related every bit of her experience of the 'birth of a plant' to the whole class in detail. Techie had the class in fits when she described how she opened up the radio at her home to look for the person speaking from inside. Millie sang a poem of her own making about nature. Geekay informed the class about his observations of ants and how they work so hard just to carry one grain of sugar. Cuebee's grandmother narrated to an enthralled classroom the story of a king from long ago, who won back his kingdom through his genius rather than through war. Arty's mother, a nurse in the nearby Primary Health Centre, interacted with the class on the need for self-hygiene and public hygiene. The active minds of the children would remain occupied with so many different forms of stirrings that their energy levels seemed to have doubled beyond repair.

The Head Teacher had indeed called for a staff meeting, and the Teachers knew better than to expect monotony in these meetings. Even in the face of unending deficiencies that the Head Teacher presumably possessed, that is, if one were to believe the senior grade teachers, his meetings were always extremely democratic. Whatever turbulence of mind or mettle one might be experiencing at that point of time, they had the right to speak, as much, or as approximately, in all meetings chaired by him.

'I am keen to actively engage with parents in the education of their children,' he started. 'It is very important for parents to know about the desired learning levels and where their children actually stand. Therefore, let us arrange a parent–teacher meeting—a PTM—where we will have a workshop-cum-demo for parents.'

'But sir, most of the parents are illiterate. We cannot get across to them; it will be a complete waste of time,' was the quick argument of the Language Teacher.

'The very fact that a parent has decided to send their child to school goes to show that they understand the criticality and far-reaching impact of education, and it also implies that they have certain expectations from the school.' The Head Teacher loved a good argument.

The Maths Teacher knew that the Head Teacher could only be won over with logic. 'Illiterate parents won't be able to help their children and educated parents will teach children in a manner that is different from how we teach them. *That*, sir, is a recipe for confounding the children,' she said, while seemingly occupied with an intriguing maths puzzle.

'In any case, parents hardly even join the regular PTMs. Why would they willingly plunge into one where we inform them about all the additional work they have to do with their kids at home,' the Science Teacher was emphatic.

'Think of the child. Think of the parents' need to see progress in their child's learning levels. Put the two together and viola, it amounts to a good parent–teacher workshop,' said Rainbow Teacher vigorously, for she could no longer keep herself away from the developing argument.

'It's alright for you to think so. Teaching Grade 3 is no great shakes. Tell a few stories, play catch-catch and you are done for the day. We in the senior grades have to toil to complete the textbooks. Think of us,' said the Language Teacher as if coming back to life from the pages of history, with a start.

'Had we not worked on their literacy and numeracy skills, how would you have taught them literature—or for that matter anything?' Buddy Teacher wanted to be in her own good books by standing up to such stuff and nonsense.

The Head Teacher was democratic, but only to a point. Beyond that, he just relied on his own seniority and the authority that accompanies such a status, to take decisions unilaterally. Therefore, without receding from his initial position, he solemnly continued as if he had not heard any of the burning arguments in between his last sentence and the one that was forthcoming.

'It is our responsibility to involve parents and guide them to be part of the school and the learning path of their children. I can give you multiple examples in many of the schools of this district where the interventions of parents have resulted in high achievement of their children. I insist on the involvement of the whole family.'

'The business of education, undoubtedly, is turning out to be a series of compromises,' Alphabet Teacher muttered under her breath and was almost about to deliver her signature stomping-out-of-rooms-and-situations, when a senior grade student came running to the staff room, informing of the commotion at the school gate as the 'police are here and they are asking for the Head Teacher'.

The Head Teacher, strangely unperturbed at the prospect of rack and ruin at the hands of the police, left immediately but not without giving a parting shot.

'So, we shall have a PTM next Saturday, in a new and engaging format. Prepare well. We must not disappoint the parents.'

Alphabet Teacher was brimming with the news of the police party and perhaps already imagining the crimes that the Head Teacher may have committed—swindling, cheating, burglary—leading to his 'timely' departure from the 'business of education.' She decided to skip her class to watch, for she, I presume, may have been engulfed by the desire to cheer the process of arrest and humiliation that was about to be exhibited for the first time on the school precincts.

At the gate stood a tall and trim young man in uniform, rather well groomed, conveying courage and confidence in the most subtle of manners. He was flanked by three other policemen, with gazes transfixed on their superior in wonderment at what could have brought him to a school teeming with juveniles and harmless teachers. The Head Teacher reached the site of commotion, and his eyes travelled straight to the tallness and trimness that stood before him. They both smiled and suddenly with the swiftness of a breeze, the Head Teacher went forward and hugged him. To a biased eye, it may have appeared to be an act of begging for forgiveness for multiple crimes committed but, in fact, it was an act loaded with warmth and love. Shortly after, the young man in uniform managed to extricate himself from the tight hug, and dove down to touch the Head Teacher's feet. Hundreds of pairs of eyes that were watching this spectacle were struggling against the conviction that if not crime, what really had the teacher gotten himself into.

'I was passing through and when I came to know that you are the Head Teacher here, I could not help myself from seeing you.'

'I am so glad for that. Come on in. Let me show you around and introduce you to the children.'

'That was my intention,' the young man said in all gladness.

As they walked towards the classrooms, the police officer felt two tiny sets of hands materializing in his. He felt a mini presence, one each on either side of him. He looked surprised at the two kids who had voluntarily lent their hands to him. They happened to be Cuebee and BeeTee.

'Are you my guides for today? Will you show me around?'

'No. We just want to make you comfortable so that you are not scared.'

'Why would I be scared?' he said with a laugh.

'Because almost everyone is scared on their first day at school,' Cuebee said earnestly.

He was struck with amazement and mirth, but he exhibited only the former emotion in deference to the two kids, and thanked them profusely for taking such good care of him.

Meanwhile, the Head Teacher introduced him to the Teachers who had collected in the corridor, few with curled lips, some out of curiosity, and others out of reverence.

'Meet the new Superintendent of Police of our district. He was my student in one of the schools where I served for ten years.'

'Sir, I see you have graduated to a car now. In our time, it was an old TV, a motorcycle and a music tape player,' said the police officer surveying the playground.

'You remember that?'

'Sir, that is what made learning so fascinating for me. I can never forget how you made school the most exciting place for us kids.'

The officer spent close to two hours at school that day, chatting with the children and answering all their questions.

'What are those stars on your shoulders?'

'Where is your gun?'

'How many criminals do you catch every day?'

'Do you chase them on foot?'

'What food do you eat?'

'Can you do somersaults?'

'My parents force me to eat green vegetables every day. Can you please arrest them?'

'What colour is your uniform?'

'Khaki? Is that a colour or the name of your pet?'

'Are thieves scared of you?'

'What are you scared of?'

The Teachers, particularly those teaching the senior grades, cowered beneath their skin, feeling somewhat mortified but chiefly ridiculous, for whatever else they may have expected, they had not expected the senior-most policeman of the district to find the Head Teacher not only palatable but worth admiring. They probably put it down to flippancy of the district's law and order administration or just a disagreeable episode, because soon they left the common area and went their way to begin preparations, whatever little, for a PTM that was not really a PTM in the true sense of the word.

After one week, Butterfly Teacher gave invitation letters to the children and explained, 'Even though school is closed tomorrow, being a weekend, we will have a PTM and all of you should come with your parents. We are going to have a lot of fun.'

'But Teacher, Amla's elder brother is in Grade 4. He told us that parents are called by class Teachers in these meetings to complain about us. How can that sound like fun?' Yoga was sincerely unable to fathom.

'But our class is different, and I am not the complaining type. In fact, I have planned something special that all of you would love.'

'Is it a game, Teacher?' Millie was piqued.

'You shall see and experience for yourself tomorrow,' the teacher informed them with a mysterious twinkle in her eye.

'Can I also bring my grandmother?' asked an over-excited Cuebee.

'That is a great idea, Cuebee. Of course, you can. If any of you also want to bring your grandparents or siblings, you are most welcome.'

The class burst into loud cheer and excitement even though the combination of parents, grandparents and fun did seem a bit odd to some of the kids.

We classrooms met briefly that night. Most of us spoke eloquently but with a sense of intrigue about the ongoing preparations by carefully avoiding the subject of the simmering clash of views and personalities amongst the teachers. Hitherto, we had been completely sheltered from the possibilities that a PTM could present. To us, PTMs represented the most unpromising of developmental material for the kids, and parents were just adjuncts who appeared and disappeared at rapid pace during these meetings. But people, places and things were changing. Our precincts were about to experience a curated and garnished PTM, something of which we had not the remotest idea. We awaited the assemblage and assortment the next day with open doors and windows.

Despite the instructions, some Teachers decided to continue with the routine PTM. In this format, the parents enter the classroom with their child in tow and in pleasant expectation. The teacher is seated behind a sheaf of papers looking her formidable best. Before the parents can be seated or get comfortable, the teacher blurts out a series of problems and challenges related to their child and sums it up with the infeasibility of imparting education to such a child. Throughout this performance, the parents assuage their guilt at not taking better care of studies at home by staring hard and unblinkingly at the child, while the child in turn looks askance at the teacher, wondering all the time whether she really is such a beastly, uncouth and uncivilized learner. The parents leave the classroom thoroughly disappointed in their offspring, while the child's self-esteem hits rock bottom. And then this whole performance is repeated for the next combination of parents and child. It is a simple system, no complications, and one-sided, therefore very easy to execute.

But I really do not want to focus here on those who take their own protesting sweet time to adjust to the changing environment. While a couple of teachers appeared to be brooding over the mortality of the erstwhile PTMs, others seemed optimistic and wedded to the new art and design they had created for the day. We classrooms were delighted to see that these teachers made varying degrees of efforts to make this PTM more engaging for the parents. As Cuebee and her schoolmates began pouring into the school that day with their families, I could, even at a distance, catch their exhilarated anticipation. Some of the teachers stood just outside their respective classrooms to welcome them.

Butterfly Teacher was particularly genial that day; she had planned for it meticulously. As parents, grandparents and siblings streamed into her class, they noticed the six glasses arranged in a circle containing a liquid each in different colours, placed on a table just outside my door.

'What is that supposed to be?' Cuebee's grandmother could not contain her curiosity.

'Oh, that is water walking from one glass to the other,' Cuebee replied.

'Water flows, it does not walk, Cuebee.'

'Let me explain, Grandma. This is an experiment we did.'

'What is an experiment?'

'It is a way of learning science through conducting tests, and I love it.'

'What test did you do?'

'We took six glasses, poured clear water in three glasses, red dye in one glass of water, blue in another and yellow in the last. Then we arranged them alternately in a circle, one clear-water glass and one-coloured water. Then we made bridges between the glasses by putting folded paper towels to connect two neighbouring glasses on both sides of the glass.'

'And then?'

'And then this is what happened. The coloured water walked over the bridge and went into the clear water.'

'So, this is science?'

'No. This is what we call observation. The science behind it is called capillary movement, and we are going to learn about it next week.'

While Cuebee was intently explaining all this, her parents and several others had joined Grandma and were ceaselessly emanating sounds of fascination in the form of 'oohs' and 'aahs' at the whole experiment idea.

'She is my daughter,' said Cuebee's mother, swimming in the ocean of pride, pointing out at her from the midst of the crowd. All heads turned approvingly towards the glorious mother who had given birth to a child who knew all about walking-water!

The parents also noticed several kitchen utensils, ceramic bowls, pans, plates, spoons, earthen pots, tin storage boxes, etc., lined up neatly outside my space in the corridor. They were naturally curious. At last, Butterfly Teacher rounded them up and requested them to walk into my space and be seated anywhere they wished. After a warm and cheerful welcome, she explained to the expectant audience the details of the PTM she had planned.

'I have planned several activities for you and your children together.'

'But how are these activities going to tell me what Techie is really up to in school? Yesterday, she opened up the entire plumbing in the house. Is she learning all that here in school?' piped up Techie's father.

Butterfly Teacher was used to dealing with these fast-paced deliveries and had a knack for fielding them.

'Techie is a curious child like every other child of her age, and I am so glad you as parents indulge her curiosity. This is what shall build her character as she grows up, but do guide her around the house.' Techie's father, on hearing about his larger-than-life role in building a strong character for his daughter, fell silent and was congenial for the rest of the day at school.

'We are doing these activities to help you understand what they have learnt so far, how kids learn best through play at this age, and how important it is for them to get exposed to a variety of stimulation even in their home environment.'

'Are you giving our parents homework, Teacher?' asked Imli hopefully.

'Well Imli, I am sort of giving them ideas for building a learning environment at home.' She paused for a bit and then said, 'I guess you could call it homework for them.'

Everyone laughed and relaxed.

'So, let's all go to the playground together and start the day,' Butterfly Teacher said.

'The meeting is in the playground?'

'Well, a meeting of sorts shall take place in the playground. There are many activities that children and their family members can choose from; however, some activities will be common for all.'

'What type of activities are there? We did not come prepared. I really cannot run around in these shoes.' One of the mothers expressed her concern at what seemed to be developing into classwork as well for the parents.

'Perish all your doubts, please. These activities do not require any kind of preparation. We have clay dough, fireless cooking, some games and picture-matching activities planned for you; and for those of you who are up to it, we even offer a three-legged race with your child for you. The icing on the cake is that your child can help you choose the activities and who among the family members shall join her for those activities. You can do one, two or all of them. Trust me, you shall not be squandering your energies in aimless pursuit. In fact, it would be rather invigorating.'

'Teacher says we are learning all the time while doing activities and playing games. Mother, you will also learn something new today. Come with me,' said the child of the doubting mother, pulling her away towards my exit to proceed to the playground.

At the playground, after assuring all parents that her aid and presence was at hand, Butterfly Teacher explained the activities.

'In the fireless cooking area, a mix of ingredients shall be available. As a team, you and your child shall have to prepare something that is of high nutritional value and creative, without too much wastage, and in a neat and clean manner. You can help your child understand the nutritive values. When the Head Teacher or any of the other parents or I visit you, your child has to narrate and present the recipe and how it is good for the body.

'For the three-legged race, one leg each of the parent and the child shall be tied together. You succeed in the race if you plan out and coordinate the run well. Once you reach the other end, you pick up a number slip from the basket lying there. Your child has to pick up that many pebbles from the same basket and place them in the cloth bag lying next to the basket along with the number slip. That will help you understand your child's numeracy skills. You return the same way and reach back to where you started along with the cloth bag, as that also happens to be the finishing line.

'At the clay-making area, children and parents are free to make objects of their choice but after completing that, the child also has to make alphabets of her name and her participating parent's name from clay.

'In the picture-reading area, you will find lots of letters inside a box. Exhibit each picture to your child. Your child should then name the picture and make the spelling from the letters available in the box.

'There is a storytelling corner inside the classroom. As soon as you finish your activities, you can go back there. We will have a draw of lots and the name picked in the draw shall have to tell a story to the whole class. Parents and grandparents, please be prepared.'

Alphabet Teacher had been stealing sideways glances at the goings-on in the playground from her classroom window, while grilling parents and children in her fire. 'When my time comes as class teacher of these kids, I shall teach these ignoramuses a thing or two about real education. Until then, patience, please help me,' she said to herself as she took this decision, whose ramifications were to be felt acutely, though a little later.

As for Grade 1 students, it was as if the entire day was constructed exactly as per the specifications laid down by them. In situations that may have overwhelmed many other kids in the school, these little ones were all fleetness, briskness and dispatch.

'Which activity would you like to do, and who would you like to do it with?' Cuebee's ever-curious grandma said.

'I want to do all the activities, one with Mother, one with Grandma, one with Father and one together as a family. I will go for the three-legged race with Mother, clay making with Father, fireless cooking with Grandma; and we will do picture reading together.'

Cuebee's response echoed the standard response of all the children. All children ensured that their families participated in all activities with them.

'What will we make from clay?' her father said.

'We will make an ocean full of fishes and plants.'

The spirits of Cuebee's mother, a lively lady in her late thirties, dainty, yet a picture of good health, soared unstoppably. 'Come on, let's go for the three-legged game first.' Cuebee and family happily ran towards the scene of action.

After an almost intoxicating couple of hours of games and fun, the children began strutting back to class with their families, though in instalments. Whatever else the activities may have been, there was no doubt that for most parents it was love at first sight of this methodology of learning. They now had a fair idea of what their children had learnt in school so far. They were bustling with ideas about how they would soon be transforming their homes as a play and learning space based on the inspiring turn of events in the PTM.

'I shall no longer count the clothes being returned by the *dhobi* after ironing. My daughter shall.'

'I am going to teach my son how to clean and cut vegetables.'

'My daughter can read. Now she will read all the wrappers of packed food items, and understand their content. Perhaps, I can also learn a thing or two.'

'My son shall help me prepare grocery lists before I go shopping for them.'

'I am thinking of devising a treasure hunt of letters written on paper chits that I can hide in the house in different places. And we could form words with all the letters found in one minute.'

'I never realized learning could be such fun. I want to become a child again!'

Short of yelling each other down with their novel ideas, the parents behaved exactly as if it were their first day at school. Though Butterfly Teacher did add herself to the audience for a moment, the commotion called for a cease-and-desist order.

'I can sense the thrill that all of you have just experienced, but it is time now for storytelling.' She spoke with firmness and authority.

The class went quiet. She had that effect on them, but only summarily.

'What will my child learn from storytelling? It is just a piece of fiction after all.' One of the parents speculated audibly.

'Storytelling shall spark your child's imagination and curiosity, and also help her develop the ability to focus or concentrate. And if she is telling the story, then nothing better than that to develop her communication skills as well.' Butterfly Teacher was adept at fielding all googlies.

'Teacher, who will tell us a story today?'

'Here is the box containing names of all parents and grandparents on paper slips. Yoga, come here. Pick one slip.' Yoga did the needful.

'The name on this slip is that of Cuebee's grandma.' The announcement was greeted with loads of clapping and a ten-second wiggly dance performance by Cuebee and Yoga.

Grandma was taken completely unawares. But the good sport that she was, she got up from her seat and walked towards the front of my room with folded hands.

'I am only semi-literate, therefore do bear with my methodology of telling a story,' she addressed the adults in the room.

'Storytelling is an art and no one does it better than my mother-in-law,' beamed Cuebee's mother, once again staking claim for all the inspirational talent that her family members were blessed with.

'I couldn't agree more. Do go ahead Ma'ji,' Butterfly Teacher said.

'Parents and children, today I am going to tell you a story of four friends. Children, you decide and tell me the characters who will play the four friends,' Grandma started.

'A deer.'

'A crow.'

'A mole.'

'A tortoise.'

The children swiftly chose and Grandma developed her story around them as she spoke with immense poise.

'A deer, a crow, a mole and a tortoise were the best of friends in a green and lush forest. You must be thinking that they are so different, how could they be friends. Their colour, shape, structure, walking style, eating style, everything is different. But they were indeed very good friends because they believed very strongly that these differences were only superficial. It is the meeting of minds and hearts that is important. So, they would meet each other every day at sunrise under a banyan tree, and over time their bonding became very strong.

'One day, the crow, mole and tortoise reached the banyan tree at the usual time but there was no sign of the deer. They waited for a while but as the day progressed, they began to worry about the deer not showing up. They discussed and decided that the crow should go look for the deer.

'The crow flew over the trees peeking below at the ground, and soon he found the deer trapped in a hunter's net near the lake. The deer too spotted the crow hovering above and informed him that the hunter was about to come back, hence there was no time and no way to escape. The crow told him not to lose hope and flew speedily back to his friends.

'He described the whole scenario to them. They thought about it a bit. They realized that though the deer had thirty-two teeth, the front portion of his upper jaw had no teeth, like any other typical herbivore. He certainly could not cut the net with his mouth. Hence, the mole knew exactly what he had to do. He asked the crow to pick him up and grip him with his beak and take him to the deer. The two then asked the tortoise to reach there and after reaching, his only job would be to somehow alert them if he saw the hunter approaching.

'As soon as the crow and the mole reached the spot where the deer was trapped, the mole began to diligently cut the net with his teeth. Moles have several types of teeth like us humans. Their incisors are pointy and sharp and the incisors in their upper jaw are rather long. Their canines and molars are used for cutting and chewing their prey. They have a total of forty-four teeth.

'While the mole was busy breaking, chewing and cutting the net, the tortoise stood guard at a distance looking for any signs of the hunter. When the net was almost cut, the tortoise noticed the hunter moving towards the deer. He quickly alerted his friends and attempted to distract the hunter. It was a huge risk he took for his friends, but as soon as the hunter began to stealth towards him, the tortoise glided into the lake. Meanwhile, the deer got free and scampered away, the mole hid himself by burrowing in the soil and the crow flew away.

'The next day the four friends met as usual at sunrise and expressed their happiness at getting back together again and thanked each other profusely for taking care of each other.

'And that is the end of the story, So, children, now tell me, what did you learn from it?'

'We must help each other.'

'Nobody is big or small. Even a small mole could help the larger deer.'

'Every friend has a unique quality and is different from us. We must respect our differences.'

'Forty-four teeth can fit even in a small body.'

'Hunting is bad for the animals.'

'If our friend does not come to school on any day, we must go and check if the friend is alright.'

'During a crisis, every friend can play a different role in accordance with their abilities.'

'During a crisis, the kind of teeth you have can be crucial. Therefore, know your teeth.'

'Animals too have intelligence. We should respect them.'

The effect of the story was magical. Butterfly Teacher and Grandma were overjoyed to hear the observations of both the students and their family members. As the PTM was drawing to a close, the parents felt that they had just been through the proceedings of a day that was very well spent. Now that they were enabled to have a much closer, pleasanter and exceptional look at the whole teaching–learning process of their children, they had begun to notice the smaller as well as the larger details. They were consumed by their free and unbridled power of parental concerns leading to a volley of unaddressed questions.

'Shall we also spin stories like Grandma did, or should we be reading out stories to them from books?'

'My daughter loves the work you are doing with the children through the medium of the car outside. Why don't you take a class or two for us parents too on the parts of the car?'

'How do we satisfy our children's curiosity, if we do not know the answers?'

'I am not good at devising new games every day. How do I follow this method?'

Butterfly Teacher's face was a study of amazement mingled with admiration of the unfettered enthusiasm among the school's most important stakeholders. She requested the parents earnestly for active engagement in their children's cognitive and holistic growth. She informed them about the learning goals that they should expect their children to achieve this year. She also explained some activities which parents could do at home, like counting similar vegetables, writing the first letter of the name of the vegetables to refine their basic literacy and numeracy skills, reading a story or telling an impromptu story, polishing their communication skills by giving topics to the children to describe, such as their favourite toy, any picture or drawing, etc.

'And if you don't know the answers to your child's questions, please tell them the truth. And perhaps, you can make it a game where all of you look for the answers together or arrive at one,' she summed up but not before asking, 'Would any of the parents or grandparents like to volunteer to assist the class in various activities?'

The first hand that shot up was that of the doubting mother, who was by now an increasingly absorbed parent. Her hand was followed almost simultaneously by that of most other parents and grandparents.

'Tell us, what do we need to do?'

'I will need volunteers for assisting us with the field visits, exhibitions, class wall magazine, annual function, help with organizing more such PTMs, and much more. We want the professionals among you—carpenters, masons, nurses, homemakers, mechanics, etc.—to interact with the children and expose them to the vocations that help build our society.'

'Unbelievable!'

'We will also have one parent as our class representative, by rotation every month. The class rep can liaise with other parents to inform them of all the developments in the class in that month. We have one hour of unstructured class every day. Parents are free to come over and conduct any new learning activities they may have been devised, during that one hour—of course, with advance information,' continued Butterfly Teacher.

This elaboration by Butterfly Teacher convinced the parents that they were at the crossroads of parenting, and unless they chartered the territory laid down by the teacher, life may offer them only banana skins to tread upon, and fate thereby shall elude their offspring in totality. The clapping, cheering, and offering of services that followed gave her more than sufficient confidence of the parents' more than adequate engagement. Butterfly Teacher knew that this could go on for hours together, if it remained unchecked. Concluding the PTM, she announced a surprise performance by the class, prepared exclusively for the parents. The kids suddenly jumped up from their respective positions next to their families, walked out of the classroom, and each one of them, except Millie, returned with one utensil or the other.

They arranged themselves, some standing, some seated on the floor, some seated on their tin boxes, others ready with vessels, bowls, spoons at hand. Cuebee came forward to explain the wonderment that the parents were about to witness.

'We are here to give you a musical performance, based on the percussion music *Jal Tarang* or "Water Waves". It originated in India. In this system, we have ceramic bowls filled with water, each bowl filled at different levels. When we strike these bowls with a spoon, some vibrations are produced. These vibrations travel through water and then through surrounding air to produce music. Today, some of us have bowls of water for *Jal Tarang*, while others will produce sounds such as drum beats on tin boxes, or other sounds with other vessels. Millie will sing a silly song that she has composed, along with our music and beats.'

When something like this falls in your lap from a clear blue sky, what do you do? Well, you are dumbstruck and tongue-tied and do nothing but gape and gloat. That is what happened that day. Parents, loaded with awe and sentiment, awaited the feat with bated breath. The performance started with the beautiful sound of *Jal Tarang*, and picked up pace with drum and vessel beats. Millie would sing two lines intermittently with only the drum beats. Her words were about what they were learning in class, somewhat like this.

We learnt ABCDE, GPTV XYZee
We learnt 1,2,3,4, La la la la la lore
We love the car in blue, Tulu, gulu, julu, shoo
We used the toilet flush, Gush, gush, gush, gush
We love to dance and sing, Ting a ling a ling a ling.

After every two lines, the *Jal Tarang* would perform. Even though the song was fairly silly, it was very informative, and the music was so well synchronized that the whole effect was that of perfect harmony. It ended with a standing ovation, not only by the parents, but also by the crowd of other parents, children and teachers from the school who had gathered outside the classroom as soon as the music had begun to flow in the corridors. They would not have missed this, at any price.

As night fell, we gathered our brick and cement voices together for our own diagnosis of the PTM. Leaving aside our foundation of good breeding, we unabashedly exhibited overt inquisitiveness about what each of us classrooms went through.

Frontal: My day today was magical, full of fun and surprises.

Temporal: Why, didn't you have a PTM today?

Frontal: Yes, I had a PTM but it was not the run-of-the-mill one.

Cerebellum: I don't wish to talk about my day or of the PTM that took place in my premises.

Brainstem: Even the unwished for PTMs deserve some recognition in our tête-à-tête.

Temporal: In that case, let me enlighten you about what I went through.

Hippocampus: I am ready to risk your banter, if I achieve enlightenment in the end.

Temporal: Your enlightenment is a near impossibility. But I shall carry on regardless. Well, the class teacher was in some strange combative mood today. She had a go at every parent and child today, sans fists. Not a single act of normal courtesy came out of the teacher today.

Parietal: Rather unpleasant, I say.

Temporal: Unpleasant is an understatement. It was horrific.

Occipital: My experience was very similar to that of Temporal. And I am still trying to gather the scattered pieces of my faculties.

Cerebellum: I have begun to wonder why humans interfere so much with life's opportunities.

Frontal: Well, maybe they like to prepare a repository of the past to get boasting rights about it in the future, only because they have nothing better to do!

Parietal: It was a dose of rational enjoyment in my case. Parents of each child entered one by one and the teacher had a detailed discussion with them about the progress that their children had made academically, their social skills, psychomotor skills, scientific temper, computational skills, etc. The teacher was rather resourceful today, and I could see the glimmer of satisfaction in most parents.

Amygdala: You know, we tend to delete families from the list of things that matter in school education. It surely is a mistake.

Hippocampus: Mine was similar to that of Parietal's. But I heard a great deal of noise from your classroom, Frontal, almost as if a carnival was in the offing.

Frontal: With all the modesty at my command, let me declare that, yes, it was nothing less than a carnival. Through fun and games, Butterfly Teacher struck her ingenuous arrow at the soul of the parents, stirring it up, and they gratefully hit the realization that a family's participation in their child's learning process is crucial for their growth and development. The crowning glory was the storytelling session by Cuebee's grandmother. What an amazing orator she is! She could engage not only with the children, but also the adults through her voice intonations and role play in her storytelling.

Cerebellum: Frontal, I have to tell you this. Though I did go through rough times spread over at least three hours today, the only good feeling I had was when the wonderful music began to flow out of your four walls.

Parietal: All this incredible stuff happened within such a brief space of time?

Frontal: Oh yes. Perhaps because it was very well planned. And you ought to have heard the observation of Cuebee about the story told by her grandma.

Temporal: Really, what did she say?

Frontal: She said that everyone is unique in their own way, and we must respect the differences.

Temporal: If even half the adults understood this, most of the problems of this world would be resolved.

Hippocampus: Off late, it appears that a vast emotional upheaval has materialized in certain quarters.

Frontal: Are you, even if inadvertently, hinting at the rumblings that seem to be consuming some of our teachers?

One moment, it was as if all the positivity experienced that day was the centre of attention, but the very next the focus had shifted, and it was as if all that was discussed that night suddenly ceased to generate any further gusto. The general enthusiasm for the day became dilute, and the nasty conflict that was taking shape put us all in a thoughtful mood. Negativity has a way of seeping in, but only if the mind is left unguarded.

5

Street play, earth and the car

CUEBEE, HER CLASSMATES AND THEIR PARENTS WERE relieved—relieved and delighted, in that order, to know that Butterfly Teacher was to continue as class teacher for this lot of kids until Grade 3. By the end of Grade 1, all the students had won their way to her warm affections and the term 'vice versa' was truly applicable in this context. She had resumed the system of one hour of unstructured learning every day as soon as Grade 2 began.

It was a bright sunny day. Cuebee had already spent a fortnight in Grade 2, and the car had been wax-polished just a week before. It was shining, and the rays of the sun were reflecting from the car's body into the classroom, as if inviting the children to come out. The car of course was no longer a thing in the front yard of the school; it had grown in stature to become a personage!

Cuebee hadn't forgotten that Butterfly Teacher had asked her to wait for Grade 2 to look inside the open hood of the car. She had waited with just that sufficient bit of patience and modicum of eagerness so as not to succumb to questioning, and even though her pleading looks could melt glaciers, they were few, but not far between.

Butterfly Teacher had not forgotten either. The independent travelling of the mind was something that she had encouraged in the children. And what better way to do that, than expose them to newer stimulations. In the third week, Cuebee's father was invited to the class and introduced as the Special Teacher of the day, who would help demystify what lay beneath the hood of the car.

If there was one thing Grade 2 students prided themselves on, it was the swiftness with which they responded to instructions from Butterfly Teacher.

'Let us assemble outside around the blue car for your next lesson on its working, by Cuebee's father.' She had barely uttered these words when the class had already departed towards the car in readiness to run around, climb on top of the car and even each other, all spruced up and alert to the possibilities of more knowledge. Butterfly Teacher smiled and perhaps thought to herself, *the Head Teacher is correct in his assessment to never underestimate the capacity of children to learn.*

Cuebee's father, who had reached the car first, was standing at a vantage point of about 2 metres from the car. He retrieved himself from the study of the beauty that the machine in blue was, and transferred his gaze to the bundle of children headed his way. He assumed a business-like stance and requested the children to arrange themselves around him as he stood at the front of the car.

'I will now open the front part of the car. It is called the "hood". All of you should spend time observing the multiple machine parts under the hood. I will tell you some basic parts and their functions. After that, you attempt to draw whatever you have observed,' said Cuebee's father in his capacity as the teacher for the day.

Excitement, chitter-chatter, peeping and poking, and a general din followed. Cuebee's father pointed at and gave names to various parts of the machine, and after some time withdrew himself from the troupe and awaited their return to the classroom. The kids returned after half an hour, along with the several chaotic figures and lines on paper in happy display, and their unstoppable mouths shooting off what they observed. Cuebee's father braced to tackle them and their curiosity with the help of his own figure that he drew on the green chalkboard. The children stopped short when they saw his drawing. It depicted the machine under the hood so well. They looked at their own drawings and knew exactly how to make the corrections. But Cuebee's father stopped them.

'Let us first understand what each of these parts are.' Then he proceeded very systematically to explain the enigma that was the car.

'The largest part you saw, this one in the centre, is the engine. This is what turns the wheels and moves the car.

'The rectangular box here, in this corner, is the battery of the car. You must have noticed a red-coloured and a black-coloured part coming out of it. They have a charge on them.

'There were cylinders too containing petrol. These cylinders each have their own spark plugs, which light up the petrol, which in turn moves the engine.

'Here, right in front of the car is the radiator. It helps in cooling the engine.

'Then here is the alternator. It helps to keep the car battery in running condition. Sometimes, the battery does not work, but if you push the car, it jump-starts. That is because the alternator is still working.'

Butterfly Teacher realized that too much information would flood the capacity of the kids to absorb. She very gently guided them towards relating their experiences that day with their daily lives. The kids of course took very readily to any new action or enterprise.

'If we were to relate the car parts to our body parts or our behaviour, how would we do that?' she said.

'I know how to do that. Teacher, you had told us that our heart pumps blood in our body, and that is what keeps us going. So, we can say that the engine is like our heart,' said Cuebee.

'Then our blood could be like the petrol in the car!' Millie added.

'Can we say that our energy is like the battery of the car?' asked Yoga.

'And the Head Teacher is the radiator,' announced Cuebee.

The teacher looked quizzically at her; she clearly had not understood this relationship.

'That is because he can cool down Alphabet Teacher any time!' Cuebee explained to a class that broke into cackles of laughter. Even the teacher was finding it difficult to hide her mirth.

With the consent of Cuebee's father, Butterfly Teacher eventually gave the students a group activity to work on. Each group was to do a role play by assuming the role of various parts of the car. They were given one hour to do this exercise. At the end of the day, when parents and family members came to pick up the kids after school, the description of the day's activities must have stayed long with them.

'I am the wheel of a car. To turn left, I swing left like this, and to turn right, I swing like this.'

'I save lives. I am the seat belt.'

'I am the brakes,' said another kid, stopping short in his tracks abruptly.

The following week, a new kid joined the class. Bullie was a bespectacled boy with a countenance that somehow smacked of a well-oiled conspiracy combined with stratagem. Butterfly Teacher asked Jadoo to show him around the school, which Jadoo did, but returned a trifle disturbed. Though he was not able to pinpoint or label his feelings at the time, he did share later with Arty that Bullie was 'different' for he tried to destroy the kitchen garden by uprooting a few plants and never repented it!

Bullie was indeed different. He appeared to derive pleasure only from activities that were aimed at changing the present status of the object that caught his attention. At every opportunity that presented itself with no lookers-on, he would pick up a pencil and draw lines on the class benches and walls, change the seating plan of any one of the group tables, leave the tap open in the washroom, or run to the kitchen garden and pull out plants. However, he was not much of a talker. In fact, he was rather pensive and did not seem to make friends easily.

New ideas come to some teachers gently and almost imperceptibly; they creep up by their side and nudge them into acceptance. But for Butterfly Teacher, they seemed to arrive with the suddenness of lightning, and like a storm that sways everything that it touches, they would galvanize her into instantaneous action. Her latest idea appeared to stem from her belief that the role of a school is not only to provide academic inputs but also to make the children responsible citizens. The proclivities of Bullie had to be handled sensitively, so she decided to take her class for a study visit to the kitchen garden in the school's backyard. She asked them to move around and 'observe' for five minutes. All but one did just that.

Bullie once again sought out a group of healthy greens and attempted to uproot a tomato-bearing shrub. He even appeared thoroughly pleased with his life and initiative. Cuebee noticed him doing it. She tried to argue it out with herself. At first, she told herself that he was doing so without thinking, as if out of habit. Or maybe, that he had a taste for tomatoes and could not help but eat them straight from the ground. Next, she pondered whether he was by nature restless. Each argument, though more fascinating than the previous, led her to more confusion. When she saw Bullie apply unnecessary force on the plant, she could not decide which of her three theories was the most applicable. Meanwhile, The Head Teacher had joined them.

'Can any of you tell me what is that one thing without which we cannot survive for more than a few minutes?' the Head Teacher said.

The answers ranged from parents, house, school, television, clothes to water and food, until Cuebee with an introspective look on her face said, 'We can survive without everything, including food and water for at least some hours. But without air and oxygen, we cannot breathe, and we will die.'

'Very good Cuebee, and from where do we get oxygen?'

'From plants and trees.'

Bullie suddenly stopped short in his tracks from the act of deracinating, and looked up, though only half-interestedly, to catch the conversation.

'Children, air, water and soil are very important for our well-being, as we need clean air to breathe, potable water to drink and good soil for growing vegetables and cereals.'

'But who looks after it for us?' asked Yoga.

'Each one of us has to look after it. Can anyone tell me how?'

Not one to be awed by authority, the children took a shot at several answers.

'We should not waste food.'

'We should put waste only in the dustbin.'

'We should also never waste water.'

'We should keep the soil clean and not poison it with dirt.'

'My father told me that cars emit greenhouse gases like carbon dioxide that causes air pollution. We should not use vehicles for travelling small distances.' This one came from Cuebee.

And then just as Butterfly Teacher was preparing herself to add her own learnings to the understanding of the kids, as if torn by the exigency of Bullie's act, she saw Cuebee casting a quick sideways glance at Bullie, as she asked, 'Teacher, do water, plants and soil have feelings?'

Butterfly Teacher winced as she was struck by this question for the second time. Cuebee had earlier asked something akin to this in Grade 1. She was experiencing a moment of stupefaction, which so often is experienced by teachers the world over when they are clean bowled by a query that they have never given any thought to. Nevertheless, with all the intensity at her command, she attempted to explain, for she had grasped Cuebee's intention. Cuebee wanted Bullie to be sensitized.

'They do not exactly have feelings, but possibly can sense several things. Have you noticed how many flowers close their petals after sunset? That's because they sense light. Similarly, plants can sense the presence of water too.'

'So when we add water to soil and it absorbs it, then does it mean it senses it too?'

'Possibly.'

'What about water? Does water have feelings?'

'There are experiments by a Japanese scientist named Dr Masaru Emoto, which may or may not be scientifically proven, that water responds to our emotions.'

Geekay, meanwhile, was there and not-there.

'Does water have feelings too, Teacher?' Geekay asked, even though Butterfly Teacher had just finished explaining the answer to this very question.

While the teacher began patiently explaining again, Bullie burst out into derogatory guffaws at Geekay repeating the same question again. His whole body was shaking with laughter, and he had his finger pointed at Geekay as if to confirm the source of his mirth. Tears welled up in Geekay's eyes as he looked away quietly. Cuebee's face, constitutionally incapable of hiding her emotions, was a study in anger over Bullie's reaction and her own concern for Geekay's feelings. Before Bullie could be reprimanded by any of the adults present and listening, Cuebee swung around to look at Bullie eye to eye and hit out sharply without blinking an eyelid.

'Geekay cannot hear us. That is why he repeats questions sometimes. You have hurt his feelings. Does that even bother you? Plants and animals must be more sensitive than you!'

Several things happened simultaneously thereafter.

Cuebee realizing the folly in her language, followed up her outburst with an apology. 'I am so sorry, Bullie. I should not have spoken like that. Now I have hurt your feelings. Please forgive me. I promise never to speak like this to you again. I am really sorry.'

Bullie was stumped into silence, but just for a moment. He too uttered a meek 'I am sorry' to Geekay and found a spot on the ground next to his feet where he fixed his gaze.

The Head Teacher was gripped with the sudden realization that the reason for Geekay's reticence was finally identified by a human sample less than 4 feet tall and with less than seven years of life and experience on planet earth!

Geekay was looking in the general direction of the sky and talking to himself. 'Cannot hear? What is "hear"?'

As for Butterfly Teacher, though she received the frothing of Cuebee seemingly without much agitation, her usual cheerful composure and disposition were certainly ruffled.

Almost without warning, the rest of the children appeared to have each arrived independently at the decision that it was time to return to the classroom, and they generally trickled away. A flummoxed Head Teacher, a nonplussed Butterfly Teacher, an apologetic Cuebee, a bewildered Geekay and a mellowed Bullie too found their way back to the classroom.

On reaching there, the Head Teacher asked Cuebee to accompany him back to his office. Cuebee happily complied.

She had always found that her interactions with him gave her enough food for thought to last for days. All of us classrooms had a wall each abutting the backyard, and therefore were the mute but captivated spectators of the happenings that day. You can imagine why the classrooms were compelled to enthusiastically pester me for the events that unfolded subsequently. We together beseeched the roof too to join in that night. How else would we know what had transpired between the Head Teacher and Cuebee?

Frontal: Back in the classroom, Butterfly Teacher got her tongue back, and told the children how to participate in creating a clean environment. She said that they would all learn to respect the environment a few steps at a time. To begin with, she has asked all students to ensure that while going to the market, they and their family members use cloth bags because plastic cannot be recycled and it is a huge source of both water and soil pollution.

Roof: What is recycling?

Frontal: Ha ha. Ocean asked the same question. Well, the teacher explained that recycling means that you can make new products using the older material. The plastic which cannot be recycled is called single use plastic. These are not biodegradable, which means that it does not decompose naturally to soil. It will remain as it is for years and will pollute soil and water, and harm the animals and climate.

Roof: Ah! I know what you are talking about. All these lightweight plastic bags that keep flying around and littering the surroundings must be single use plastic.

Hippocampus: Right you are! I have heard this being explained by the Science Teacher.

Amygdala: Can we desist from the expert comments, please? I am really keen to know what happened in the Head Teacher's room.

Roof: You lot are always chivvying for action. I don't know whether to appreciate it or depreciate it.

Occipital: That is your prerogative to decide. But for now, please do tell.

Roof: Well, the Head Teacher asked Cuebee as to how she had arrived at the conclusion that Geekay cannot hear. Cuebee explained her observations in great detail about how Geekay responds to voices only when he is facing the person and lip read. I must say that to all intent and purposes, it was like hearing a conversation between two concerned adults.

Frontal: It is all so incredible! I think I have loved this child from before she was born! She was just a thought earlier, now materialized as a human.

Cerebellum: Yes indeed! It is as if I am returning to consciousness after having been stunned!

Frontal: Yeah! Now that it has happened, consciousness might make something of you as yet!

Parietal: Cerebellum, do not rush unsuspectingly towards your fate by offering a response to that statement from Frontal!

Cerebellum: What fate?

Parietal: Where you tempt Frontal to pull your leg or as we know it, your foundation, and we laugh at your expense!

Geekay's parents were called the very next day and conferred with. They too met with Cuebee to hear her keen observations and felt none the better for having missed out these signs themselves. Geekay must have been taken to a specialist doctor, for within a fortnight, he was sporting hearing aids and jumping astonished at every sound. He would discuss every sound with his group of friends—the sound of voices, running water, leaves hustling in the breeze, the pressure cooker at home, and so on. He went around school with stars in his eyes for months on end. His diction too began to improve and he discovered his love of talking, chatting, communicating, even when he was supposed to only listen. It took very sensitive handling by Butterfly Teacher for this amazing child to settle down well with his new-found ability of hearing.

After a few weeks of 'trying' to take the 'first steps' to keep their environment clean of single use plastics, the children began grumbling about the insularity of response from their home turfs. Butterfly Teacher sought counsel from the Head Teacher and also Buddy and Rainbow Teachers. A joint idea took shape. She soon informed the class that students of Grades 1, 2 and 3 would perform a *Nukkad Natak* at three different sites in the village, and that the Sarpanch was willing to organize an ample crowd at each venue.

The play was prepared jointly by the teachers and children; in fact, many of the characters and their dialogues were decided by the kids. All the students of Grades 1–3 had some role or the other to play in it—a few were the actors, some took on the work of costume designing, yet others wrote the dialogues and developed the sequences. A group of them set up the venue of the play, and another set of about 7-8 students directed it.

I was privy to the *natak* as all the practice sessions were held in my space. I narrated the interesting parts of the rehearsals to my dear classroom friends.

Cuebee (rather unapologetically): Hello everyone, I am single-use plastic. I live forever.

Techie (human adult who can hear all objects speak): Ha ha. No one and nothing can live forever.

Cuebee: Ha ha yourself. Try me. Even if you throw me, I will remain for years to come. If you throw me into the soil, your animals will eat me and become sick. If you throw me into the water, fish and other marine animals will die. If you keep on using me, I will pollute your soil, water and air. One day I will capture this earth and live here alone and peacefully. Ha ha.

Techie: No, no, please don't do this. Our planet earth is meant for humankind and flora and fauna, not for plastic. There must be a way out.

Yoga (a child): Our teacher has shown us the way out. We must simply stop using single-use plastics from now on. We must only use materials that are recyclable. That is why I was insisting that you take your own cloth bag for shopping, and carry your own bottle and container for water and food wherever you go.

Techie: That can be easily done! We start today!

Cuebee: Ha ha. Single-use plastic does not go away by a single person's disuse. Unless you spread this idea everywhere, you just cannot escape me. And I am sure you are least interested in doing that.

Techie: I will tell and request everyone in the village.

Cuebee: I sincerely hope not! In any case, what I have noted of you human beings, is that your spirit may be willing, but your actions do not mirror that.

Techie: Strange that we humans have to learn lessons of survival from a piece of plastic that can be blown away by one strong exhalation of mine! Single Use Plastic, I hereby declare that your time is up! We will boot you out and make you a tiny blot on our horizon, if only as a reminder to never permit you on earth again!

Cuebee (stomping): What a beastly day it has turned out to be!

Techie: Oh, I can hear water coming my way! And water is talking to me! What did you say?

Zouzou (acting as Water): That was a brave decision! And it has given me the confidence that you will take care of me too.

Techie: Of course! Tell me what I need to do.

Zouzou: Stop wasting me. I am not endless. Catch me when I fall as rain. I am important for life to continue on earth. Conserve me. Recycle me. Use me well.

Techie: I am so inspired now! I have a sense of duty. I am ready for anything. Thank you, Water, for taking such good care of all that lives. I promise not to persist rashly with wastage. I will conserve you, my friend!

Yoga: Look there! What are those things moving towards us?

Millie: I am the peel of vegetables and fruits. But you have made me useless.

Techie: How can I make you useless? You are already useless!

Millie: But I can be used as compost. In fact, I can turn into very useful organic compost. I am easily biodegradable.

Techie: And what is my contribution in making you useless?

Millie: You insist on mixing me with dry waste. That is how I become useless.

Techie: I apologize sincerely. I understand now. I will keep separate containers for dry and wet wastes. And hello, who are you?

BeeTee: Hi, I am a scooter, a two-wheeler. Since you are on a comprehending spree, do listen to my woes too. Many people use me for going short distances that are easily walkable. But why do that, when you know that burning fuel causes air pollution?

Techie: Listening to all of you, I feel like I have been placidly sitting on my haunches and viewing the crisis of pollution as something on which everybody else has to act, while I need do nothing.

Cuebee (pointing to the audience): And all your fellow-dwellers in the neighbourhood, have also been doing the same. You all are the reason for my life and happiness! Come on, shout with me: Single use plastic, Zindabad, zindabad!

Techie: No way! It all ends today and now! And hey, Scooter! I promise not to use any vehicle for short distances. Walking is good for health anyway.

BeeTee: Well, it appears to be a very well-guarded secret!

Techie: What secret?

BeeTee: The health benefits of walking!

Techie: I apologize for not acting earlier. But this is the time, and we are the people!

Millie: Now I call upon all of you present here to take a pledge. Are you ready?

Cuebee (as Cuebee, addressing the audience): Our pledge is a small poem that we all have written together. Please speak after me.

Where we take birth, that is our Mother Earth
She gives us many things for free,
water, soil, air, animals and trees
Let us not harm her, let us not grill her
Let us not injure her, let us not kill her
No single use plastic from today
Dry and wet waste, we will separate
No wastage of water, rainwater we will store
We will use less fuel, and walk much more
We promise you, Mother Earth, we will help you restore.

Not ones to let the grass grow under our feet, right after my narration that night we debated about the benefits or otherwise of *nataks* at *nukkads*.

Parietal: It is indeed a very well-crafted play.

Hippocampus: But how does it help learning?

Brainstem: You seem to have a poor opinion of human creativity. Well, have we not heard that creativity is one of the twenty-first-century skills? This is creativity at its best!

Occipital: It is communication at its best!

Cerebellum: I can only imagine how this will inject even more confidence in our kids to work for society.

Frontal: This is truly multidisciplinary teaching at its best!

Hippocampus: How is that?

Temporal: There was language, science, environmental awareness, communication, problem-solving, all in one!

Frontal: I expect suspicion in humans. That is their nature. But you, Hippocampus, take the cake!

Hippocampus: When Cuebee asks questions by the dozens you dote on her, but when I do, you talk about cake!

Parietal: Ha ha! Jealousy, thy name is Hippocampus!

Hippocampus: God forbid! I could never be envious of or compete with such sweetness and brightness as Cuebee!

Grade 2 kick-started on a compelling note. Aside from learning to read fluently and with comprehension, the focus was on basic numeracy too. The kids in my classroom spent a lot of time playing games about numbers, words, sentences, basic numeric operations, pattern recognition, measurement, art and craft and sports activities, and generally looking at their young lives as a series of happy events. Butterfly Teacher introduced them to the idea of picnics, walks in the nearby fields, visits to local monuments, interactions with local craftsperson, class wall magazine, speaking in the morning assembly, personal hygiene, cleanliness of surroundings, etc.

The children discovered many of their hidden talents and strengths in the process.

One day, when the weather outside my space was more inviting than my protective four walls, Butterfly Teacher decided to take her class outside and under the sky to have a balloon race in pairs. Kids were asked to choose their partners. Cuebee and Millie, BeeTee and Yoga, Techie and Geekay, Imli and Amla, and so on paired up and geared up for the race. Each pair was given one balloon to inflate. They were to face each other and put the balloon between their faces and trudge, walk, or run from the start line to the finish line without dropping the balloon and without using their hands to balance it.

Butterfly Teacher called Buddy Teacher to help her demonstrate. The children clapped loudly and cheered for their teachers. The Teachers tried their best but could not complete the race to the dismay of the children, who were certain that they would set examples. The two teachers summed up their inability to complete the race by warning that unless the participants synchronized their speed with their partners and listened to each other, they would end up uncoordinated.

Cuebee and Millie were the first ones to complete the race. They had noted with a great deal of seriousness the whole idea of communicating with each other. They kept on talking to each other and adjusting for each other. BeeTee and Yoga's balloon fell down midway as Yoga decided to run fast to finish the race early. BeeTee looked sad. He tugged at Butterfly Teacher's sleeve, gazing disappointedly at her.

'We did not stand first. I am feeling very sad.'

Butterfly Teacher asked all the children to crowd around her.

'Did you enjoy the game?'

'Yes!' shouted everyone.

'Did all of you win the race?'

'No!' they shouted again.

'But even then, you enjoyed it?'

'Very much!' they all agreed.

'BeeTee, that was the idea! Rather than winning, participating in the race is important, and even more important is to enjoy it and learn something from it. You saw Cuebee and Millie also struggled half way but they talked it out and resolved it. So next time, you must remember that in a team game, your partner is equally important. Now let's clap for all of us for participating and enjoying the race.'

Their claps could be heard in all the classrooms.

'So can we call Cuebee and Mille as "Kings of the day"?' BeeTee asked in all gladness.

'But there are no kings now. Teacher, why don't we see them now?' Cuebee was not going to let a questioning moment pass, and Butterfly Teacher was not going to let a dose of random learning pass by unacknowledged either.

'Cuebee, in earlier times, we were ruled by kings but now our country is democratic, and we have a prime minister who is elected by citizens through voting in elections. Remember we learnt to vote in Grade 1?'

'Oh, so in a democracy there are no kings?'

'No, Cuebee. Kings are not selected by the people. They are mostly there due to their family members having been kings earlier. But in a democracy, people have the right to elect their own leader. It is always good to have the right to choose your leader.'

'Teacher, can I also become prime minister one day?' asked a speculative Cuebee.

'Yes, you can, but you have to work very hard to get there.'

I have a feeling that Cuebee and the other kids may not have fully grasped the meaning of democracy that day, but they did understand the importance of having a choice or a say in selecting things. They had embarked on a spree of giving their called-for and uncalled-for opinions in class on what activities they liked and must be continued, and what needed to be discontinued forthwith, chief among them being homework!

Towards the end of the year, but well before the last month of school in this academic session, the Head Teacher called for a staff meeting on how to take forward the assessment of students of Grades 1–8. The Teachers collected in the staff room and indulged in an animated banter about the agenda of the meeting.

'I thought that I had that much prerogative and autonomy to decide how I do assessment of my class,' remarked Alphabet Teacher sarcastically.

'I find autonomy overrated. But at the same time, the old way of doing things may not always be right!' the Maths Teacher said emphatically.

'Our Head Teacher's so-called zeal for reforms remains unsatisfied, whatever we may do!' burst out the Language Teacher.

'I don't think he has the remotest idea of the difficulties we face each time he introduces something "innovative"', the Science Teacher said thoughtfully.

'Being closed to new ideas—aside from incompetence and a taste for procrastination—is quite the worst characteristic that a teacher can possess.' Buddy Teacher appeared as if she could not take in any more.

A war was about to break out in the staff room when the Head Teacher walked in. There was a suspension of hostilities immediately, even if temporarily. He had heard the last bit, but he could exercise considerable self-control in the face of odds to give a semblance of undisturbed visage and character.

'Tell me,' he started, 'does the report card teach anything? Is it really so important? Is it too early to introduce this judgement for a child in early grades? Is it not acting as a hindrance to creative learning? How does a child react to a report card?'

'In my view, it is the most interesting as well as the most disheartening time of the year,' said the Maths Teacher.

'That's so true. I have seen that after their first experience, they fear this day all through their school lives! That is why with your permission last year, I only wrote a long letter to each of the parents on the unique abilities of each child, rather than giving a report card,' informed Butterfly Teacher.

'There is a perceived sense of injustice by the children of being judged,' remarked Rainbow Teacher.

'May I say something?' the Sports Teacher said rather shakily.

'Of course! Why do you hesitate? Why do you ask?' the Head Teacher said.

'Because I am the Sports Teacher, and unlike the rest I do not teach academics.'

'Exactly! And you feel judged, because you take classes outdoors and we may not be treating you as equally as we should. This is exactly what is happening with our children too. Go ahead. What did you want to say? To me, we are all equal,' said the Head Teacher, who was by now emotionally charged.

'Well, rather than relying solely on external indicators, the children must develop metacognitive abilities—the mental habits required to assess their own progress,' the Sports Teacher said.

'Brilliant! You are right! Studies have shown that when students are encouraged to evaluate their own contributions and work, they improve their abilities. This perhaps was not possible in Grade 1, but a notion that you are your best judge can be very subtly imbibed in the children at least from

Grade 2 onwards. This will be in addition to teacher and parent assessment. For Grade 1, we continue with Butterfly Teacher's experiment,' added the Head Teacher. 'You all have the autonomy to decide your own methodology of self-assessment, teacher and parent assessment,' he said, wrapping up the meeting.

Butterfly, Buddy and Rainbow Teachers jointly decided how they would encourage self-assessment in literacy and numeracy. In literacy, for example, a grade-appropriate passage was given with some standard text with many words missing, spelling mistakes and a few illogical conclusions. It was a somewhat meaningless text and the children were expected to make their own meaning out of it by filling in the blanks and giving the correct text. The act of completion was the only goal. The assessment was just this and no more. By being their own judge very early in life, they received a lesson in self-evaluation without knowing, bothering for, or resenting the other's performance.

'Teacher, will you not check what I have done?' asked Sky.

'Why should I do that? Why do you feel the need for it? You have to decide and be satisfied that you have the correct answer in front of you.'

'I am worried, Teacher … suppose I don't know that I'm wrong.'

'Sky, you will know, if you do it carefully. Are you scared of finding out that you were wrong?'

'Yes, Teacher. I am afraid to check my own work.'

'You are too young to feel that way, Sky. Does anyone have the same feeling?'

There was initially an awkward silence. A few of the fence-sitters tried unsuccessfully to go back to what they were doing. But the moment passed, and almost the whole class raised their hands in confirmation.

'Children, you are fearing a self-evaluation because you are not sure of yourself. That is because you think you have not learnt well. Right?'

'Yes, yes, Teacher,' they all exclaimed, nodding their heads.

Cuebee's was the only head in vehement disagreement. 'I like this activity; I made several mistakes the first time, so I did it again. And now I know it well. Teacher, I think my friends don't want to repeat the task.'

As is natural for young blood in a young classroom, they began booing her. 'No, no, she is wrong!'

But then a spirited Millie got up amidst the commotion and said, 'Cuebee is right. I didn't want to repeat the task.'

I sensed a wave of covert agreement and overt denial by the whole class. But, soon enough the idea of review and reflection caught on. It was just what was required to complete the self-evaluation. Small and energetic humans learnt a new lesson that day, in fact, a life skill. Lessons that adults can't learn over a lifetime, they did it so subtly. This system of self-evaluation, self-understanding, self-correction soon became one of the most popular activities and children's appetite for it touched sky-high as they never tired of asking for more.

We classrooms met every night as usual, but always with a purposeful air to discuss and debate on the innovations we were witnessing for the first time—each class had adopted its own method of self-evaluation, ranging from role plays, quizzes, to project work, group work, even peer assessment, etc. Though it appeared as if there was a forbidding wall between some teachers and the Head Teacher's 'new ideas', classrooms reported that even the protesting teachers were regaling in private how the suggestion had turned out to be not bad at all!

Towards the end of the academic session, the parental assessments started pouring in. They were much more constructive this time as compared to the ones they gave the previous year which had led to a certain consternation in our minds too. Last year the assessments were more akin to drawing battle lines between the parents and the rest of the world. But this year the threat had completely abated. Butterfly Teacher read out many of the parental assessments to Buddy Teacher. Instead of judging their children or labelling them as 'smart' or 'slow', many of them had written about the skills and competencies acquired by them. The families were indeed getting around to contributing to their children's cognitive growth. To add to the delight of Butterfly Teacher, at least three grandparents, including Cuebee's grandma, had submitted their grandparental assessment too.'

Now this turn of events deserves a proper account. One day, almost into the third month of Grade 1, I narrated a curious incident to my classroom mates.

Butterfly Teacher was singing a poem related to the solar system, which included the names of each of the eight planets.

'Earth is the planet we live on,' she informed the class as she completed her song.

She had the globe in her hand.

'Why is the earth mostly blue in colour? Does it appear blue even from outer space?' Cuebee's imagination had just taken off.

'We have huge oceans full of water on earth, that is why the earth appears blue from space too. In fact, earth is also called the blue planet.'

'What are these other shapes in different colours?' Cuebee asked, pointing at them on the globe.

'These are different countries.'

Cuebee began to point out different countries, and the teacher began telling their names to the whole class.

After two or three days, Butterfly Teacher and I noticed Cuebee and Millie sitting together with the globe and Cuebee was pointing at different countries and correctly telling the names. Butterfly Teacher was astonished, because Cuebee was yet to learn spellings. How was she able to read all this?

'Cuebee, how do you remember all the names of different countries and their location?'

'Oh, when you were telling the names of different countries on the globe the other day, I noticed that the shapes of all these countries were different, and they were also represented by different colours on the globe, so I identify them by associating shapes and colours to names,' Cuebee said to a stunned Butterfly Teacher.

'And who taught you this?' she said on recovering herself.

'My grandmother. She knows all the parts of a car. She cannot read too well, but learnt the names from my father by associating names to shapes and colours.'

While I saw Butterfly Teacher's forehead retreat under her graciously ponytailed hairline that day, I knew that she was not one to let a learning experience slip out unnoticed. In consultation with the Head Teacher, towards the end of Grade 1 itself, she had added a nota bene to her written request for parental assessments—'Grandparental assessments are welcome too.'

Well, that year, not even a single grandparent participated. I put it down to an unexplained hesitancy, for it appeared, at least to me, contrary to all rules of etiquette of a family fully engaged in the child's overall development. But in grade 2, we had three grandparents participating in assessment. We classrooms could not but help admire the genius of Butterfly Teacher and her disposition towards constant innovation.

We wrapped up the proceedings of the last day of the academic session with my narration and our typical banter. The three sets of grandparents were solemnly added to the meagre and motley list of our favourite persons.

Parietal: Life is worth living after all!

Frontal: Here I am telling you about how families too contribute to random acts of learning, and you are philosophizing about life!

Parietal: Pleasure before business!

Frontal: Ha ha. You are crazy!

Occipital: And so the Frontal contingent marches into the lines, armed with stories, impatient with classrooms, but ready for a laugh!

Temporal: Class dismissed!

6

Food web, mouse and Millie-is-cool

THE HEAT OF THE SUMMER THIS YEAR WAS APPALLING. Amidst the severity with which the weather was treating the village, starting the academic session ought to have been grimness personified. But not so, for the newly promoted Third Graders. As the school reopened in mid-June, early in the morning every day, with the usual spring in their step, they were often found chit-chatting or playing with the agility of one who was experiencing rather fair weather and temperatures.

Meanwhile, Cuebee continued her daily morning question–answer sessions with the Head Teacher.

'Why do mosquitoes and other insects even exist? They don't seem to have any use, and they render our sleep useless by coming out in hordes and biting us in the night!'

'Well, everything in nature has its use. Guess what birds eat or what a lizard living in a desert does to survive in an environment where humans, if left alone, would not survive for even two days?'

'But do we need so many mosquitos? It was me against fifty of them last night.' Cuebee was not convinced.

'That is nothing. In reality, the number of insects is at least double, if not more, as compared to the entire human population. And if we combine the populations of insects, beetles and arthropods on this planet, it is estimated that it runs into quintillions.'

'What are quintillions?'

'It is a huge number—ten followed by eighteen zeros. You will learn about it in higher grades.'

And so began Cuebee's fascination with the zoological world and new unpronounceable words. She delved deeper and deeper into the study of the food web and the interdependence of living things on each other. She learnt heavy words for a child her age, such as prey, predator, ecosystem, ecology, amphibians, mammals, etc., and would use them randomly to the delight of the other children. Even if only vicariously, her classmates too were picking up words and their meanings through the process that Cuebee and the Head Teacher went through every day. Statements such as the following were splattered through the school days.

'Ours is the only food web that has *mithai*, *golgappas* and *papdi chaat* in it.'

'I am the predator and I shall prey on the mid-day meal.'

'Yoga is an amphibian. He lives on land but plays with water all the time!'

'Plant a tree, develop your own oxygen plant.'

'Our logic must always be bio-logic too.'

'I love mathematics in quintillions!'

'You are my favourite earthworm, because you are helping recycle waste.'

'If you don't want rats in the house, then stop felling trees.' Cuebee was asked by her friends to explain this one. She happily obliged her classmates.

'On cutting trees, many insects lose their homes, and with it so many birds and squirrels also lose their food. This in turn drives away eagles and bats from there. There are not enough eagles and large birds to eat the rats, therefore they thrive. The increase in rat population means that they will look for more places to eat and survive. Best place is our homes. So there, that is why, do not cut trees.'

This divulsion led to several experience-sharing sessions among the children. Millie described how her mother was being troubled by a mouse at home.

'The mouse is so naughty and destructive. Mummy is very upset. It has spoiled a lot of food.'

Butterfly Teacher overheard her, and accustomed to such conversations by now, she decided to intervene with information.

'The mouse is an animal that lives where humans do, and it is dependent on the food of humans for survival. Tell me, what do you think can be done?'

'Use the mousetrap. Let us kill the mouse. Ha ha.'

'Have an eagle as a pet to hunt it down.'

'Or even a cat might do.'

'Just swat it with a bat!'

'No, why should you kill it?' This one came from Cuebee.

The teacher persisted. 'Let us try something interesting. Why don't we write a letter to the mouse on how each one of us wants to deal with the mouse?'

The idea appealed to the kids. Each of them was by now able to read and write well, though with lesser vocabulary than they would have desired. Limitations notwithstanding, they were able to express themselves with prolific abundance.

> Dear Mousey, please become my friend. I will keep you in my pocket.
>
> Yoga

> Don't feel very important because we are all writing about you. Just stop troubling Millie's Mother, or I will hunt you down!
>
> Bullie

> Dear Mouse,
> Why do you trouble humans so much? We keep food for you in one corner, but you don't like to eat it there. You always like to bite it off from fresh food, so that we can't eat it anymore. Please dear mouse, don't trouble our parents. They work very hard to get us good food. I don't want to hit or kill you, because you also have a life. Just come over to one corner of the house every day where I promise to give you food every day.
>
> Cuebee

Everyone was asked to read out their letters in class. Most of the children had written about killing the mouse, hitting it hard, using repellents, traps, etc. But Cuebee, and to some extent Yoga, were clearly outliers. Finding Cuebee's letter the funniest yet the most adorable possible alternative to hunting it down, the whole class had a good discussion around animals and their right to life.

The universe must have had some extremely wise purpose in creating Grade 3, but it was quite inscrutable at the start. Soon it dawned upon Butterfly Teacher that the children had begun to exhibit passionate interest in the new subject, science, and she was struggling to cope with it. Butterfly Teacher sought the Head Teacher's counsel on how to nurture this interest.

'What you need is the help of the Science Teacher.'

'What I really need is to get an undergrad degree in physics or something, but the support of the Science Teacher shall do very well for the present.'

Following a long and detailed discussion with the Science Teacher, they came to the conclusion that an introduction to logic and critical thinking could be initiated by posing an intricate question to the kids, such as how can you prove that the earth is round?

'If you all keep walking straight, across forests, hills, water, etc., where do you think you will end up?'

All this while, the children had been honing their curiosity, and they were basically prepared for anything. It just needed a perfectly framed question, such as this one, to set them off. Several hands shot up to respond.

'No, do not be in a hurry. Here is a map of the world. And this is where we are all located. Ponder over it in your groups for ten minutes. And then we shall love to hear from you.'

One voice, then two, then the whole lot joined in. Soon, thirty voices were rising with excitement. After ten minutes, there was just noise and wild gesticulations, and both teachers knew that it was time to bring back peace and quiet in the classroom.

'Class, now tell us, what conclusion you have arrived at.'

The children had a strange expression, as if they had discovered something sensational. They all decided to speak at once and together, in an attempt to drown each other's voices.

'We cannot walk that much.'

'We will definitely fall into water at the end of the earth.'

'Are we all going to fall down, if we keep walking?'

'We will fall off the edge of the earth into a hole.'

'Earth looks flat as far as my eyes can see. Beyond that, I think I will fall deep down somewhere.'

Cuebee remained unusually quiet throughout this ample display of the power of vocal chords. The teacher turned to her. 'What do you think?'

'The question is not correct, Teacher. Something is missing here,' she said almost dismissively.

'Ha ha. Cuebee is saying that because she doesn't know the answer to the question.'

'Both Cuebee and I think that the earth is not flat. But we are unable to prove it.' Geekay came up in support of Cuebee.

'And why do you think so?'

'You had shown us a globe earlier. Now you are showing us a map. I feel you are trying to confuse us deliberately,' Cuebee replied.

This was the cue to begin an experiment. The Science Teacher left the class momentarily and came back with a large gym ball in his hands. He placed it on the desk. He asked each child to then place their cheek on the bottom of the ball on one side, with their eyes almost level with the ball.

'What do you see? A flat surface or a round surface?'

'A flat surface.' This was the response of every child.

'You see a flat surface, because the closer you are to an object, the flatter it seems. Now I am moving a pen from the other side of the ball to this side. Continue to keep your cheek next to the balloon. Can you see it?'

'No.' None of the children did, until the pen moved to the horizon.

'I saw the tip first, and slowly as you moved the pen, the whole pen came in full view.'

'I got it. The earth is round indeed!' Geekay was jumping with joy at this discovery.

'Because we stand on it and are so close to it, it appears flat. And we will never fall off. We will just go to the other side of what looks like the horizon.' Cuebee too could not stop herself from solving the problem for her class. The rest of the students also got very excited at the solution and agreed with Cuebee and Geekay wholeheartedly.

The Science Teacher started clapping.

'I don't know why I am clapping, but I am so happy that you all caught on. Yes, that is right, and you have made my task so easy, Cuebee.'

'Now I know why Cuebee is your favourite student.' The Science Teacher quietly said this to Butterfly Teacher.

Butterfly Teacher froze. Realization hit her like a solid asteroid crashing unannounced on a planet, that she was indeed indulging in favouritism. Why had she not surmised this herself? She always considered herself as a teacher who loved all her students equally, without ever crowning a favourite child. Even if she did have one in her mind, it was never to be expressed to the class. But the typical weakness of the human mind must have displayed its undesirable form to the discerning Science Teacher. She made up her mind to do course correction.

She braced herself to treat every child with the equanimity they deserved.

From that very day, she began to encourage all her students—not just Cuebee—to ask questions. In fact, a couple of times, Cuebee felt as if she was being neglected. After several joint sessions with the Science Teacher, Butterfly Teacher had caught the spread and flow of how to teach science. One day as she entered my space, she surveyed the classroom and its little occupants, just as an artist would her art, with modest pride. She picked up the chalk and began to write on the green chalkboard: S-C-I-E-N-C-E. If a person's character were to be deduced from chalk writing, I would say that on the other side of the chalk was a very determined young lady, energetic and well-informed.

'What is this classroom, you, the car outside, your pencil, everything around you made of?'

It was impossible for the kids to remain entirely undisturbed when a provocation in the form of a question was thrown their way. Several hands shot up eager to respond.

'Matter! You told us about it in Grade 1!'

'And …'

'And matter is either solid, liquid or BeeTee's gas,' a few said with a giggle.

'Hmm. Now listen carefully. All matter is made up of molecules. It is the smallest particle of a substance that has all the properties of that substance.'

'Even matter has property? I thought only our elders could possess land and property.'

'By property, I mean characteristic. Like your characteristic or property is that you jump too much.'

'And Imli's property is that she has dimples.'

The class was now consumed by the idea of having characteristics and properties. Such statements by the teacher had an inherent magnetism and they attracted a lot of chatting. Butterfly Teacher would invariably allow them their moment of fun before she would bring back peace by the tapping of the duster on the table. But not this time. It was Millie who drew the attention of the class this time.

'Why is it called "molecules" ? Why not Millie-is-cool or something like that?'

The teacher smiled and answered. 'There is a logic behind every word. Every word has an origin. The word molecule in Latin language means extremely minute or tiny particles.'

'If all matter is made up of molecules, what are molecules made up of, Teacher?' Cuebee was asking a question and a good question at that. The teacher could not possibly ignore her. But she did.

'Does anyone else have any questions?'

'Yes, please answer Cuebee's question,' said Zouzou.

'Well, molecules are made of A-T-O-M, atoms. There was a scientist named Democritus, who lived in Greece (she pointed out this country in the world map). He named it based on an ancient Greek word that means uncuttable.'

'Do they move, the molecules, Teacher? Is it because of them that we move?' Cuebee persisted.

'Any other questions?' the teacher persisted too.

'Like Cuebee asked, so if the car outside is still, are its molecules also still? Do the molecules start moving to move the car?' Techie jumped in.

Before the teacher could take the discussion any further, the school bell rang with the force of an announcement that school time was over.

'Wait for the next class. Until then, all of you think about it!' Butterfly Teacher said, smiling almost mysteriously.

While the rest of the class were inundated with wonderment, Cuebee felt increasingly unsettled. When Grandmother came to pick up Cuebee that day, she found her granddaughter in a strangely pensive mood. When she attempted to enquire why she was so thoughtful, all she got was a 'it's nothing' from Cuebee. A vivacious child who had earlier shown interest in everything that life presented to her, seemed to be in the throes of some form of disturbance within, almost like a foreboding. Grandma caught the anguish but deemed patience and non-persistence to be the correct course of action for the present.

The next day's discussion was to be on the subject of whether or not molecules move. Butterfly Teacher entered the class with a glass of water and some colouring agent. All eyes were on her and her accompaniments.

'Okay children, what do you think is happening inside the glass? Is water moving?'

'No, Teacher, it is still,' said all in unison.

'Okay, what do you think will happen if I drop colour into the glass of water?'

'It will just fall down,' said Arty.

So, Butterfly Teacher dropped one drop of indigo colour into the still glass of water. The colour spread and dissolved in the water. The children were not expecting this.

'So children, why do you think the colour moved in the water?'

Excited as he was, Mindesh remarked, 'Because everything moves down.'

'But here, it was spreading in all directions, and it even went up,' Butterfly Teacher pointed out.

There was pin-drop silence as the children tried to process this information.

'This little experiment shows that something in the water was moving, and these are the molecules. This is a basic principle of science; molecules are in constant motion. Isn't that interesting? So, now can you understand that even inside you, all the molecules are moving.'

At exactly this juncture, an unpredictable event stirred its unexpected head. Bullie grabbed the bottle of colour from the teacher's desk and poured it on Amla's uniform.

'What do you think you are doing, Bullie?' Butterfly Teacher half yelled.

'Teacher, just checking whether Amla has molecules,' Bullie replied spaciously.

'Out of the class! This is wrong! Go get some water to help Amla clean her clothes.'

'But she doesn't have molecules. See, all the colour just flowed down and did not spread,' responded Bullie dubiously.

While Cuebee too appeared to be pretty disturbed by the whole episode, she did not jeer at Bullie for his uncalled-for behaviour like the rest of the class did. Before Butterfly Teacher could take stock of the situation, Cuebee took over.

'Bullie, you are doing all this to make a friend. Right?'

'Perhaps many friends,' exclaimed Bullie in a burst of peculiar imagery.

'Well, you just lost many friends with your silliness.'

Bullie was taken aback; in fact, rendered tongue-tied. Butterfly Teacher looked at Cuebee with honest admiration and whatever came over her next, led to her giving Cuebee an impromptu hug and telling her, 'That, my dear Cuebee, is resolution in the face of an oddity.'

Seized of his silliness, Bullie felt the need for a public apology which, in turn, had a strange impact. From that day onwards, Bullie became the fourth member of the former trio of Imli, Amla and Simla.

Cuebee was not one to let the series of incidents go unacknowledged. One day, after school, she stayed back in class and met with Butterfly Teacher at her desk. There were just the two of them, and solemnity seemed to have descended upon them like a haze. They stood awkwardly for a brief moment.

'Teacher, have I hurt you in any way?' Cuebee said, her young face overcast.

'No Cuebee, it is my foolishness that I am behaving so awkwardly.' Butterfly Teacher looked at Cuebee with a maternal gaze and candidly explained her predicament about not wanting to appear to have favourites in class.

Little teardrops that lurked beneath the surface of Cuebee's utter sunny nature, escaped the corner of her eyes and found their way to her cheeks. That upset Butterfly Teacher to no end. She too let go of a stream from her eyes, warmly hugged Cuebee, and told her in no uncertain terms, 'I have hurt you Cuebee, and I am really sorry for that. It will never happen again. I promise. And I also promise to make my classes even more participative.'

That day, when Grandma came to pick up Cuebee after school, the spring in her step had returned along with the twinkle in her eyes and the gladness in her speech. Cuebee's earlier thoughtfulness had been the one jarring note in Grandma's life. Though, for her emotions were not a thing that anybody could effortlessly turn off or on, Grandma was relieved that for Cuebee it had all happened so fast.

That night as we collected ourselves and finished narrating the day's events, the discussions veered around the reconciliation between Cuebee and Butterfly Teacher.

Amygdala: A person with any sense would not have hurt Cuebee in this manner. I expected the teacher to do better than this.

Parietal: Put that mortar mouth of yours to better use. Appreciate the fact that teacher and Cuebee could talk to each other as two logically thinking adults would.

Occipital: The combined age of Cuebee and the teacher is less than forty. I had quite forgotten that sense and sensibilities can take care of any conflict between two sets of people at whatever age. I must have become fossilized.

Frontal: Yes, you must have. I can almost see the headlines: Promising young classroom found to be a remnant of Jurassic Park.

Brainstem: If you ask my opinion, this should be set as an example for conflict resolution for the whole school.

Frontal: But who's asking? For your opinion, I mean.

Brainstem: Ha ha. That does not deter me. I am consoled by the fact that even if we classrooms are 'still born', it is possible for my atoms, molecules and matter to be happy over small reflections.

Well into Third Grade, one of the topics of science that had to be dealt with was of the concept of evolution and the evolutionary history of human beings. Initially, Butterfly Teacher adopted the typical system being used by the school since decades of exhibiting a large chart with several figures named as *Homo erectus*, Neanderthal, *Homo sapiens*, and so on. At first, the children had a hard time with the sudden onslaught of unfamiliar and tongue-twisting words.

'I wish to goodness that we did not have to evolve in such a complicated manner,' Anxy remarked.

Butterfly Teacher had been given this chart by the Science Teacher who claimed to have rendered this topic successfully on at least five separate occasions. However, what met her eye in her own class was boredom imperfectly combined with an unmet curiosity. The last straw was when Cuebee let out a suppressed yawn.

'That's it. No more of this chart business,' Butterfly Teacher exclaimed and sent the class for a five-minute recess while she scurried to the Head Teacher for advice. As expected, when two creative minds, passionate about teaching, meet, there is bound to be an ingenious lesson plan.

Butterfly Teacher started the next day by giving a survey form with five true/false statements that all the students had to fill in. The statements were about the idea of evolution.

a) I as an individual can undergo evolution.
b) We humans have not descended from chimpanzees.
c) Non-living things can undergo evolution.
d) When milk becomes curd, it is evolution.
e) Every day some new evolution happens.

After a few minutes she collected the forms. She took the help of a few students and about five minutes to collate the results of the survey. All the students had marked all statements as 'True'.

Then she began the class. She asked the students to give her examples of things around them that they find are changing.

'The trees are growing.'

'The car is rusting, unless we take care of it.'

'The school building needs repair.'

'Grandma is growing old.'

Then, the teacher asked an unsettling question. 'These are all changes happening around you. Let us discuss the changes only in living things.'

'Teacher, Sky did say that Grandma is getting old.'

'Well, are these changes physical or will these changes be inherited by the whole population of trees and humans? So, will their next generation of trees and humans have these characteristics from birth itself?'

The kids were tongue-tied.

'No, I don't think so. I think these are just small changes that happen all the time.' Cuebee had mulled over it before answering. The class agreed eventually.

'Exactly! These are changes and are not evolution, because individuals do not evolve. It is the whole population that evolves.'

'How does that happen?'

'Well, our living system keeps generating new characteristics or traits that can be inherited by the next generation, or they can have that characteristic from birth itself. Nature selects certain traits that we get by birth and decides to continue with those, while discarding others for entire populations. That is how entire populations evolve into something different.'

'Teacher, please give examples.'

'Have your parents ever taken or given you antibiotics to treat illness?'

'Yes, Teacher.'

'Antibiotic drugs are used against bacterial infections. "Anti" means "against" and "biotics" means "related to life" as bacteria are living things. Due to too much use of antibiotics, humans are no longer affected by several of them which have become useless in curing illnesses that they earlier cured. Why do you think that happened?'

'Because we generated a new trait to accommodate the antibiotics and the bacteria in our body to live in harmony with each other?' Geekay said.

'That's right. Now let us come to human evolution. We have evolved from chimpanzees.'

There was a huge round of protest at this statement. The chimpanzee seemed to have become an almost tangible presence in my class and impacted different kids in different ways.

'Not possible, it has no brains.'

'It is too fat.'

'Am I a chimpanzee inside of me?'

'If we were chimpanzees earlier, then when will all the chimpanzees in forests turn into humans?'

'I don't like bananas like chimps do.'

'Is that why I love jumping around?' This last one had the whole class, including the teacher, bursting into uncontrolled fits of laughter.

'Well, nature slowly selected traits such as a straight back, bigger brain, better grasp, lesser hair to evolve chimpanzees into humans. But it took a very, very long time.'

'Teacher, please give us more examples.'

'Hmm. Let me see. Yes, I have one. Our skin colours. Our skin has a pigment called melanin. In different parts of the world, the sun, and therefore the temperatures are either harsher or milder in comparison to each other. Wherever, the sun is harsher during the day, such as in the African continent, the melanin helps to make the pigment darker to act as a sunscreen.' Butterfly Teacher pointed to the globe while saying this.

After almost three full periods of discussion, I witnessed what I think was the height of cuteness. Next morning before Butterfly Teacher came to class, the students had an internal meeting. They appointed Simla as their representative to make an earnest request to the teacher.

'Teacher, all of us have a request.'

'Sure, do tell me.'

'We realize how wrong we were in our understanding. Therefore, may we do the survey on evolution again, please?'

'Ah!' Butterfly Teacher must have thought to herself, as she smiled, *Why wouldn't I love them all till death do us apart!*

One day, towards the middle of the year, Butterfly Teacher and the Science Teacher entered my classroom together. As conversation ceased, she informed the class that their much-awaited wish was about to be fulfilled.

'Last year, you discovered many things about the car. Did you get all your answers?' The Science Teacher literally threw a bait in the class.

Conversation was unstoppable thereafter. The Teachers, for a moment, could do nothing to dispel the excitement until Millie piped up and everybody else continued the thread.

'Yes Teacher, we remember many things. I had many questions. I even got the answers, but each answer led to more questions. It confused me.' No sooner had Millie laid down the context, the kids decided that shooting more questions at the Teachers could possibly be the only logical corollary.

'Why do we use only petrol to run the car and not water?'

'I am puzzled as to why we fill petrol at the back of the car if the engine is in the front.'

'Isn't the car a very dangerous thing? It can kill people.'

'Why is it made of steel, why not wood or plastic?'

'Why can't the car have three or four rows of seats?'

'How does the car move? When will we be able to take a ride on a speedy car?'

'Why are there so many wires and pipes inside the car engine?'

'How does the car turn?'

'Why is the shape of the car different from that of a bus or truck?'

'One by one, please. I understand that you have more queries than the number of parts in the car!' Butterfly Teacher was clearly exasperated. She seemed to be ready to hunt for a bombproof shelter. But the whole class was in splits at her remark. They found it extremely funny. It took a while before she finally managed to bring in a semblance of peace in the class.

'The car is a complex thing, and it may be difficult for you to grasp everything about it right away. But we will certainly try to clear your cloud of doubts and queries.' The Science Teacher was able to quell the next round of questions with a twist. 'But before I do that, I want all of you to do your own research on how a car works and perhaps even try to answer some of the questions raised. You can work in your own groups. And tomorrow each of the six groups shall make a presentation before the class on the understanding they may have arrived at.'

'Teacher, how do we do research?'

'Well, you can do any of three things or a combination—read books, ask experts or your family members, or go observe the car engine and develop your own theory.'

'My father says that answers to every conceivable question that pops up in the human head are available on the Internet.'

'That may be so. But for this exercise, these are the only forms of research that are permitted.'

The next day, class began with palpable enthusiasm. The first group emphatically established that the car by itself is not a dangerous thing. Its safety on the roads depends upon the people who use it. Another group demolished the idea of having three or four rows of seats in a car because then it would turn into a minibus! A third group that had preferred to undertake research through keen observation, surmised that even the sundry-looking wires and pipes had a huge role to play. They candidly accepted that they had no idea why they cluttered around the engine, but as the Sports Teacher had told them that even if one wire or pipe snapped, the car would not work.

Cuebee's group did their research by relying on her father's expertise. Techie, Yoga, Millie, Geekay and Cuebee presented before the class. Yoga went to the green chalkboard and drew parts of the engine as they had understood it.

Next, Cuebee, Techie and Geekay explained each part first. 'Inside the engine are these kinds of cylinders as you see on the board. There are four of them. The spark plug is used for lighting up the petrol inside the cylinder. Cylinder is the place where the petrol gets ignited or lighted. The piston moves up and down with the help of the connecting rod and crankshaft to increase or decrease the space within the cylinder.'

Then Millie presented a silly poem.

The car engine has many parts,
Shoom, shoom, shoom
Cylinders, piston, spark plug and crankshaft
Woom, woom, woom
Wires and pipes are also there
Poom, poom, poom
Filling up the front and also the rear
Room, room, room
Together they make the engine vroom
Making the car run zoom, zoom, zoom.

Cuebee summed up their presentation with the look of a person shrouded in doubt. 'This is all we could understand,' she said.

'All of you have done amazing research. Let's clap for all of us.' The applause on the stated directions of the Science Teacher could be heard in all the classrooms as I was told later that night.

'First, the cylinder has to suck in a mixture of air and petrol. For this, the crankshaft pulls the piston down and provides space in the cylinder. As the piston goes up after that, it presses the mixture of petrol and air in a smaller space. It is called compression. At this time, the spark plug ignites the mixture. On getting ignited, this mixture expands and pushes the piston down. But since the crankshaft is moving continuously, the piston goes back up. This time, it pushes all the waste or burnt fuel out of the engine. This kind of movement gives energy to the axle to move the car.'

I am only summing up the Science Teacher's discussions that day. He patiently explained the working of the car and answered each query to the utter satisfaction of many of the question-bearers. But the continued looks of perplexity on many other faces prompted him to become a counsellor of sorts.

'As you go to higher classes, you will understand many concepts. Please don't get troubled if you don't understand everything at once. Learning is a gradual process, keep your eyes and ears open. Just never lose your ability to question.'

'But I still don't understand why cars are not made of wood or plastic. Will it not be easier and cheaper?' Sky kept at it.

'The first cars were like powered tricycles, then came some covered ones, with thick cloth or fabric. And as the car technology became more complex and the speed increased, it became important to make the car stronger. Wood is weaker than metal; it can rot very soon. A plastic body may not be safe in case of a crash. Metal is easy to mould and repair; it doesn't tear very soon. But many cars had a roof made of a kind of plastic, which is also known as convertible. Does that satisfy you?'

The Science Teacher then displayed several types of car models that he had collected for this class. It was a very enriching experience but it left the children with another binge of questions, such that they refused to pay heed to the last school bell of the day.

Butterfly Teacher came to the rescue.

'We will have one more class next week on the car. Meanwhile, I have a new activity for you.'

At the mention of the word 'new,' all conversation stopped. Eyes to the front. Body alert. Attention caught—hook, line and sinker.

'From today we will all maintain our personal diaries, where we will note down all the questions that arise in our minds, in class, in school, outside school, at home, anywhere. This diary of yours, will remain with you till you leave school. It will be the story of your journey of learning. It will also be a constant reminder to be curious, to never hesitate to ask questions. Let us call it the "Forever Diary".'

'Teacher, why "forever"?' asked Cuebee.

'Forever, because it will be with you, always.'

The glimmer of hope of another week, and another lesson on the car did comfort the children in the intermittent period. On the appointed day, exactly a week later, they wanted what they had waited for. However, the Science Teacher was too caught up on that day in some administrative matters and could not make it to their class. He informed them that the session on the car would now be held next week. Butterfly Teacher knew that the children were in no position to face the interregnum resolutely, unless given a task that would occupy their restless minds.

'To be able to participate in the next class, you have to draw a bus, a truck and a tractor. Also, please do a bit of research on what the three pedals at the bottom of the driver's seat are for.'

By now, 'research' was a popular word in my classroom. In fact, the kids had been flaunting their research capabilities to the higher classes, the Head Teacher, and as I overheard, even at home. In school, in the last one week, they had already offered their expert research abilities for checking on why one of the fans in the school was not working; why men wear pants and women *salwar-kameez* or *sari*; what would grow best in the kitchen garden; why kids in the neighbouring classroom always sat in pin-drop silence; why children should be allowed to eat chocolate, and so on. They wore their faculty with the confidence of being able to eclipse a PhD student, no less.

When the Science Teacher entered the classroom next week, hungry minds and eager tongues were ready to drown his discussions. He managed to raise his voice above the others, and asked each group to make a two-minute presentation on their exploration. Their presentations were indeed well-researched. One group did a role play where three children sat crouched on the floor acting as pedals, one acted as a driver, and a fifth narrated the mechanism. Cuebee, meanwhile, was unable to control her excitement about her group's understanding of the mechanism of the three pedals which her father had explained to them the previous evening.

'I will explain our research with the help of a poem that was written by us with Millie's ideas,' she said.

I am the Aksa-le-ra-ter, To add speed to you.
I am the Brake, I will stop you.
I am the Clutch, To add power to you.
Three of us A, B, C, Make the car go.
To start press C, To stop press C.

Press A, leave B, Press B, leave A.
C-A-B, Remember me!

The whole class clapped almost hysterically.

'Teacher, we want to go to the car, no lessons inside today!' they shouted.

And they were allowed, of course. It was part of the new process to occasionally allow children to decide the course of the class. The Science Teacher took a chart paper along with him. He laid it on the ground next to the car and asked Cuebee's group to draw the three pedals and mark them in sequence.

'What happens if I press all three together, Teacher?' asked Bullie.

'That's a silly question. Do you have three legs to press all three pedals together?' Seerie's statement led to mirth in the class.

'I can use two feet and one hand.'

'Yes, that is certainly possible. But if you press all three when the car is still, there will be a loud noise in the engine and the car will not move at all. And if the car is already moving at speed, then the car will suddenly stop and the engine will make a lot of noise in this case too.' The Science Teacher was very patient with Bullie.

'But why?' insisted Bullie.

'Can I answer?' Cuebee asked. On getting a nod from the Science Teacher, she tried to answer Bullie's query.

'From what I have learnt, the clutch connects the running engine to the axle which moves the wheels. The aksa-le-rater gives more petrol to the engine to run faster. So, if you press all three pedals, the engine starts running faster without moving the car!'

'Yes, that is a simple explanation. There are some more parts in the car, which I think we should leave for higher grades. And if you ask anything more, you are going to scare the wits out of your Teachers.' The assumed ignorance of their teachers as expressed by the Science Teacher drew many chuckles from the kids.

'Nothing is clear to me. What burns, where, how can fire move a wheel, why are there so many wires inside, what is the battery used for? This car has baffled me. Look at my Forever Diary. It's full of questions. Teacher, I need the whole lesson again.' Imli was visibly disturbed.

'Imli is so foolish, she understands nothing. Teacher, I can teach her if you allow.' Bullie was clearly boasting.

'I read somewhere that fools seem to know it all!' murmured Mindesh almost under his breath. Bullie definitely heard it and perhaps gauged the strength of the remark too, and just as he prepared to pounce on Mindesh, Anxy and Millie quickly stood between the two like an oasis of peace in a desert of conflicts. If my memory serves me correctly, this episode ended the car session on that day, and Cuebee took it upon herself to help Imli understand the car better. Mind you, none of this was a part of any of the textbooks assigned for study by the class.

We classrooms, as you know by now, were frequently tempted towards speculation on subjects on which we had little or no expertise on. In this series, the colossal role of textbooks was often the subject of our tête-à-tête.

Temporal: When the car, globe, birds, playground, kitchen garden and even toilets are being used to teach the kids new things, should a new textbook not be designed based on all this?

Hippocampus: Or should there be textbooks at all?

Parietal: It is not as if the textbooks are not good. They are excellent. But it all seems like a fairy tale to children, as if they are happening elsewhere and to other people. Unless they experience it themselves …

Occipital: Yes, it appears that real-life experiences, doing things yourself, are the key to sustainable learning.

Amygdala: How can you say that? What hands-on experiences do we classrooms have? We don't have hands in case you have forgotten. Do you mean to tell me that we have learnt nothing?

Occipital: Experiencing is also living through events and happenings. I think we too are learning.

Hippocampus: So, coming back to textbooks, do we have any answers?

There were none. And we secretly did feel that it seemed too wanton and needless to destroy, even if with the help of a conversation, a system that had delivered pretty well in the past.

7

Democracy, aristocracy and a car ride

THE FIRST THREE GRADES FOR CUEBEE HAD BEEN riveting and engaging without an ounce of superfluous. She seemed to have acquired an extensive taste for research, observation and experimentation, Millie-style poetry writing, *nukkad nataks*, peer learning and group and collaborative work. She was all of nine years old, looked forward to her double-digit age, and had a general air of gladness about her. One would have assumed that nothing, really nothing, could modify this status, and nothing could tempt fate to do so within the confines of a school, tucked away in a far-flung corner of the earth. After all, we knew the ropes, and ropes don't change easily.

The school had a system wherein the children who joined Grade 1 in a particular classroom, continued in the same classroom till the end of their schooling here. It was only the number plate outside the room that would announce a change in the grade level. The Head Teacher was convinced that the children had so many more things to adjust to in life, so one less thing to adjust to could only be helpful. A good system or bad, well, I really cannot comment. All I can say is that not altering the scenery where Cuebee was playing the lead role, worked to my benefit. My bricked life had begun to revolve around that of Cuebee.

On the first morning of the new academic session, the sun was as relentless as it ought to be in the middle of June. The plate on the wall outside my door now proudly proclaimed 'Class IV'. After the morning assembly, Cuebee and classmates, bright-eyed and high-spirited, walked into my good old space with the same spring in their steps that I had got so accustomed to seeing. The furniture had been rearranged to have the age-old three-column seating plan, with all the students facing the board. Each of them felt a pang I am sure, but such tiny setbacks were not going to deter them from making best of the grade.

They settled down with anticipation, awaiting an introduction to their new class teacher. Minutes later, Alphabet Teacher entered the room with a sheaf of papers and a bundle of small books in her hand. Without uttering a word or even directing a welcoming smile towards the expectant faces, she dumped the stuff on the table, and with her back to the class, she started writing on the green chalkboard: D-I-C-T-I-O-N-A-R-Y.

The children cupped their palms and tried to speak into each other's ears in low murmurs. I could see their eyebrows were finding it hard to settle in their prescribed place on the faces. Such was the mood in the class.

'No talking,' Alphabet Teacher said in a stern voice. 'We will learn about the use of a dictionary today.'

'Are you our class teacher this year?' Yoga could not suppress his curiosity any more.

'Yes, I am.'

'Then why were you trying to hide this information from us?' Bullie butted in.

'There will be pin-drop silence in the classroom when I teach. Only when you are asked to, you may ask questions. Is that clear?' Alphabet Teacher half yelled her diktat. Bullie's query had not gone down well with her.

'But Teacher, we want to be introduced to you,' Millie persisted.

'I said no more questions or chit-chat! Is that clear?' she thundered this time.

Alphabet Teacher achieved her goal within the span of barely a minute or two. The class fell silent, and faces appeared as if they were experiencing great difficulties in extricating themselves out of a war-torn area.

But the teacher continued as if nothing had happened. She distributed the tiny books, one on each table. She taught them about the dictionary, about nouns and pronouns, and introduced them to division—all packed into a single day. The children continued in a state of shock and never spoke a word until the end of the day. I could see that the reason for their silence was that they were wounded, and not because they preferred to be quiet.

That is the way it went, class after class, day after day in Grade 4. Most of the kids looked on askance as the teacher would declare one topic completed after a couple of periods. They just did not know how to deal with the increasing pile of lessons they did not comprehend. The Forever Diaries of almost all the students had a spate of furious entries every day. Cuebee, Techie and Geekay took it upon themselves to help some of the other kids through peer learning. They had learnt about its mechanism when their seating plan had facilitated group work in their earlier grades. It was not as if they had grasped everything either; it was just that their faculties were pretty active as they had embarked upon self-learning.

Cuebee, despite all efforts, was unable to disentangle herself from a growing feeling that classes would from now on continue in the same monotonous manner and that her happy days had come to an end. One morning, Cuebee and Techie were early to school. They went straight to the class and sat down quietly. I could see Cuebee's eyes welling up with tears as she looked longingly outside towards the car.

Techie walked up to Cuebee and said in a very reflective tone, 'I am not saying that I am smarter than the others, but if I have to keep looking after other kid's needs, will I ever become better?'

Cuebee thought for a moment, and unhesitatingly said, 'I also think I am better than the others in many activities. But my mother tells me that we live in a society where each person is different. We must learn to live, like and work with people even if we feel that they are not as good as us. That is life.'

Techie half-agreed. 'I don't think we have a choice till we grow older. I will work very hard to study in the best place in the world. But yes, I agree with your mother, she is very nice. I will try harder to like everyone.'

Mindesh had entered the room exactly when the two girls had begun their serious chat. He listened quietly and joined in uninvited, 'I really like the way both of you talk. And Cuebee, you used to ask so many questions. But see how fast we are completing the syllabus, now that there are no discussions. And I am getting enough time to cram up too. After all, we are not expected to understand everything, are we?'

Cuebee and Techie were startled and aghast on hearing Mindesh's words. They suddenly felt that the school was too small to run away from such obviously 'different' assemblage! Cuebee's mother had certainly not prepared her daughter for this!

Alphabet Teacher announced that day that the objective of the next lesson was that children should be able to differentiate between objects and activities from the past and the present. She very briefly gave examples of transport used in the past and the present. And then she did the most unheard, unseen of things. She drew a table on the chalkboard, wrote 'transport', 'currency', 'houses', 'clothes', 'tools', 'skills', etc., in the first column, and then gave examples for each in the past and the present in the next two columns, respectively. After finishing, she whizzed around as if in a hurry and announced, 'You may write this down in your notebooks and learn them by heart. I will give you a test on this tomorrow.'

Planting 'learning' on young minds in this manner was a first for the class. Most of them were appalled. There was something about this teacher that sapped a student's determination to learn. Cuebee could take it no longer.

'Teacher, can we learn all this through an activity?'

'Why would we do that?'

'That way all our questions get answered, Teacher.'

'Cuebee, I appreciate your questions, but with the answers you tend to generate a whole new set of questions. We have limited time in class.' Alphabet Teacher explained patiently at first. Perhaps, in her own way, the teacher wasn't wrong, but Cuebee's face fell with disappointment written all over it.

'Teacher, that's what I keep telling her. Finishing the syllabus in the textbook is more important than idling away our time doing endless activities.' Mindesh was feeling unusually independent and spoke in a loud and clear voice. He was always dazed by Cuebee's inquisitiveness. I considered Mindesh a very sincere student, but he did not appear to have the critical thinking faculties of some of the other kids like Cuebee, at least not yet.

'Mindesh, you are a good student.' The teacher showed her favouritism openly, and in the most qualmless of manners.

Cuebee was already in a reduced state of affairs. 'But, Teacher, I thought learning was all about understanding what is going on, and not memorizing without understanding,' she quipped.

'That's it! No more of this utter nonsense! I do not like students speaking back at me! Now hold your silence or I will turn you out of the class!'

There was nothing Cuebee could do except sit down and brood for the rest of the day. But this was not a child who gave up easily in the face of odds. Next week, Alphabet Teacher was teaching the students about democracy and the right to vote. Something strange must have come over the teacher, for she directed a query towards the class, almost as if interrogating the witnesses to confirm that they were in attendance at the scene of teaching.

'Any questions?'

'Why is democracy better than other systems?' Cuebee's repressed emotions suddenly erupted.

'Because it gives a choice to citizens to elect their representatives who form the government.'

'But you said that the majority wins in democracy.'

'Yes, that is the beauty of the democratic system.' Alphabet Teacher appeared to be in an enlarged mood as she continued to field Cuebee's questions with just a hint of annoyance.

'What if the majority also holds the wrong point of view?'

'What do you mean? Give me an example.'

'Like, if you ask in the class right now whether we want to study or play, the majority would choose to play, but that may not be appropriate at this time.'

'Cuebee, you use too much of that coconut between your ears for your age,' said the teacher, clearly exasperated by now.

'But you did not answer my question.'

'I am teaching you as per your syllabus, and you are not supposed to know more than that.'

'If democracy is so good, why can't we decide what, when and how we should be taught in school. Why is our viewpoint not considered?' Cuebee was in no mood to comply,

'Cuebee, you are a kid; you can't decide things in school. Even the right to vote is given after eighteen years of age.'

'Do children have any right or not, can't they express themselves freely?' an offended Cuebee continued to assert.

'Cuebee, you are testing my patience now. Just sit quietly now and let me finish my chapter. Never forget, that I am in authority here, and not you.' Alphabet Teacher was infuriated.

Disappointment and hurt were so visible in Cuebee's eyes that day. It saddened me. I was having a foreboding that things would only get worse from here. I had a deep urge to discuss this matter with my classroom friends. I poured out the whole set of events.

Cerebellum: For the last three years we have seen the other end of the spectrum, where the curiosity of this child was nurtured.

Occipital: And it is quite a challenge to retain the curiosity of a child and not suppress it forever.

Temporal: The Head Teacher is so conscious of this fact.

Frontal: How can you tell a child to not ask questions! How will she understand the concept? It will only promote rote memorization.

Hippocampus: Well... the teacher does have the responsibility to complete the syllabus, otherwise parents may object.

Frontal: Well, yes, but still, is it the done thing to discourage any child from being curious? Is it not a natural and inherent quality of every child? Can we get past their education by suppressing these innate aspects?

Hippocampus: You have a point. I need to be more sensitive to the other point of view.

Frontal: What I like best about you, dear old friend, Hippocampus, is your ability to remedy your ideas with changing times. I only wish Alphabet Teacher was more like you!

Well into Grade 4, the Head Teacher had become acutely aware of Cuebee becoming distant and unusually silent. Her morning set of well-thought-out questions that she would pose to him, were now few and far between. One morning he accosted a deep-in-thought Cuebee in the corridor.

'Cuebee, why are you so silent nowadays? Is your question bank empty?'

'No, I am alright,' she said, almost disconnectedly.

'I sense a despondency in you. What is it, Cuebee? Let me help you.'

'I had asked a question the other day about what happens if the majority views in a democracy do not reflect the right perspective. Teacher told me that I ask too many unnecessary questions and that I should focus on what is written in the textbooks. I am trying to do that, but the textbook does not have all the answers for me. Is it wrong to ask questions, Teacher?' It all gushed out like free-flowing water suddenly let out of a hose pipe.

'Unless you ask questions, how will your mind be more open to see connections in the world around us? You will not find learning meaningful. Every time you ask a question, and understand the answers, you are building your learning skills, Cuebee.'

They continued to talk like two adults sharing their innermost fears, until the bell for the morning assembly rang. The whole exchange must have had quite an impact on the Head Teacher for he walked in unannounced into Grade 4 the very next day.

'So how is your class coming along?' the Head Teacher asked Alphabet Teacher.

'Sir, we are trying to complete the syllabus on time,' she casually replied without stopping whatever she was writing on the chalkboard.

'And how are you ensuring that children are learning all the concepts?'

'Sir, I am taking regular class tests and also asking them questions once I complete a chapter.' This time she let go of the chalk, turned around and replied in an assertive tone.

'I am not quite in agreement with your approach. We have discussed this several times. Please change your pedagogy to one that is activity-based,' the Head Teacher almost whispered in her ear. It was clear that he did not want the children to hear this part.

'Sir, we will try to follow your advice, but the children ask too many questions, and that is a real wastage of time,' Alphabet Teacher said loudly, uncertain of her own commitment.

'Well, since you want it so much, I will myself initiate activity-based learning in your class tomorrow,' said the Head Teacher as if he had not heard the last bit.

Next morning, the children cheered with genuine enthusiasm as the Head Teacher entered the room.

'Good morning children, today we are going to learn about the difference between aristocracy and democracy through an activity.'

Then he suggested that the class be divided into two groups.

'One group will be led by a king and another group will choose its leader, and both groups are being given a few common issues to decide.'

Through a lottery system, two groups were created. Bullie became the king in one group with Imli, Simla, Mindesh, Anxy and others as team members. The other group with Cuebee, Millie, Yoga, BeeTee, Techie and others was asked to elect their leader; they all decided that Cuebee would be their leader.

Then, the Head Teacher explained the rules.

'Being the king, Bullie, you can decide things as per your wish, with or without consulting anyone. Cuebee, you should decide things on the basis of the majority's opinion, but do not forget to address the concerns of classmates who are not in majority, and to the extent possible, try to bring about a consensus on important issues.'

Next, the Head Teacher proceeded to the blackboard and wrote down four common issues to be decided upon by both groups.

1. What should be the desk arrangement in the class?
2. What should be the assessment procedure for the subjects?
3. What should be the timetable of the class?
4. What should be the homework policy?

Meanwhile, the Social Science Teacher had also joined them. The Head Teacher indicated with a flourish of his hands to him and Alphabet Teacher to withdraw from the centre of the class and be seated in one corner to keep a close watch on the developments in both the groups.

Bullie's group worked in a jiffy.

'Oh, these are easy issues. I am the king. I will decide quickly. The desk arrangement will be in theatre style; there will be no homework, duration of school hours will be reduced, and no assessment for any subject.'

Bullie finished and announced to the Teachers that all his decisions as king were taken. His group members looked visibly disturbed but decided to keep quiet about it, as they knew that they were not supposed to have a voice in aristocracy. Mindesh still went ahead and raised some objections.

'With no homework and assessment, our parents will not be able to know whether we are learning or not, and curtailing school hours is not a good idea.'

'I am the king and no one is allowed to oppose me. And you, Mindesh, better yield to my decisions, unless you want to be banished from my kingdom!'

Bullie was deep into the act. Mindesh knew that these were not good decisions, but simmered down to get into the skin of the role-play as a submissive subject to an aristocrat.

On the other side of the room, the group led by Cuebee was in heated discussions over the desk arrangements.

'I don't like the present seating arrangement; we can have round tables and face each other,' said Millie.

'Can we have two long desks so that we can be seated facing each other? This will reduce the groups to two, as opposed to too many round tables.'

Techie did not agree with Millie.

'Why can't we continue with the present theatre-style seating? How will we see the blackboard properly in round tables or large table seating?' Yoga was obviously not very pleased with the suggestions and wanted to maintain status quo.

'Techie and Millie, why do you want to change the present seating system?' Cuebee initiated her arguments to resolve the issue.

'Because, the present system does not pay enough attention to backbenchers,' Millie said.

'I agree. And also, it's too boring to sit in this style every day,' Techie added.

'What about the concern raised by Yoga?' said Cuebee.

'They are also valid concerns,' Techie said after pondering on it.

'I am suggesting a possible solution. Let us have a flexible seating pattern in our classroom. If we are working in large groups, we will follow Techie's pattern of conference seating in two large groups. For smaller groups' work, we will follow the round-table pattern suggested by Millie. If the chalkboard is being used, then we can have U-shaped seating to ensure proper attention to each child.'

'We agree!' was the response in unison to the complete surprise of the Alphabet Teacher.

Cuebee felt confident now and moved forward to deliberate on the pattern of assessment.

'Should we have class tests, or annual exams or some other method of assessments?'

'I don't like tests. I find it very difficult to write so much text in a short duration of time. Also, I hate surprise class tests.' Yoga was categorical.

'I don't like to memorize things for tests without knowing their logic; I would rather know and understand things in depth,' Techie said with a sideways glance at Alphabet Teacher.

'We should have a no-tests-and-no-exams policy,' said Millie, without really believing in what she was saying.

'If we have no exams or tests, how will we know whether we have learnt the prescribed syllabus or not. But I don't know the substitute.' Cuebee reflected on the problem.

'Can we not make exams interesting?' said Techie.

'Yes, how about exams and tests being conducted in a manner that we don't find them boring and scary,' Sky added.

'Till the time we decide on the exact form of assessment, we can have oral presentations, and the teacher can ask questions in the class to assess whether we have learnt or not?' This was BeeTee's opinion.

'Teachers should also see whether or not we are helping our peers; whether we are reading books available in the library, whether we know of things that are not related to the textbooks,' reflected Cuebee.

'All these things should be made part of our report card. Right now, they merely depict the marks in subjects; let us redesign our report cards. My report card should show my love for animals,' said an overjoyed Yoga.

'And my love for art,' said Arty.

'So, in conclusion, Teachers please pay more attention to what we do in the classroom every day, rather than holding one-time examinations,' said a seasoned Cuebee. She also suggested that Yoga and BeeTee 'work on redesigning assessment and report cards', if they wished to.

Of course, they did!

The next topic was very close to their hearts.

'Why can't we have no-homework days twice a week?' Yoga initiated the discussions.

'We all have our hobbies, and we need time to pursue them, so no-homework days in a week is a good idea. What about the quantum of homework? Should it not be reduced considerably?' Cuebee asked.

'But will our parents agree? I think they will raise objections to everything we have decided until now. They will certainly point fingers at us thinking we are looking for excuses to not study.'

Millie was suddenly not too sure of the whole process.

'This is a real problem, I think we need to convene a PTM to explain and convince them about the decisions which we have taken,' exclaimed Cuebee.

The timetable was also similarly discussed and it was decided that one hour of flexi, unstructured learning must be continued in all grades. The Head Teacher was conspicuously elated with the discussions.

'So, children, now I leave it to you to decide which system is better, aristocracy or democracy, as we explain these terms further to you,' saying this, the Head Teacher and the Social Science Teacher began to explain the tenets of the two systems. I am sure that the Head Teacher was secretly convinced that by this simple activity he had managed to shatter several illusions and upturn multiple beliefs that may have been closely regarded by Alphabet Teacher.

My classroom-mates were awaiting my account of the day, all agog. As soon as I finished describing it all, they tried their best to emulate a standing ovation, simply by announcing that their Millie-is-cools—we had renamed 'molecules' after Millie's idea—were clapping inside, and loudly so.

Temporal: So, when children are given the responsibility to decide upon seemingly adult issues, they are capable of pragmatically deliberating over it.

Brainstem: Yes, and how much we underestimate them.

Cerebellum: It is almost as if they have the intellect of adults.

Frontal: But definitely free from their vices, I say!

But then, our worst fears came true. The expected change in pedagogy did not happen. Alphabet Teacher continued, regardless of all that had transpired earlier. Cuebee was unceremoniously put down each time she raised a hand to clear a doubt. In fact, it almost felt as if Cuebee was being targeted by the teacher as the propagator of all her woes with the Head Teacher. All the happy memories that I had stored up so far were quickly dissipating in the face of what Cuebee had to deal with every day. The life and soul of the little girl must have been in turmoil, for she would be mostly found sitting still and quiet in the classroom, as if every mitochondrion had been extracted from her cells.

Mindesh, on the other hand, continued to flourish as the favourite of Alphabet Teacher. She did not even deem it fit to hide her proclivity. In fact, she was ever pleased with him, as she sincerely appreciated his disgruntled reaction whenever some out-of-box activity, such as the car, was imposed on the children.

'This group-work kills the initiative of the best,' she discussed with the Language Teacher.

'These new pedagogical practices are detrimental and may lead to very bad results for the school in future.' The Language Teacher was in complete agreement.

'Low-level achievers and middle-level achievers who are involved in a heterogeneous group activity may do better in tests, but the best would be scaled down to their level,' surmised Alphabet Teacher in gloomy satisfaction.

They were discussing all this within my hearing distance. I wished I could knock some sense into them. Since I could not, I contemplated, broodingly though, on the wreckage that their views could leave behind. Cuebee was almost becoming a shadow of her old self. After witnessing the methods of the Head Teacher, Butterfly Teacher, Rainbow Teacher and Buddy Teacher, even the Science and now the Social Science Teacher, no one could convince me otherwise from my sturdy belief that all groups of students benefit from the important social skills they develop by working together in groups.

I looked forward to the car lesson, which had been the first science lab for children, as I knew that it would be the only saving grace in the tumultuous sea of rote learning this year. But the car lesson took place almost at the end of the academic year after the winter holidays. The Head Teacher had got a mechanic to repair the car, charge the battery, restore the lights and put another coat of wax polish. The car looked dashingly handsome and remarkably priceless.

Meanwhile, the Head Teacher carried a mysterious air about him, as if he had something interesting up his sleeves. Even the teachers were not aware. As he sauntered into the Grade 4 classroom that day, a large poster in hand, the children gathered around him, tugging at his clothes, asking what was in store for them. The first thing he did was shifting the furniture to the sides of the room with the help of the kids and Alphabet Teacher. Then, he unrolled the huge poster he was carrying on the floor of my classroom. It contained the outline of a car in three views—front, rear and side view.

'Oh! It's the car lesson!' exclaimed one excited kid after the other. They could not believe their eyes. Their admiration for this lesson was boundless, and they made it a point to exhibit their emotions.

'Children, first we will recall our previous learning. Each one of you shall name one part of the car on the chart itself. As I call out your names, come to this side, and write the name.'

'And after that, Teacher?'

'After that, there is a surprise for all of you.'

A wave of exhilaration swept through the class, though Alphabet Teacher, and to some degree Cuebee standing quietly in one corner, appeared untouched by it. Since suspense was not something the kids had learnt to withstand as yet, the car parts were named in a flash. Activity completed, the Head Teacher advanced towards the car, children in tow. He opened the front door of the car, sat in the driver's seat, put the car keys in the keyhole, and lo and behold, the car started!

And that was not the end of the suspense. He then invited six kids at a time so they could be taken for a joy ride around the playground.

The children were not necessarily new to car rides, but the magnetism of the ride was such that every child rolled out of the car starry-eyed, verging on a state of stupor! The Head Teacher gathered them back in the class for discussions. But as soon as the kids awoke from the inertia of the stupor, they drowned the room in the cacophony of experience-sharing and questions for the Head Teacher who tried his best to answer each of them.

The horn of the car was the fascinating topic of discussion that day.

'What is the need for a horn?'

'The horn in any car or vehicle is mandatory by law. It serves as a loud warning to alert pedestrians and other vehicles. It is also frequently used to warn other drivers.'

'How does the sound come out on pressing the steering wheel?'

'That I will check and tell you tomorrow.' The Head Teacher was always candid in admitting his ignorance.

'How is the sound produced?'

'We can hear sound because it is made up of vibrations, or sound waves. When these waves reach our ears, they cause the sensitive skin of the eardrums to vibrate.'

'What is a wave, Teacher?'

'Waves are a type of motion pattern. Through this motion, energy is transferred from one location to another without exchanging matter. There are various sorts of waves. We can hear sound because sound waves travel through air. Water waves move on the surface of the water. Light waves travel through space in straight paths. Before you get confused let me show you something.' Saying this, he took out a six-foot-long rope.

'I will show you a wave; just hold this rope from one end, Bullie.'

Bullie held the rope and the Head Teacher tugged at it with an upward and a downward movement; the rope had an oscillation.

'This is a wave, and it is called a sine wave. Remember this and write it in your Forever Diary for future understanding.'

The class was awestruck. Science had its way of confounding much more with every answer given! Meanwhile, Alphabet Teacher felt her precious life slip by as she was left hanging on to a hopeless class in the hope that better sense would soon prevail over the humankind that she was dealing with.

Mindesh was intently observing the class. This was the only out-of-syllabus lesson he enjoyed. But somehow, though the car did fascinate him, he whispered to Cuebee, sitting quietly, next to him.

'Something stops me from asking questions, although my mind is full of them.'

'But why? Why don't you ask?' She finally broke into a friendly smile.

'Because the Teachers also get irritated and most of the time, they don't have the answers anyway.'

Cuebee fell silent again, and she turned away with a faraway look in her eyes. The Head Teacher had noticed the signs of permanency creeping in to the changes in Cuebee. He felt that he had misjudged her whole situation and needed to work harder on bringing the child back to her inherent nature.

One afternoon after school hours, the Head Teacher called for a staff meeting. There was no doubt in his mind that this meeting was just what the doctor had ordered for some of the Teachers.

'I have called this meeting so that we can all prepare a good pedagogical plan for all the teaching ahead, consisting of interesting and age-appropriate activities for all grades.'

'Sir, I don't want to oppose your ideas, but I am not yet convinced of this method of endless questions that are the tag-alongs for all activity-based learning. It seems to me that children are asking for the sake of asking rather than genuinely seeking answers. They have, in fact, started enjoying the questioning, as if we Teachers are in the witness box and guilty of not knowing!' Alphabet Teacher almost detonated in cold respectfulness.

'Look, is your problem more that the prescribed syllabus is getting left behind, or that you can't answer the queries of the children?' the Head Teacher almost lost it but quickly resumed his calm composure.

Alphabet Teacher was caught unawares. 'Sir, it is both in a way.'

'The term "classroom" is becoming obsolete by itself. These are learning spaces and the future has arrived. The classroom should now include flexibility and collaboration or we are already living in the past.' The Head Teacher tried his best to explain.

'Then sir, are all the methods that we had followed so far, completely and absolutely wrong?' Alphabet Teacher was not convinced easily.

'The earlier methods are not wrong. They may even have been alright for the context in which they took birth. They just need continuous modification to suit the needs of the day. They simply cannot support changing requirements; in fact, they may end up obstructing new habits and activities.'

'Sir, I am bound by conduct rules to follow your orders, and I will do so. But I have serious reservations on the sustainability of such a model.'

'We, the Teachers, teach children to read, write, manipulate numbers, observe and record their world experiences, and give them experiences that stimulate their imagination and broaden their horizons. Let them ask, let them be happy, even if it is about our ignorance. It will compel them to explore, ask more. Please believe in this, and you will thank yourself one day for being part of this reform.'

The staff meeting turned out to be a bilateral negotiation between the Head Teacher and Alphabet Teacher, with no signs of either side diluting their position to accommodate the other. None of the other teachers got a chance to get in edgeways. The Head Teacher may have eventually decided that a staff meeting may not have been the best solution to the problem at hand.

While Cuebee was in the earlier grades, I would often forget how time just slipped by and the academic session would be over in a flash. But this year turned out to be slow and painful, for both Cuebee and me. I think the impact of Cuebee's despondency was such that I had practically lost my sunny side, which, I had firmly held, was responsible for making me the universal favourite amongst the classrooms. Cuebee came out of Grade 4, a quiet, unexcitable, uninquisitive child, crestfallen that learning was no longer an engaging and joyful affair.

On the last day of school in that grade when Grandma came to pick her up, Cuebee directed an odd question at her.

'Did you decide to discontinue your education after Grade 5 because you disliked school?'

Grandma was stunned. She looked at Cuebee with warm eyes. Her grandchild had something really bleak about the way she delivered the question, almost as if she had swallowed a tsunami before speaking.

'No, my dear child, I loved my school. In those days, we girls were married off very early, and that is why I had to leave school.'

'Good for you, Grandma! Maybe you should marry me off too!' Cuebee spoke fiercely as if she belonged to a pro-child marriage society or a league for the suppression of school education.

This really upset Grandma. She knelt down, held Cuebee by the shoulders and looked her in the eye.

'Cuebee, listen to me. Life will never be a bed of roses. There will be ups and downs. Let that never deter you from acquiring knowledge. If one door closes, look for another door to seek knowledge. Don't give up so easily, Cuebee. You are stronger than that!' Grandma had tears in her eyes. The Head Teacher had kept her informed of the impact of Grade 4 and its classroom transactions on Cuebee. She realized only now, how badly her poor dear little grandchild was hit.

'I cannot see you like this, Grandma. I promise that I will not let anything come in the way of my learning,' Cuebee said, as she wiped away her own as well as her grandma's tears with the edge of her skirt. The two of them then tightly entwined the fingers of one hand each and ambled away, not to be seen for the next forty-five days of summer vacations.

Meanwhile, we classrooms spent the entire vacation discussing threadbare the advantages and disadvantages of rote- versus activity-based learning, and arrived at our own conclusions, faulty or otherwise.

Parietal: Do you think The Head Teacher is being impractical? Is he obsessed with the idea or experimenting with the children?

Temporal: The kind of rich and varied learning experiences that activity-based and experiential learning can provide, rote learning is no match.

Occipital: And do not forget that the school is responsible for transforming a solo learner into a social learner. Without collaborative work, how will it happen?

Amygdala: Even if I agree in principle with you, Parietal has managed to sow the seeds of doubt in my mortar. It is driving me insane.

Temporal: Some bit of insane behaviour is imperative for change. I think you are finally changing, Amygdala!

Hippocampus: Do you recall we had left our discussion on textbooks hanging, as we had no answers then.

Temporal: We don't have answers now either.

Hippocampus: Well, I feel textbooks need not be as unversed with the ways of the world of learning as they are made out to be.

Frontal: Yes, I too have been thinking on those lines after seeing how Alphabet Teacher worships every word in them.

Amygdala: Do you have any bright ideas?

Parietal: All bright ideas must take reality into account. If we want the millions of our children in schools to get good quality education, then the millions of teachers also need support and guidance about what to teach.

Frontal: Well, I was thinking that since the majority of the teachers go by the written word, perhaps there should be a system of developing and prescribing resource books to teachers for teaching each topic, just as we prescribe textbooks to students. The resource book will give a suggested list of experiential learning and activity-based interventions for each topic. This way, the teachers who love to, can stick to the written text on the one hand, and the syllabus is also completed in an engaging manner, on the other.

Cerebellum: Hey roomsters! I am sorry I am late. Wassup?

Temporal: While you were late in materializing into our chit-chat session, Frontal seems to have hit upon the solution of this century!

Cerebellum: Is it reasonable to assume that your lordships shall tell me about it of your own volition, or do I have to wring it out of you?

Frontal: We prefer it to be squeezed out of us by a classroom that is static and stationary in perpetuity. Do try!

8

Pulse, music and speech

6.25 a.m.: The Head Teacher and few other teachers enter school through the side gate.

6.30 a.m.: Main gate of the school creaks wide open.

6.31 a.m.: Cuebee, Millie, Yoga and Geekay bounce into school.

6.33 a.m.: The four kids drop their bags in my classroom now marked 'Class V' and rush to the car in the playground.

6.35 a.m.: They are all over the car, with Millie on top of it, singing a song from the latest Bollywood film, and the rest doing some form of a twirl-and-whirl routine, perhaps hoping for it to be recognized as a dance form.

6.45 a.m.: The Head Teacher joins them. He sings along at first, and then answers several questions posed by Cuebee and feigns ignorance about several others.

7 a.m.: A surge of small humanity begins to enter the precincts of the school in waves, as if suddenly let off from their caged confinement.

7.15 a.m.: The school bell rings for the first morning assembly after a well-earned summer vacation.

It was once again the month of June and the sun was a bit unsure that day, you know, whether 'to-be or not-to-be' scorching. Cuebee and her friends were in their element as they entered their revered classroom with great promptitude, soon after the assembly. Their elements lasted but briefly on encountering Alphabet Teacher already standing in class, hands on hips. The children knew too well from past experiences at home and in school that the specific stance of hands-on-hips was never the harbinger of good tidings! Barring Mindesh, most faces fell to embrace melancholy. Bullie attempted to imitate Alphabet Teacher's pose as he walked in. But she stared so hard, long and fast at him, that he decided to take up the battle of hips in more favourable times and dropped his act.

Without waiting for all the students to be seated and settled, Alphabet Teacher wrote on the chalkboard 1-0-0-0 and started teaching.

'We will learn the mathematical operations of four-digit numbers in Grade 5 along with fractions, measurements and many other things. Let's start.'

'Are you going to be our class teacher once again?' a beaming Mindesh got up to ask.

'Yes I am, Mindesh,' she beamed back at her favourite student.

'Teacher, would you like to know my name too?' Zouzou got up from the back row to ask with genuine concern. It was her second year with this class teacher, and she was almost getting used to being addressed as 'kid-in-the-last-bench'.

'Now, no more questions! Remember to speak only when spoken to, otherwise you can go and stand outside the class!'

The teacher then returned to the chalk on her desk and devoted the rest of the time before meal break to the pleasure of hearing her own voice mingled with mathematics.

Post the break, Alphabet Teacher ushered in the Language Teacher before entering the class again herself.

'Children, a few of your classes in Grade 5 shall be taken by Language and Science Teachers too,' Alphabet Teacher informed her students.

The entire class let out a sigh of relief together, almost like teamwork.

'What was that?' she said, immediately suspicious—raised eyebrows and all.

'Nothing Teacher, a cool breeze just hit us from the window,' Bullie explained.

'It managed to hit all of you together at the same time with equal force?' She did not relent.

'Yes, Teacher. That is the chief property of a breeze!' Bullie retorted. Of late, in the face of the difficulties posed by Alphabet Teacher's unyielding nature, Bullie seemed to have developed a quick wit and sarcasm to the utter delight of the class.

Alphabet Teacher thought better than to engage with the little ruffian. She had obviously taken umbrage, for she walked out of the classroom rather rapidly.

'We will learn many things in language this year, including, reading and comprehending newspapers and other text aside from textbooks, taking dictations, crossword puzzles, language through sound and music, and much more,' the Language Teacher said.

'Teacher, will you also explain why our voices are different, and why are there so many languages in India?' Millie was already curious.

'Teacher, why do some people sing so well, and why am I so different?'

As Seerie expressed his limitations, the whole class sniggered. Seerie truly was no singer. Whenever he opened his mouth to sing, his intentions, throat and voice box appeared to be at war with each other. He always ended up yelling the lyrics on top of his voice, more like a new politician addressing a large crowd demanding votes in the upcoming elections.

'Hmm. Full of questions as I was told. Fine, we will start with the topic of sound, language and music, but give me a moment,' the teacher said and momentarily left the room. She returned armed with two empty glasses, a bottle of water and spoons.

She called Millie to her table and asked her to pour the water from the bottle into the glass very slowly, while Seerie was asked to continuously strike the glass with a spoon. The glass went ting, ting, ting, ting. The sound pitch became lower with a deeper tone as more and more water was poured into the glass. The Language Teacher buzzed around the two performers in the legitimate hope that this would clinch the lesson. But it took only the next question to dash her hopes.

'Teacher, what is new about this? We have known how to do this since Grade 1,' said one of her students.

And then came the barrage.

'Teacher, what if we poured milk instead of water? Will the sound change?' said another.

'If we hit with two spoons, will it sound the same?' enquired yet another one.

'What if the glass was made of metal, then what would happen, Teacher?'

And so it went on for an uninterrupted ten minutes. The teacher suddenly felt alone in the midst of a teeming crowd. She was not prepared for such an onslaught. She had come prepared with a basic lesson on sound. The students sensed her bewilderment and whispered to each other about her inadequacy, but loud enough to be caught by her. The moment of victory was shared by the whole class as was evident in their conspiratorial bearing and twinkling eyes; first day, second class, and teacher was clean bowled and declared 'Out!'

A bit of a digression here, to put things in the right perspective. The present Language Teacher was but a shadow of her old self. The quondam Language Teacher would have argued her head and heart out to discipline these kidlings who did not show adequate respect and diffidence where they should. But very recently, she had somehow been convinced of the ways of the Foundational Grade Teachers and was ready to experiment. Whatever else she may have been, there was enough substance in her. Not one to be daunted easily, she continued regardless, 'I will ensure that your Science Teacher answers all your queries. And I shall now proceed to explain the beauty of sound and language.'

As she eased herself into the area of her expertise, she relaxed.

'You are not born with a language on the tip of your tongue. But you are born with an extremely active brain that catches all external interactions and stimulation and processes them. As a newborn child, the first words or language that you hear are your mother tongue. It is this language that helps you make sense of the world around you,' she said.

The children found the class gripping—very informative and rather different. Thirty minutes flew past faster than they cared for. For the first time, they enjoyed a solo act by any teacher for an entire session. The Language Teacher noticed their keen interest. She must have landed high in her own scroll of fame that day.

The next morning started with a quick visit by the Head Teacher to the class.

'So how was class yesterday? I believe you did not get all the answers to your scientific queries from the Language Teacher. A little bird has told me how happy it made you that she didn't know?'

A bit of giggling followed by a confused quiet and perhaps an internal conflict: Did we do the right thing?

'Don't be afraid, it is your first lesson today. It is natural to feel victorious when you can ask questions that can't be answered. But children, that will not help you grow or learn anything. The spirit of enquiry should be used to acquire new skills and information and not to show your superiority.'

He then turned to the unusually quiet Cuebee, 'Cuebee, so what is the right way? You pose so many questions to me every day. Is it meant to show me down or to quench your curiosity?'

'I question only to know more, to find out more. It satisfies my curiosity. It makes me happy,' Cuebee said, apologizing with her eyes.

'Well, you were happy with what you all did yesterday too?'

'I don't think it was happiness. It was an unjust attitude at the expense of another person. Sorry, sir. It will not happen again.'

This last statement came surprisingly from Bullie. All eyes turned astonished towards him and all hands joined together in clapping. Bullie's initial carriage was indeed turning out to be rather deceptive. It had not gone unnoticed by the children that Bullie never hesitated to apologize, and always meant it.

As promised, the Science Teacher did show up a few days later and give explanations for the questions knowingly or unknowingly released into the Language Teacher's basket. Like dropping back a lost child in the waiting arms of her sobbing mother, he handled the whole explanation part very sensitively, without admonishing the children any further on their past follies.

'Milk instead of water will make the sound marginally different.

'The sound of water in different metal containers or even ceramic will certainly be different.

'If you hit the glass with two spoons at a time, the sound would be somewhat shriller and may not exactly be musical.'

Though in respectful attention, the discussion had whet their palates, and many kids wanted to know more about music.

'Fine, let's first learn to feel your heartbeat by locating the pulse.'

'What does heartbeat have to do with music, sir?'

'A lot. Be patient. Now close all your four fingers together like this, and place them about an inch inside on your wrist from the side where your thumb is located. Yes, like this, and gently. Can you feel your heart beating?'

In sheer excitement at discovering their pulse, Arty, Seerie and Sky actually climbed on their benches, declaring to all and sundry that they were alive!

'Settle down, please. Now tell me, is there a rhythm to your heartbeat?'

'Yes, there is! It is beating at the same pace all the while.'

'Well, that is the basis of music. There are seven notes around which all music is made. In India, these notes are *Sa*, *Re*, *Ga*, *Ma*, *Pa*, *Dha*, *Ni*, *Sa*. Each note is different from the other in its pitch.'

'Yes, we noticed that in *Jal Tarang*. So, we can actually make music with a beat in the background and hitting one spoon on seven glasses filled with different levels of water, Teacher?'

'Certainly! But please create music only after school hours.'

'You are so funny, Teacher!'

'And here is where I stop. You need to wait for a few years before you can learn about the science of music and sound. Let us now proceed to understand your favourite part of the body—the speaking machines! Now tell me, which part or parts of your body do you use to speak?' The Science Teacher continued with generous vigour.

'My mouth.'

'My lips.'

'Tongue.'

'Teeth.'

'The brain, Teacher?' That was Cuebee, unsure of herself, as if she had spoken all right but did not know if she ought to have. She seemed to have entered into quietude, of late, or rather into a state of shrunken defeat. I could gauge that there were words on her lips and thoughts in her mind but silence had imperceptibly penetrated her entire being.

'These are perfectly wonderful answers!'

The Science Teacher then drew a caricature of a child on the chalkboard, with very large ears, larger teeth and his tongue hanging out.

Chortles from all directions.

'I am going to name and draw the various parts of the body that participate in helping us talk.'

He drew and labelled the lungs, vocal chords, voice box, tongue, teeth, lips, mouth and the brain. I certainly was not expecting an artistic portrayal of the speech parts, but this was more like a comedy in chalk.

'There are so many parts of our body involved in speech. Now, do you realize how complicated speech is?'

On Techie's behest, and with painstaking efforts, the children spent a number of days thereafter focusing torchlights into each other's mouths, while activating the speech machine and looking for the mechanism behind. With open mouths, tongues held out, obviously there was no speech, just a great deal of ear-splitting 'aaaaaa' sounds. It took the rasping glares of Alphabet Teacher to put an end to such enterprise.

The Language Teacher followed up the very happening science class with the sound of letters and how the mouth is used to emanate that sound.

'Each letter—A, B, C—uses different parts of the mouth in a unique way. Come on, now say O and then E.'

'OOOOO ...' they said gleefully.

'Look at each other while saying "ooo". What is happening to the mouth?'

'Teacher, BeeTee is looking like a duck!' Zouzou was in splits.

'And so are you, Zouzou.'

This had the class in splits.

'Now let's all say "eeeee". So, what do you observe this time?'

'All of Millie's teeth are on exhibition,' Geekay said with a laugh.

'And ...?'

'Nothing seems to stop my speech, not even the wind! It is so amazing!'

'And ...?'

'For every letter, a different part of my speaking machine is used.'

'Good work, children.' The Language Teacher clapped for them. 'So, here's the homework.'

'Eeeeee, Teacher!'

'Nooooo, Teacher!'

'You need to do a bit of research.'

'Oh, yes, Teacher, we love doing research.' The Language Teacher had got them all lock, stock and barrel.

'For the next one week, observe what you do with your mouth for each of the twenty-six letters. Write it down. Start associating the connection of the mouth, tongue, lips, airway, etc., to sounds.'

'Can we observe each other too?'

'Of course!'

For the next one week, students of Grade 5 were pretty certain—even if it meant looking silly to others—that they had to practise the facial twists and turns to deeply comprehend vowels and consonants in their full glory. After all, that is what research was all about. In every corner of the school, there was a Grade 5 student practising alphabet sounds, with a tiny notebook and pencil in hand, furtively noting down the results of such 'action research'. If you heard an 'eeeeeee' from behind the car in the playground, or a 'beeeeee' near the beehive, or even a 'peeeee' from the confines of the washroom, you were not to assume that a child was in distress; instead, you were supposed to appreciate how the students had embraced the idea of experimentation at such an early age.

Even though on the outside you might consider us classrooms to be holders of plastic emotions, you will never know how hilarious we found these episodes. Each of us had come across some child or the other in our vicinity performing delightful theatrics of the countenance and voice box, and had stories to tell each other, every night. Our nights had become colourful. At this juncture, the joint request of us classrooms may at least be heard, if not entertained. We believe that alphabet sound exercises breed happiness, even if there is no reason for it! We recommend you try it. You, the reader, may once again find the child in you. We did our own research, and found that this exercise led to a respite, even if temporary, in Cuebee's cloud of despair.

The Head Teacher had called for a staff meeting. He wanted the teachers to understand how crucial it is that every child attains the skill of being able to learn; basically, every child should learn how to learn.

'Let us attempt to instil the spirit of a child being its own teacher, you will just be the catalyst,' he initiated the discussion.

'Then we might as well close shop. What is the need of teachers if they will self-teach?' said Alphabet Teacher half scornfully.

'The classic way of learning remains relevant. First, supply facts and pictures to students, then some logic to organize the pieces of information. Finally lead them to find conclusions,' said the Head Teacher ignoring the jibe.

'I realize that one has to become as childish as they are, as innocent as they seem. This is the key to understanding them and penetrating their thinking. But the questions! They are exasperating when they take off,' lamented the Language Teacher, though good-naturedly.

'It's like a test of our understanding. But I am in total agreement that this is the most needed skill in every child,' concurred the Science Teacher.

'Yes, we need to find ways and means to motivate them to become self-learners,' summed up the Language Teacher.

'I have found that children really lap up praise, and it encourages them to do better at learning,' Buddy Teacher said.

This last statement led to immense discussion back and forth.

'But praise may not always be suitable.'

'Yes, true. Children rapidly see through the automatic praise, regardless of the work, effort, or behaviour, and it loses its impact. Only suitable labour, effort, or behaviour should be rewarded with praise.'

'My experience with adolescents is that many of them feel embarrassed by praise, especially if it is given in front of their peers. In fact, they do not respond positively to it.'

'I think I took the implications of praising to the other extreme when I began to ignore Cuebee for not being touted as my favourite.'

'There are some students like Mindesh, who work hard to get good grades in their homework and complete the syllabus on time. They do deserve open praise, in my view, even if it means that they might be considered teacher's *chamcha*.'

'I use a system of feedback to inform children about their progress and encourage them to keep going. When feedback is combined with praise, I find that a child is more likely to learn successfully and act correctly.'

'We need to use discretion when doling out praise. Praising a child who is misbehaving may be perceived as rewarding poor behaviour, thus motivating the child to misbehave in order to get attention. Children have a unique psychology. Narrative is very important!' The Head Teacher was very cautious yet democratic in his advice to teachers.

'As your professional expertise and judgement grow, I am sure each of you will figure out how best to use praise to drive their learning,' he concluded.

Days turned into weeks, and weeks into months. My classroom-mates had begun to notice the absence of Cuebee's antics in our portrayal of the events in the school, and my related and growing sadness. Almost 7-8 months into Grade 5, I had steadily begun to discern a modicum of change in the classroom transactions of Alphabet Teacher. Though her haughty and firm demeanour did not show any signs of delayed sublimity at that point, there was certainly something that was changing in her approach.

Take her class on fractions, for example. Erstwhile, Alphabet Teacher would have written some stuff on the chalkboard, entered into a monologue with the children about fractions and the multiple ways in which they can be deduced, and left the room after a full forty-five minutes convinced that she could tick off one more box in the syllabus. But this new avatar of Alphabet Teacher seemed to have thrown all caution to the wind.

'We will study fractions today. Fractions are nothing but a part of a whole. Let me give you an example.' She raised her palm with three fingers folded. 'How many fingers do you see?'

'Teacher, two.'

'Good. Two out of how many in this hand?'

'Two out of five, Teacher.'

'That's right. So, we are talking about two parts or two fingers out of a whole that has five parts or five fingers in one hand. Therefore, when I raise my palm like this, two is a fraction of five.'

'Teacher, if we consider all fingers, should it be two as a fraction of ten?'

'Very good! That is correct. Now let us think of some real-life examples.'

'We are in one classroom out of eight in the school.'

'*Shabaash*! Any other examples?'

'Teacher, whenever Cuebee decides to smile these days, we can see only a fraction of her teeth. Maybe six out of thirty-two.' Bullie with his sardonic sense of humour was getting increasingly better at making the class happy.

'What else?'

'Teacher, when we buy groceries, then half kilogram means one half part of 1 kilogram.'

'Excellent! How do you know this?'

'Teacher, I sit in my father's shop every day after school,' said Sky to the unconcealed amazement of the teacher.

'That's a good start. Let us all find out the ways in which your Ma and Papa use fractions in their daily life.'

That was the beginning of the free flow once again of unfettered minds.

'My mother divides the food into four parts when she serves us dinner.'

'My father got only four out of the ten answers correct, when he was guessing while watching *Kaun Banega Crorepati* last night.'

'My mother counted and sent nine clothes for ironing, but only eight out of nine returned,' Cuebee joined in.

Can you even believe this? The same children who held earlier that if they were to open their mouth in Alphabet Teacher's class—even if to take an extra dose of fresh air—an attack was imminent, were now bestowed with the confidence to not only participate, but keenly so in active learning. I was plainly, absolutely and verily intrigued. Even Cuebee had begun to open up somewhat to my unqualified surprise. The mystery had to be solved. That night, as the eight of us gathered our quantum of energy for our daily chat on school life's particularities, I was itching to register my stupefaction at the turn of events.

Frontal: Has time healed the wounds or is this a passing phase? What do you think Alphabet Teacher is up to? I suspect she is up to no good.

Hippocampus: You seem to be totally unmindful of the ways of Alphabet Teacher so far. Her ex-students have unhesitatingly recognized her as a good teacher.

Frontal: No, this is unlike her. I would do anything in my power to get to the bottom of this.

Occipital: Anything?

Frontal: You seem to know something. Come on, out with it!

Occipital: That is not the answer to my question.

Frontal: Fine! Anything!

Occipital: Thank you very much. I want you to fall in love with Alphabet Teacher, like you did with Butterfly Teacher.

Frontal: You do not seem to comprehend the ghastly and outrightly offensive nature of your demand!

Temporal: At least hear Occipital out.

Frontal: Go ahead! Unmake my day as well as whatever is left of the night!

Occipital: It seems Alphabet Teacher's fame is not limited to our school in more ways than one. The education inspector, having heard of our school, had requested the Head Teacher to send one of our teachers to take lessons on innovative pedagogies for teachers from the cluster of neighbouring schools. And guess who he sent?

Temporal: Alphabet Teacher! I can't believe this.

Occipital: And guess what she went and spoke about to the audience of teachers?

Hippocampus: Come on! My walls are about to fall down with all this aching suspense!

Occipital: She spoke about the need for introducing randomness in learning and the need to connect all learning to real-life situations and making classroom transactions more engaging. And …

Hippocampus: And what?

Occipital: And she discussed something so powerful about mathematics—how can something be taught to children that does not even exist in nature and cannot be observed. There are no numbers in nature, no calculations, no perfect shapes. Just can't see it anywhere. It is all artificial and unnatural construction in the pages of our textbooks. Yet, it defines reality, and every law of nature. She told the Head Teacher that she would attempt to connect reality with mathematics in her classes hereon.

Brainstem: And how do you know all this?

Occipital: Well, I overheard her discussing all this with the Head Teacher and how well her talk went off, and that she felt guilty of not practising what she preached.

Parietal: What integrity, I say!

Amygdala: I have a growing suspicion that this was the Head Teacher's creative methodology for reforming her, knowing that she has it in her to improve her own classroom transactions.

Brainstem: Indeed! This promises to leave the deepest possible impression on me.

Occipital: Well, Frontal … you appear to be struggling to retain the possession of your dismembered faculties. But a promise is a promise, my room!

Frontal: What promise?

Occipital: To add yet another human to your several love interests!

Alphabet Teacher indeed was practising what she had recently preached to a group of impressed teachers who felt that she was perhaps the last word in education.

The Science Teacher's classes, meanwhile, had managed to pique the imagination of the children endlessly. One day, while teaching about the world of animals and plants and its interconnectedness to all living things, including humans, he decided to sensitize the kids through a novel method.

'We are going to prepare a Biodiversity Register for the school.'

'What is that?'

'It will be a register that will record all living things in the school.'

'Oh, that is such a simple thing to do, Teacher. There are trees, a few plants and us.'

'Hmm. Are you sure?'

'Umm, there are the rats, the birds, vegetables in the kitchen gardens, the stray dog, grass, butterflies, spiders and such other insects … Teacher, actually there might be too many things!'

'Correct! And do you know the names for each of the living things in school, their uses, the way they multiply, how they are connected to other living things, etc.? And by the way, spiders are not insects because insects have only six legs, while spiders have eight. Have you ever noticed?'

'No, Teacher!'

'That is why we will undertake this exercise as a class.'

'Teacher, please tell us more about the difference between spiders and insects. Please, please.'

'Well, while spiders and insects are distant ancestors, they are not the same type of animals. The family to which insects belong is called as *Insecta* while spiders belong to the family named *Arachnida*. An insect has six legs and its body is divided into three, while a spider has eight legs and its body has two parts. You don't need to know more than this right now.'

'Teacher, if I get angry, can I call the person in front of me an *Arachnida* or *Insecta*? Will it be considered foul language?'

'Well, you may do that, provided you allow me to call you *Mammalia*.'

'What is that?'

'Find out! Until then, no calling each other names!'

The Science Teacher went on to debunk certain myths, such as everything that crawls is an insect; two earthworms will grow of one earthworm if it's cut into half; all animals and plants can be seen by the naked eye; snakes are out to get you, and many more. He then carefully explained how to prepare the biodiversity register—by identifying the living thing, its location, and drawing it. To find out its local name and uses, if any, the children were free to interview their elders. He promised to discuss more details about every living thing they identified.

The Language Teacher decided to join in this exercise, as it gave her an opportunity to observe the children's creativity, communication and reflective skills. The children did make a register with arduous labour and extraordinary eye for detail, and engrossed their agencies in a fairly deep understanding of the delicate balance that exists in nature, such as in the predator–prey relationship, human interference leading to collapse of ecosystems, need for conservation of every organism, etc.

My appetite for such genius lesson plans was quenchless. I would wait for something or the other to change or snap, or be mined out or excavated from some part of the school, just so that a series of winsome learning interventions could be introduced in my class. So, on days when nothing interesting was whipped out, I wished that the Head Teacher or Butterfly Teacher would just take over the entire school! So far, no one could surpass their competence in conjuring up some livewire classroom transactions.

It had been days since something new and exciting came my room's way. That is why my gladness knew no bounds the day the fan stopped working in my classroom. The Science Teacher had just walked in immediately after the morning assembly and announced that the next three days would be spent hovering physically or mentally around the car.

'We will discuss today who invented the car; rather, who made the first car.'

'I know, Teacher, it was Benz from Germany,' exclaimed Cuebee.

'*Arrey*, how do you know that?'

'My father told me, and he also said Diesel was the scientist who invented the engine of the car and it is named after him.'

'Yes, that's right. Thank you, Cuebee. The phases in the development of a car are very interesting. It was initially fabricated for the very rich and exclusive. Ford changed that perception. He set up a huge factory where many cars could be manufactured using standardized methods, such that each new car that came out of the factory was exactly the same as the previous ones. This model was called Model T.'

'Teacher, is there a fan in the car?' Seerie asked the teacher, a trifle agitated.

'Yes, indeed there is.'

'Can we go and sit in the car with its fan switched on? The fan here is not working.'

The Science Teacher immediately registered that he was dealing with a stand-alone issue here, but unless it could be set to rest, the class would not move forward. The electrician was not due for another hour, and children would tolerate the heat only if they knew the science behind fans. Students of Grade 5 had a reputation of sorts for insisting on such academic footnotes.

'Let us deal with fans first. So why do you think the fan is able to cool a room?' asked the Science Teacher.

'It creates air and wind, and the wind cools us,' replied Jadoo.

'That is okay, but Teacher, how does it give wind and why?' Cuebee was beginning to get into her niche.

'Scientifically, the fan does not cool the room. It only circulates air. The blades of the fan are designed in a manner that they throw air downwards.'

'Teacher, if the blades were just straight then what would happen?'

'No air will be thrown back. In fact, it is interesting that if we reverse the fan rotation no air would be thrown down!'

By now, all heads were looking upwards, literally editing the blades and imagining the effect.

'Teacher, why are there only three blades in this fan?'

'After some research it was found that three blades are most suitable in Indian conditions. More blades increase the force needed to rotate the fan, but do not add to comfort. In North America, the fans mostly come with four blades and can operate in the reverse direction too. But don't ask me any more questions, else your Language Teacher, who is waiting outside for the next class, will get angry,' he said laughing.

Now that the Science Teacher had endeared himself to the kids the previous day by 'fanning' their questions, and the electrician had done his job with Techie in focused attendance, the children were happy to participate in the resumption of the car session the next day. He explained the concepts of time, distance and speed with the help of the car.

No sooner had he started explaining that speed is all about how fast any object is moving, Bullie dashed out of the class and disappeared in a *whoosh*! To the casual and uninitiated observer, it might have appeared as an emergency visit to the restroom, but the Science Teacher knew better! Before he could recommence, Bullie dashed back in.

'Teacher, I just gave a demonstration of speed. Did you like it?'

'Yes Bullie, that was quite a display, now sit down, please,' he smiled. 'Now try and imagine the connection between the speed of a car and distance and time. What would it be? Yes, Cuebee?'

'A car at higher speed will cover more distance in less time.'

'Spot on! Hence, speed is nothing but the distance travelled over a period of time.'

'But how would the driver know the speed of the car?' asked Awey.

'Remember the speedometer on the dashboard of the car? It has a dial from 0–160. That indicates the speed.'

'But Teacher, does that mean a car can go at any speed up to 160?' Cuebee was doing a lot of mental maths.

'No, it does not. It only indicates the maximum and minimum speed possible. Can you imagine how the speedometer measures the speed?'

'No, Teacher.'

'Well, the rotation of the wheel is measured. It is very easy to convert the number of rotations to distance travelled on ground if you know the diameter of the wheel. Let me show you what I mean by that.' The Science Teacher then proceeded to make a diagram of the wheel and marked its diameter on the chalkboard. His students immediately understood the concept and decided unanimously to float out.

'Teacher, we are going out to measure the diameter of the car wheel, using the ruler,' spoke Techie on behalf of everyone and led the way.

The Science Teacher gazed at the kids surrounding the car, some lying next to the wheels, some under the car holding out a ruler, some barking directions, some sitting on the roof of the car and enjoying the general scenery, and smiled to himself. He knew that they would be returning to him shortly, loaded with many more questions, for which he was prepared like the parched earth is for the coming of the monsoons.

It was nearing the end of the academic year. Alphabet Teacher's popularity was steadily rising in the school charts, and she was veritably pleased about it. She was often and unexpectedly found in the midst of groups of Teachers, doling out unsolicited advice on how to make classrooms more engaging. Cuebee, who earlier appeared to be at the brink of a precipice, had meanwhile retrieved the gleam in her eye, the spring in her step, the curiosity of her mind and the hunger within for learning.

A month prior to the summer break, the academic session appeared to be peacefully drawing to a close, when the Head Teacher announced that the school was about to get ten computers to set up a computer lab. Within a week they were there, and the lab was set up in the empty room next to Parietal's classroom. Computer classes started in earnest, for grades 7 and 8.

This development had a strange impact on Cuebee. Her inestimable curiosity had got the better of her, and she was attracted to the computer room like a piece of metal being unable to resist a runaway magnet. She would be often found lurking aimlessly in the corridors near the room. She would skip lunch just to stick her face on its glass door to catch a glimpse of the machines and contemplate upon them. She once even mustered up the courage and asked for permission to learn, but was curtly denied as this was meant for higher classes. She was pretty disappointed but she accepted the rule.

She, instead, went to the library and found a set of books on computers, mobile technology, programming, artificial intelligence, etc. The Maths Teacher was the library in-charge and was amused and wondered if Cuebee was equal to the task of devouring such books. In two days, the teacher was so persuaded by her reading capacity, that she informed the Head Teacher of the phenomenon called Cuebee.

'What excites you about the computers, Cuebee?' The Head Teacher met her in the library and asked her.

'I read in this book that we are living in an age of computers, and that one day it will replace us. I really want to see what is inside the box that can do what we do.'

'Do you believe it is even possible that computers will replace humans?'

'I am yet to explore that, only if I can touch a computer,' she chuckled, but her eyes were appealing.

'Not just touch, you are allowed to use the computer. Go ahead Cuebee, learn and enjoy the computer. You can continue during the summer break too, if you like.'

Cuebee was deeply stirred, her face turned pink with the glow of joy and she ran towards the Head Teacher and hugged him.

As for me, how do I describe it? I was stunned as a rush of respect and tender admiration for the Head Teacher and Cuebee flooded the heart of my brick being. That summer, Cuebee diligently attended her computer classes in the mornings in the room abutting Parietal, and I fervently pestered Parietal every night to share every single thing that happened in the room next to it.

Love and affection are indeed an unknown quantity and their 'speed' of spread and 'distance' covered over a period of 'time' are immeasurable.

9

Timelines, commandments and civilizations

Dear Forever Diary,

In the last four months, I have grown four inches taller. How?

Why is my body shape changing? I am only eleven!

Why do I prefer to be with my friends more than with my family?

Do Grandma, Ma and Papa feel bad about it?

Why is hair sprouting from various parts of my body? At this rate, I almost might get a moustache. Is that normal?

Why does my stomach feel like a bottomless pit? Why do I eat so much? Am I fat?

Ma and Grandma have told me what to expect in terms of changes in my body, as I grow up, but why am I so scared?

Yours,
Petrified Cuebee

It was once again the middle of June, and I could not cease to be astonished at the manner in which the sun exercised its autonomy over mankind by changing its stance over the deployment of its rays as per its fancy. Today, the sun was hiding behind grey clouds, not really in a mood to engage with the civilizations below. The new academic session was set to start, and the Teachers assembled in the playground eagerly awaited the children to gather for the morning prayer. The longish hiatus between the last day of the previous session and the first day of the new one, was utilized for transitioning the tired minds to ones as fresh as the ripest mangoes of the summer season.

Cuebee entered the school with her grandma and father as well as her little brother Joy, in tow. He seemed to be a replica of the six-year-old Cuebee—dancing eyes, dimpled cheek, skipping steps and all, though with shorter-cropped hair. It was his first day at school. Cuebee and family took him to the classroom marked 'Class I', and deposited him in the affectionate arms of Butterfly Teacher.

'Joy, she is the best teacher in the world. She will take care of you and you are not to trouble her with your unending questions, the way you trouble all of us,' Cuebee warned him affectionately.

'But Grandma says if I do not ask questions, I will never have answers,' the little one persisted.

'I can see that you are indeed Cuebee's brother!' remarked Butterfly Teacher.

'And I can see that you are Butterfly Teacher. Cuebee told me that the teacher that I would like instantly would be you,' Joy was just limbering up to a long chat.

'Joy, go find a seat for yourself.' His father directed him before the teacher had a chance to reply.

Prayer over. Bell rung. Assembly dismissed. The sun by now had worked its way through the clouds and restored its rightful place in the sky. The eleven-year-olds ran towards me; I was now proudly sporting the name plate, 'Class VI'. All eyes darted here and there and everywhere to decipher who their class teacher would be this year. After waiting for almost ten minutes, Alphabet Teacher jauntily walked in with the Social Science Teacher.

'Good morning, class. My friend here will teach you the new subject of social science. And Language and Science Teachers shall also continue like last year.'

All this waiting had a strange effect on the faculties of the children. They were especially quick to arrive at an analysis of the situation.

'Alphabet Teacher, so you are our class teacher once again!' Mindesh spoke for all of them.

'Yes, I am. And I will see you all later.'

Alphabet Teacher may have changed her pedagogy, but she still had the capacity to make you feel that your life had been thoroughly useless unless you restricted your speech to her liking at all times.

The Social Science Teacher was a pleasant sort of a middle-aged man, whose 'chief property', as the kids loved to say, was his 'length'. Six feet and three inches of humanity wrapped in a khadi kurta and pyjama—no one of average height could remain entirely undisturbed at the prospect of craning their necks against gravity only to converse with him.

'We will learn about rivers today to know more about human life. Children, can you tell me how important rivers are for human existence?' asked the teacher, almost hovering overhead.

'Rivers provide us with fresh water to drink,' Millie was quick to respond. Children on their first day of school after a long break were itching to learn.

'Rivers also provide water for agriculture,' BeeTee added.

'Good. Tap your brains a bit more. Rivers have played a crucial role in human history.'

'I remember now. I read a book in the library about how all major civilizations came into existence along the banks of the rivers,' Cuebee recalled.

'Very good Cuebee, you are absolutely right,' affirmed the teacher. 'Before I explain the emergence of civilizations to you, we are going to do a bit of maths mixed with history.'

The tallness in khadi then went ahead to explain at some length the concept of timelines. The eleven-twelve-year-olds were then given a group exercise to prepare the timeline for any set of events that they fancied, as long as the time period in years was specified and the intervals of change were defined. After twenty minutes he called out each group to present their timelines. One group exhibited timelines related to seasons, while another one prepared the timelines of Amla's family showing birth years of all her family members starting from her great grandfather, who was still alive, up to her little brother. Cuebee's group presented a timeline of the new concepts learnt by them each year. Bullie's group displayed the per year increase in BeeTee's height.

The teacher appreciated the creative timelines, and only then introduced the complexity, that is, human history. He jotted down the following on the chalkboard in a timeline:

- 40,00,000–20,00,000 years ago: Appearance of hominids such as *Homo erectus*
- 3,00,000 years ago: Modern humans or *Homo sapiens*; stone tools found in East Africa
- 70,000 years ago: Humans began migrating to Europe and Asia
- 25,000 years ago: The Americas were inhabited
- 12,000 years ago: All ice-free parts of world inhabited
- 10,000–5,000 years ago: Humans settled on land and took to agriculture
- 5,000 years old: Recorded history of human civilization

The uninitiated teacher in the saddle did not know it, but a great surge of questions was imminent in the face of such riveting information. The Social Science Teacher was no novice at his trade either. Without any signs of perturbation whatsoever, he patiently answered every query.

'These ancient civilizations paved the way for republics and empires and the consequent history of war, invasion and colonization. Recorded human history is, therefore, a saga of conquest and constant warfare, leading to the rise and fall of empires across the globe,' he attempted to conclude.

But by now, the young minds were ignited beyond redemption.

'Who started colonization,' began Cuebee.

'When was the first war fought?'

'How do you define an empire?'

'What is the difference between invasion and colonization?'

Unintentionally, the teacher had sown many more seeds of pedantic discontent amongst the younglings, and there was no way he could proceed any further without the horticultural approach to teaching, that is, watering the plant of curiosity. He took an extra period to satisfy them, and they, the teacher and the taught, parted on fairly good terms that day.

Early next month, the Head Teacher called for a staff meeting to discuss a prescription that he had devised for the army of teachers to steer the academic year towards the goal of holistic growth and holistic learning.

'Here are my four commandments,' he started in a conspicuously unilateral manner, daftly opposed to his sensitive and multilaterally inclined nature.

'First, collaboration should be encouraged as a skill for the future. The classroom should not be a place for continuous mindless competition.

'Second, the teacher must emphasize and appreciate the process that the child has adopted rather than just the result. The means-versus-ends debate must start very early in the child's mind.

'Third, feedback is to be only offered about the child's work or behaviour, not the child herself, for it to be useful. It must communicate to the youngsters whether or not their work or behaviour is satisfactory, rather than whether or not they are good (or bad) in general.

'Fourth and last, help every child make connections—between science, social science, languages and maths. Introduce multidisciplinarity.'

'I could have added many more, but restrained myself knowing the huge amount of preparation my commandments shall subject you to,' the Head Teacher culminated his discourse.

The teachers came out of the staff meeting unsure of how to react, or rather, whether to react at all! Under the acute guidance of the Head Teacher, most of them had reached a level of competency that made most other schools they visited seem no more than a crèche. Heads bowed in deep consternation, or more likely in reflection and rumination, they left the staff meeting wiser than they were at the outset.

The breaking news a couple of weeks down the line was the gift of a small-sized smart television to all eight classrooms by a benefactor who preferred to remain incognito. Roof informed us that the said benefactor was persuaded by none other than the ex-student of the Head Teacher, who in his present-day life was a police officer. For some children in the school, television was an alien instrument of unwarranted noise, where adults insisted on watching breaking news interspersed with long-drawn and boring serials. But as an instrument for education, it was a modern-day marvel for most of them. Soon every classroom had a TV fixed on the wall in the space next to the chalkboards. The teachers had to be quickly trained on its use and upkeep. They did not find it difficult, being already adept at their smartphones. The display of learning content through the smart TV was such a huge novelty for the elders in the village that a few of the septuagenarian and octogenarian local residents requested the Head Teacher for a demonstration on a weekend. This enterprise, of course, received the blessings of the Head Teacher.

For the time being, the Science Teacher had decided to teach discoveries and concepts by continuing with the timeline exercise that the Social Science Teacher had initiated, which was also in deference to the fourth commandment of the Head Teacher. He commenced the class by displaying on TV the major scientific discoveries, the persons behind them, their birth and death, etc. Basically, it began as a class on the history of science and progressed systematically like a dateline would.

'I was told that Cuebee and team traced the history of all the concepts learnt in the last five grades on a timeline. That is what gave me the idea for this class.'

'Teachers also learn from students!' said Bullie.

'Yes, Bullie. We do. Well, from basics about animals, last year we had reached the point where you have understood how cells make up an animal's body. Do you remember that?'

'Yes Teacher, it is still unbelievable that ultimately it is the cells acting together that make the animal run, hunt, eat,' Cuebee was fired up, 'and to know that I am also nothing but an aggregation of cells is yet difficult for me to handle!'

'We are walking, talking and thinking cells indeed!' continued the Science Teacher. 'In Second Grade you learnt about constellations; this year you will learn about the birth and death of stars. In Third Grade we experimented with water; and next year you will study the atoms and molecules that make up water. Do you remember about weights and the concept of space taught in Fourth Grade? And the laws of motion taught in that same year?'

'Yes Teacher, we now know that Bullie and Mindesh are equal and opposite forces!' Imli just had to say it. The class found this too hilarious and took a while to recover.

'Well, the timeline of studies is programmed according to your hunger for knowledge at every grade. The scientific changes from Newton to Einstein will enthral you,' the Science Teacher carried on. 'This is the journey of learning, step by step!' His own energy seemed to be at its peak by now. 'And now a group activity laced with research!'

Researching was like a splash of gulmohar under the summer sun. The class always received such activities with abundant eagerness.

The timeline of discovery was shown to students as follows:

- Ancient to 0 CE
- 0–1000 CE
- 1000–1500 CE
- 1500–1900 CE
- 1900–1950 CE

The students were to find out and write down the discoveries and inventions that they felt might have had a transformational effect on human life. They were given the flexibility to reclassify the period based on an important discovery or invention or identify a year or century of transformation. This was an engrossing exercise, and unknown to them the Science Teacher had introduced the bug of 'learning how to learn'. They took a week and came out with a number of things, ranging from the wheel, compass, zero, printing press, penicillin, warm clothing, khadi, paper currency, steel, pesticides, plastic, to cell phones, computers, cars and aeroplanes, and more. They learnt from each other's presentations and from the gentle prodding of the Science Teacher about the vast world of scientific thinking and its huge role in the evolution of mankind.

The Social Science Teacher continued on the subject of human civilizations, but in consultation with the Head Teacher he had hit upon a unique methodology for implementing all four of his commandments with one activity. The class was divided into six continents—Asia, Africa, North America, South America, Europe and Australia.

'Teacher, why have you not included Antarctica?' quipped Anxy.

'We are going to study the effect of rivers on human civilization. Antarctica has no human settlements, so we will discuss it separately.'

Each group was given a large chart. The activity was to draw a map of the group's allocated continent and mark all major rivers and all the big cities and towns, and attempt to explain how rivers were the focal points of civilization. They were to use pens for the first time and were genuinely disappointed to know that erasers are not effective with pens. The teacher had assumed that the children would find it difficult to fill the chart but fifteen minutes later the standard complaint was 'there is not enough space to write'!

The charts were then displayed in the class by the groups. They were smeared and smudged all over with overwriting, deletion marks, arrows criss-crossing, notes in different handwritings; it was like weeds overtaking a lotus pond with impunity. Though that did not bother the teacher one bit, the students themselves felt they would do better the next time. In fact, their self-feedback and peer feedback might have appeared as if they were in the order of utterances and reflections, but they were only more substantial.

Cuebee, I could make out, was struggling to cope with the fast pace of changes within her. Perhaps all the girls were struggling similarly, but I had by now become the champion of favouritism and noticed Cuebee much more than the others. Cuebee tried to distract herself by being very regular in the computer classes. She was learning coding, computer languages, etc., but as soon as she would get free from there, her emotions seemed to be playing football inside her. On the one hand she felt all grown-up when in the company of her little brother, Joy; on the other, she felt like a lost kid whenever alone in the company of her thoughts. She detected that the need to revolt, to not conform and speak her mind was growing like elephant grass within her. The other day the Science Teacher had remarked, 'We need to learn a lot more about planetary movements and stars that we see in the sky,' when Cuebee had all but jumped on him as if intending to dig in her claws.

'No point, Teacher. You are just going to tell us a few things without explaining anything in detail. Everything is left for us to research or is to be studied in the later years. By that time, I even forget all my doubts and questions.'

'I thought the study of the sun, the moon and the earth fascinated you. I don't understand why you are so upset?' the teacher asked her.

'It is just that I feel like the school, books, teachers and my parents cannot cope with my levels of enquiry and curiosity,' Cuebee had calmed down by now.

Then she feigned an energetic happy tone and remarked, 'Someone just told me that the speed of earth's revolution around the sun is 30 kilometres/second, and I feel giddy! Maybe I am also giddy because no one can explain all my whys!'

The conversation ended there that day. The Science Teacher, like all other teachers, had handled adolescence before, and knew that this phase was to be dealt with utmost sensitivity and gentleness. But Cuebee being Cuebee was so upset with her own behaviour, that she stood up in his next class and apologized.

'These days, I often do not know why I behave the way I do. I feel so conscious of myself,' she admitted.

'Me too. I feel the same way.' Imli, Amla and Simla too confessed. This was followed by almost all the other girls disclosing their odd behaviours.

'This is all natural. Do not struggle against it. I have requested Alphabet Teacher to sit with you girls and counsel you.'

That idea did not please the girls at that time, but when they did have a sitting with Alphabet Teacher, they realized how well she connected to them. The girls started meeting her regularly to understand the nature of things to come and be prepared. Alphabet Teacher was so different outside class. She would chat with them on varied topics—from films, to clothes, hairstyles, music; from careers, to the environment, the gram panchayat, their studies, with utmost freedom and candour, mostly with a joke or two thrown in here or there.

Once when they told her about their study of civilizations, she remarked, 'You have given me an idea! We will do an activity in class to find how maths helped in civilization. So, what do you think?'

The girls would give her their free and frank viewpoint on such issues as well, and the teacher would absorb it with good cheer and had the gumption to ask for more. The girls' opinion of Alphabet Teacher had swung from one extreme to the other. They began to dote on her.

'Teacher, why were you so difficult to connect with earlier?'

'Oh, that! I was in self-destruction mode!' she replied honestly and ensured that going forwards she became a butt of their internal jokes.

'Hope I seemed stern enough in class today?' she would self-effacingly ask them when they would meet after class.

'Teacher, I definitely saw you giggle at Bullie's remark when you turned towards the chalkboard.'

'Oh no! I must mend my ways,' she would feign a lamenting tone.

'And Zouzou, I always knew your name. I am sorry, if I hurt you by calling you everything else that was not your name,' she confessed openly. She was adorable, indeed!

Cuebee wrote in her diary as she sat in my space during lunchtime that day.

Dear Forever Diary,

Why is it that I find it much easier to chat heart-to-heart with Alphabet Teacher than with my own parents?

How is it that I used to dislike her so much earlier, but

love her equally more now?

Am I such an undiscerning person that I cannot even see the goodness in people under the layers on their outside?

And Diary, when do you think you will start to answer me back?

Yours
Awaitingly and questioningly, Cuebee

It was not just the girls; the boys too had become a little untrusting of their classes. The Teachers knew it was the sum total of hormones acting up and continued to treat the children with respect and dignity. In one class when the Science Teacher was explaining the stem and root, he also told them some interesting exceptions, such as the potato being a modified stem, onion being the root of a plant, tomato being a fruit, etc. And that ended up being a call for commotion.

'If onion is a root, then potato should also be a root.'

'If tomato is a fruit, then why do we not get it at a fruit shop?'

'That is the scientific, rather biological way of defining things,' the Science Teacher feebly tried to explain.

'Science and even biology are illogical. We will not accept this, Teacher.'

'Then what do I do to convince you?' He kept giving explanations and kept going deeper and deeper into the pit that he had dug for himself.

The next day, he asked the Head Teacher for help. The two came together to the class in the morning.

'I am told that you find science illogical.'

'Yes Teacher, all of us do, especially after what we were told yesterday about root, stem, fruit.'

'Well children, the fundamental approach to science lies in the way we define and categorize things. Onion is a root and potato is a modified stem is a scientific definition. Tomato is a fruit as per science, whether or not it is not sold in fruit shops is not important.'

'Teacher, does that mean we have not understood from the science point of view, what a stem or root or fruit or vegetable is?' Cuebee asked contemplatively.

'Yes, that is exactly what I want to convey. So be patient, first learn that difference, and understand why science defines things the way it does. Sometimes, science is more magical than magic itself!'

'Teacher, I think we got carried away and closed our mind to learning the science of it all,' Techie remarked.

'It happens. It is alright. But remember, the teacher will knowingly never teach you the wrong thing. Have faith. Can I expect that?'

The class nodded in appreciation. But I could hear them telling each other how they needed to educate the fruit seller outside the school to start selling tomatoes!

We eight classrooms had never followed up the period of adolescence so closely as we were doing now. We would earlier resign ourselves to a mouldy attitude in higher classes, putting it down to being a product of haphazard teaching. How the deuce had we missed comprehending it, was the topic of discussion for most days. We were now convinced that adolescent kids also sported blood in their veins, and not oodles of irresponsible behaviour as we had imagined earlier.

Such discussions added the necessary spice for us to achieve with gusto each night, the three unalienable rights enshrined in the American Declaration of Independence—life, liberty and the pursuit of happiness!

This year, the car lesson was taken up as soon as the school's winter break was over. The children were in for a huge surprise when Alphabet Teacher informed them that this year the car lesson would be taken by the Social Science Teacher for them. Given the excess hormones, the kids could not help discussing if the school had finally lost its mind.

'We are going to discuss how a car or an automobile could usher change in society. We could then discuss how so many other technologies have impacted human societies and have often transformed them for the better. Any ideas?' The Social Science Teacher was radiating positivity.

Perhaps his choice of a white khadi kurta pyjama that day had something to do with it. The topic so clearly positioned, immediately caught the attention of the hungry class.

'Could it be that it helped people to meet their relatives more often?' Anxy asked the teacher, viewing the teacher now with a kindlier spirit.

'Or that it helped them reach the hospital in time in an emergency?'

'Interesting points of view. Well, you see, in the United States especially, the car changed a lot of things, in industry, technology and everyday life. Let us look at industry first. One of the earliest industries to employ the assembly line system was automobile manufacture.'

'Were they the first to get their workers to stand in line for the morning assembly?' asked Bullie.

'No, Bullie. An assembly line is a type of manufacturing process that is extremely important in the manufacturing business. Parts are assembled and added on a product in a specific order, one after the other, in what is called an assembly line. Each worker and machine at each interval are responsible for completing only one part. All parts are then finally assembled to create the final product.'

'It is somewhat like us kids, going from class to class, and in each class a separate set of teachers working on us, to make the final product of a learned human being,' mused Geekay.

'I love that simile. You all are remarkable kids. May I continue now?'

'Yes please, Teacher. This is all so interesting.'

'People in America had more personal freedom and access to jobs and services, thanks to the car. It resulted in the construction of better roads and transportation. To meet the need for automotive parts and fuel, new industries and employment arose. Petroleum and gasoline which is called petrol here, followed by rubber and finally plastics industries came up. Fuel stations and convenience stores cropped up all over the country as a result.'

'But Teacher, the car is a very costly thing, so how could people buy it?' BeeTee interrupted.

'My grandpa told us that a car is only for the rich, and the rich exploit the poor,' Seerie informed the class.

'Teacher, so, how did this change society, if only a few rich people had access to the car?'

'The automobile provided people with jobs, housing and services. It also aided the growth of fun activities. With leisure came a slew of new services. Motels, hotels, amusement parks and other forms of entertainment, as well as restaurants and fast food, were among them.'

'Teacher, aren't cars one of the major pollutants, and they add to traffic and congestion too?' Arty wanted to know.

'Yes, the automobile or car also had a negative impact on the environment. Pollution was caused by the exhaust from vehicles. Highways and accompanying industries were built on previously undeveloped land, which led to felling of trees, dispersal of some habitation. But all development comes at some cost. Anyway, today we will focus on the car and how it helped the world, then we will discuss what to do about its negative impact. Is that okay?'

'Yes, yes, Teacher, please continue. We will keep our questions for the end of class.'

'So, this mass-produced car altered the middle class in the United States. More people were able to afford a car. In many respects, the car altered American society. People had more freedom and time on their hands. They were also able to do more in their spare time. People who lived in cities were able to escape to the countryside. People from the countryside could also travel to cities. Suburbs arose as a result of more vehicles and better roads. Suburbs are neighbourhoods that grow up around cities.

'Also, the car was instrumental in giving a sense of independence to women; they could drive and explore the world. Also, when most of the menfolk were at the war front, they had to take care of the house and family especially during World War I. So, finally, I have to say that by using the assembly line to make a standard model of automobile, the costs involved in manufacturing came down substantially, and a greater number of people were able to buy a car. That in itself was a social change.'

'That means not just cars, many other technologies would have altered our society? Any more examples, Teacher?' Mindesh asked.

'Like the cell phone has connected people to each other and a whole world of information,' Cuebee added.

'Hmm. No more examples from me. That is your group activity for the next week. Take your time, contemplate upon the technologies used for things around you, like clocks, trains, ships, aeroplanes, computers, telephones and more. We will try to write down how they have changed our lives.'

The Social Science Teacher not only guided the activity next week, he also took the opportunity to educate the young fawns on the Industrial Revolution, its huge basket of inventions and discoveries, India's surge in the field of Information and Technology, and its impact. In the end, while summing up, he introduced the impact that all this had on knowledge.

'This revolution also put a lot of emphasis on education as it promoted science, technology and the need for skilled manpower. Thus, the invention of cars and other machines also brought in sociocultural change that they had not bargained for,' he summed up.

It was brilliant! I suppose, honestly speaking, I ought to inform you that we classrooms had initially also ticked the Social Science Teacher off—before the car lesson—properly, and in no uncertain terms. We were clear that cars exude technology, and social science has no place in it, for it. But nothing in this world is perfect, least of all us classrooms! The Social Science Teacher had, in fact, ushered in a technology-

and-change revolution in the school. Soon, other teachers for Grade 6 and other grades also began to adopt this pedagogy. Take for instance, the Science Teacher. He took up the story of aluminium in my class.

'It is now used in everything from soda to space shuttles, but it wasn't always so. Aluminium is the most abundant metal on the planet, as well as one of the most affordable. However, it was once more valuable than gold. Can you guess why?'

'It was not found in large quantities.'

'Yes, that is right. Aluminium is the third most abundant element in the earth's crust, yet it also has a high affinity for bonding with other elements. That is, it isn't found as a pure metal in nature.'

'Then who made it, Teacher?'

'Bayer and several other engineers found a commercially effective process for extracting aluminium from its ore and the price of aluminium dropped dramatically by the beginning of the twentieth century and it became available to give flight to the Space Age. Aluminium alloys were used by NASA for Apollo for the same reasons that they were used for aeroplanes: weight and strength.'

'Are engineers also scientists, Teacher?'

'In a way, yes. So, children, what lesson do we learn from all this?' asked the teacher at the end of the class.

'It is important to have a lot of scientists,' said Techie, 'I will become a scientist.'

'Human beings are able to reap benefits from many things that are simply lying around on the planet,' Jadoo added.

'The cost of any item depends on how easily it is available. So, one day, even diamonds could be very cheap.' Cuebee appeared to have soaked up all this with a unique perspective as her first lesson in economics!

Soon thereafter, on a full moon night, the eight of us were together sighing—internally, of course—at the beauty of the celestial body, when Hippocampus decided to open the proceedings with a bang.

Hippocampus: Frontal, what is your position on the Alphabet Teacher now?

Frontal: Why do you ask in such an accusing tone; it is like an assault on my reasoning abilities. It is as if my intellect is being accosted, or perhaps being held ransom.

Hippocampus: I am so sorry; I did not mean to …

Parietal: I know when you are pulling a fast one, Frontal. Stop scandalizing Hippocampus!

Frontal: Ha ha.

Hippocampus: Oh, you sure got me there. I was about to retract.

Frontal: Well, to tell you the truth, my cup of love overfloweth. Alphabet Teacher is a rare gem.

Hippocampus: Isn't she? I think I now understand what it is to love a human.

Frontal: Same boat, my friend, same boat.

Brainstem: And what do you all think of the Social Science Teacher?

Occipital: Unusually good in an infiltrating sort of way. His teaching is like a paint that penetrates every nook and corner of a glass of water.

Brainstem: Well said! I too am experiencing affection for a human for the first time.

Frontal: No wonder! You are sounding your charming and festive best.

Brainstem: But when have I ever been discommodious?

Amygdala: Rooms, I seem to have got touched by a contrasting emotion. One of the kids in my Grade 5 class lost her cousin who lived with them as a joint family. He lost the battle to some deadly disease. She is devastated, absolutely inconsolable.

Temporal: Oh! That is so heartbreaking. How do you think her teachers will handle this?

Amygdala: I believe the Head Teacher has given some instruction to all the teachers for taking up the discussion on life and death, gently, for Grade 5 upwards.

It was already towards the end of the year. But this important lesson had to be learnt. The earlier the better. In all grades, the teachers allowed children to first talk about losing. The children realized how deeply they felt when they lost the things that they loved, and understood that losing a thing was trivial in comparison to losing a person.

Amygdala reported the next night that a Grade 5 teacher asked the class to write a letter to the cousin of the child who had lost a family member. The teacher demonstrated how to write a condolence letter. It was a very organized approach to writing and as an observer one would have thought that the teacher was attempting to conform them to a particular style of writing. The children were required to express sorrow in the first paragraph. Then communicate the good memories about the person who had died in the second paragraph. And lastly write a few lines on how they would miss the said person.

The same exercise was taken up in my class by Alphabet Teacher, the next day. But what followed really surprised all of us. It had not sunk into me till this day, what an extraordinarily formidable education these children were getting. They were so connected to real life. The children whom I thought might be indifferent, just the typical kind of kids you know, wrote so intently, it dug holes in my solid heart, and when they spoke about the perceived sense of loss, the teacher almost shed a tear. The students did need some structure to get started. And surprisingly the seemingly inflexible structure provided them with the 'freedom' they required to write. The Head Teacher was also quick to usurp this as a new commandment to be practised by every teacher, that is, structure and planning is sometimes good for encouraging free-flowing thought.

These exercises had an unintended impact. Children not only began to relate life and death to the plant and animal world, the evolution of human beings and the earth itself, but they also began discussing the value of life, the inequalities in society, the need for equity and justice; it all appeared to now come naturally to them. Championing social causes and accepting the cessation of all things may, I suspected, get a little easier for them as they tread the intricate path of life.

On the last day of the academic session, while everybody else was saying their goodbyes for the summer break, Cuebee was not to be seen in my classroom. I was totally mystified. She was such a vivacious child and loved her friends dearly. For the life of me I was not able to comprehend her absence from the parting scene! As soon as night fell, and we gathered, I could not contain myself anymore.

Frontal: Roomies, do tell me if you have any idea where Cuebee was at the end of school hours.

Occipital: What would you give to know?

Frontal: Not again, Occipital! What do you want this time?

Occipital: You promise to address me as 'Your Excellency' for the entire summer break.

Frontal: Fine!

Occipital: Fine, what?

Frontal: Fine, Your Excellency!

Occipital: That was so satisfying.

Frontal: Now, out with it!

Occipital: Now, out with it, what?

Frontal: Your Excellency, Your Lordship, Your Honour, please do your loyal subject the extreme favour of informing of the whereabouts of my little friendling, Cuebee.

Occipital: Sure, my subject. She was in deep conversation with the Head Teacher for permitting her to use the computer room during the vacations for the purpose of developing something she called an App. Perhaps it is a short-form for something. Do you know what that is?

Frontal: An App? How and why would I know what that is? I am hearing of it for the first time in my built-up life.

Occipital: Well, we expect you to know, because you are the brain part with the reasoning and critical thinking capabilities.

We continued the back and forth like we were performing callisthenics with a ping pong ball, and then like every other time, we parted with more than adequate goodwill. But I know for sure that on being given this piece of new information, each one of us had only one thought in our structure that night—what new meaning is this remarkable kid going to give once again to our still lives!

10

Floating ice and the omelette universe

'HEY, *HOMO SAPIENS*, HOWDY!'

'Hey *Mammalia*, how have you been?'

'My body was in a state of inertia all of summer, until the force of my mother's *gaalis* was applied to it.'

'Ha ha, I was part of the kitchen assembly line. Cutting and chopping vegetables was my responsibility.'

'My atomic weight per atom remains the same, but my body weight is up by 2 kilograms.'

'Look at my vacation photos. I look like I have been hit by a sack of potatoes. Please photo-sympathize with me.'

'I did not get even a fraction of a second free to laze around. I did some or the other work every day. My father believes in "industrious evolution" for us kids.'

We were back in the middle of June. The first bell of the first day at school was yet to be rung, but the sun was already hanging overhead, red-hot, blazing and impressive. Cuebee and her classmates were seated in the room for Grade 7 students—that is, my space—for the last half an hour. The morning assembly had been shifted to the classrooms because of the heatwave. The children, seeing each other after almost eight weeks, were chirruping and showing off their retention of knowledge thus far, with the quips I just narrated. I was listening in as usual with the indulgent air of an elder who has risen from the fossils only to admire the products of its evolution.

The blue khadi *kurta*-and-white *pyjama*-clad Social Science Teacher stood at my door, perhaps scrutinizing the class and its occupants much more microscopically this time. He was easily in his late forties, a quiet sort of a person who smiled easily. We classrooms had heard that he was a budding IT engineer in the United States, but left it all to study social sciences and teach in the schools of India. Call of the motherland, as you say!

'Good morning. Good to see your cheerful faces. This year, I shall be your class teacher, Social Sciences Teacher and IT Teacher in the computer lab, all rolled into one,' he said and dimpled his left cheek.

'What? Teacher, you will teach us computers?' Bullie was almost hyperventilating.

'Put it away, please, Bullie—your tongue, I mean.'

'But, Teacher …'

'It is a free country. You are permitted to be adept at more than one thing. Like you Bullie, I know you are good at cricket and maths.'

'Sir, he is also great at cracking jokes and his knuckles.'

'Well, no surprises there. So, let us start with ...'

'Teacher, can we start our first period on the first day of school with the computers? Please, Teacher,' pleaded Techie, before he could start.

'Hmm. Fine, let me see if that is possible.'

The teacher marched to the room full of black and glistening machines to check availability, and marched right back with the breaking news that the class was hoping for.

'Computers, here we come!' they shouted with glee and rushed to their destination as if they were about to purchase it and own it.

'Young active minds!' sighed the teacher. 'Ah, to be a young and active mind again!'

He then went on to explain what computers are. He introduced them to the hardware, monitor, keyboard, CPU and also the UPS system, etc. Then, he moved on to talking about software.

'Computers are meant for computing. For a computer, its entire world is made up of two numbers—one and zero. They use several combinations of these two digits to do all their calculations.'

'So, they work on their own. Then they can kill us?' Anxy was anxious yet again.

'No, they cannot work on their own. We need to give them very detailed, step by step, and logically flowing instructions,' Cuebee clarified.

'And that is what the software is all about. Thank you, Cuebee. Each such set of instructions that completes one activity is called a Program. And programs are written in computer languages,' the teacher summed up.

'What language is that, Teacher?'

'Java and Python, for example. For today, that is all. Let us go back to the class and do an activity to understand computers better.'

The teacher divided them into two groups. Cuebee's group would do the role play of a computer that is being given instructions, and the other group would write the instructions to direct the role play. They were to write a series of instructions or a program on completing the activity of 'how to write on the chalkboard'. Cuebee was instructed to not help, so the rest of the students could learn by hit and trial. The end result was hilarious. The instructors would assume several things by writing very brief commands, as if they were writing for humans, and not machines.

'Go to the chalkboard and write on it.'

Cuebee's group trotted to the chalkboard while continuing to face the students and wrote with their fingers in the air.

'Turn around and go to the chalkboard, and write on it.'

Cuebee's group kept whirling round and round, as there was no instruction when to stop.

It was evident that the kids had acquired a fair amount of problem-solving skills, for it was not easy to make them stop. They persevered with a great deal of reasoning, despite the fact that it took them multiple rounds of rewriting to be able to picture a program and write it step-by-step, that would be comprehensible by the role play group.

'That, children, was your first lesson on computational thinking,' the Social Science Teacher announced happily at the end of the class.

The landscape of physical properties, attitudes and behaviours for our twelve- to thirteen-year-old prominent citizens of the school was changing. The girls were filling out a bit while the boys were thinning down; the voices of many boys were cracking and some of them appeared to belong to the cat family due to the erratic and thinly laid whiskers on their upper lips. Many of the girls were taller than most of the boys in class. The difference was really stark between the twins, Techie and Yoga. Techie was almost one head above him. Even Cuebee and Millie were at least 6 inches taller than him, Geekay and BeeTee. The band of six friends, three boys—Geekay, BeeTee and Yoga—who were earlier inseparable from the three girls—Cuebee, Millie and Techie—was almost disbanded when in the standing position. The boys being exceedingly conscious of their length and breadth would be found together with the girls only in the seating position. The girls were getting thicker with each other and had this strange urge to share 'secrets' such as how a senior boy smiled at one of them, and the boys were similarly finding each other's company more reassuring than being nervous in the company of girls. Both groups of boys and girls were becoming more aware of their respective genders. While the girls continued to be counselled by Alphabet Teacher, the boys found a mentor in the Sports Teacher. Fortunately, all this had no negative impact on their burgeoning curiosity.

When you enter the habitat of singularly curious creatures, with thirty pairs of eyes and ears hungry for more food for thought, you cannot but deliver exciting cuisine to their complete satisfaction. The Maths Teacher had taken over maths lessons from Alphabet Teacher. She, the Maths Teacher, was a small person—small in height, small in weight and very pleasant looking. Cuebee was 5 feet 4 inches tall by now, and the Maths Teacher fell short of her by at least a couple of inches. She had a solemn face but only when she was not teaching maths, at which point all the energy of an entire electricity-producing plant appeared to exude from that singular face. She sported a pair of stylish glasses on her nose and it looked terribly fashionable. Apparently, she was the reason for the sudden interest in senior kids to wear and flaunt numberless glasses. She was always dressed in a long kurta, comfortable pants and a dupatta. All in all, a smart-looking woman. She was very approachable as the kids soon found out. She believed that maths could best be learnt by drawing connections between mathematics and the world around us.

'The most important aspect of maths is to learn its logic, how the whole thing fits together. It is important you find connections in maths with your lives to imbibe the mathematical way of thinking.'

'First the Social Science Teacher tells us about computational thinking, then the Head Teacher about critical thinking, and now this new thinking. Teacher, I "think" I am confused,' said Seerie.

'Ha ha, you are a quick-witted class. I already like you. Well, just to put the record straight, thinking in itself is not a skill. But critical thinking is. When we observe, experiment, conduct research and analyse our findings, and use it to solve real-life problems or apply the knowledge gainfully, then we are thinking critically. And when we apply critical thinking for computation, then it is computational thinking and when we do the same to analyse numbers, look for patterns, etc., then it is mathematical thinking.'

'So, critical thinking is the Head Teacher and the rest are various subject teachers,' stated Millie.

'Excellent Millie, that is a good simile.'

'Nice poem, Teacher!'

'Ha ha. Millie, I will be happy to hear a poem on maths too sometime.'

'Your wish is my command, Teacher. In the next class, I will recite a maths poem,' Millie happily agreed.

'Children, today we will understand some rules about the universe, and based on these rules, you will develop and prove other ideas.' Saying this, she drew a huge circle and called it the universe. She explained that right now it was a two-dimensional or flat structure, and bore resemblance to a piece of paper.

'Okay, let us assume there are three points X, Y and Z in the universe. A line drawn between X and Y, is called XY. The point Z is not on the line between XY. Do you remember what parallel lines are?'

'Yes Teacher, two lines that never cross, never meet.'

'So, if you see the universe that I have drawn here, one and only one line can be drawn through the point Z that is parallel to the line XY.'

'May I come to the blackboard and try, Teacher?'

'Yes, please do.'

BeeTee took a scale and tried making lines.

'There can be several lines, Teacher. See, so many lines do not meet this XY.' He had drawn less inclined or smaller in length lines that did not meet XY. A very natural question indeed.

The teacher then explained about the possibility of infinite length of the line. The children's runaway imagination began to conjure the vast prospects of infinite space above their heads, around them, and in faraway spaces.

'But children, in reality the universe we live in is three-dimensional. So, if we define parallel lines as two lines that never intersect, there would be an infinite number of lines in a three-dimensional universe that can pass through that point Z. These would still remain parallel with the line because they are on different planes or surfaces.'

Then she showed two sticks, the lower one hanging by threads joined at two points with the top one.

'These sticks are like parallel lines, now as I rotate the lower stick, you can see it still is parallel to the top one, but now there are infinite parallel lines in this three-dimensional existence.'

Next, she went on to explain how by changing a single postulate in the world of geometry, a whole new world is born. By now, the imagination of children was triggered to such a degree that they wanted the operation of teaching and learning to be suspended forthwith or at least adjourned to another day. They just wanted to know more about the dimensions of the universe. The teacher acquiesced and showed them a few films on the smart TV, and then doled out some solid and almost indigestible food for thought.

'Until you did not know about the three-dimensional aspect, you believed the two-dimensional aspect of the parallel lines. So, how do we know if something is true?'

'Teacher, please tell us how.'

'No, I want you all to reflect upon it. We will discuss this next week.'

In the coming weeks, the children discovered an important lesson about truth with the help of their Maths Teacher. Truth, at least scientific truth, meant something that is logically derived from the initial postulates. For the kids, these fundamental ideas would have far-reaching implications for all fields of study. Soon, there hung an aroma of intense enquiry around the kids, as they attacked their own opinions and judgments though cautiously, and also began to apply these ideas to comprehend the assumptions we make about society and our universe. I would not have picked a maths class to become the inducer of the art of philosophizing, but then I am decidedly unschooled in the ways of life!

This whole idea of critical thinking being a skill had set us classrooms thinking.

Frontal: Can there be learning without thinking?

Brainstem: How do you learn without thinking? Never heard of this one.

Occipital: Unconformity, thy name is Frontal!

Temporal: Come to 'think' of it, the Head Teacher had spoken in a staff meeting once about a book that discusses how the presumed enemies of learning—ignorance, distraction, interruption, restlessness, even quitting—can be used to work towards better learning. But first I want to understand from you, Frontal. Is there any conflict in your mind?

Frontal: Cuebee is building an application. Remember, we spoke about her app? This app seems to have gained some sort of intelligence, but I am sure it has no thinking capacity. The IT Teacher keeps on harping that the machine is not intelligent. It has zero IQ, but it can gain more capacity to do work than humans, if it is trained well.

Temporal: That is exactly the difference between human thinking and machine thinking.

Brainstem: I get the point that you are driving at. You are talking about the phase we have been mute witnesses to—when our curriculum transaction was such that our children were learning without thinking.

Frontal: I am saying more than that. I am indicating that if we are not careful, if we do not engage students in joyful learning, we will end up begetting machine-like students in many of our schools!

One day, Joy was feeling a little out of sorts, so he took permission to sit with Cuebee in class. She always had a calming effect on him. That day, the Science Teacher was taking the car lesson of Grade 7 level. He introduced the class to a very famous line by Henry Ford: 'Any customer can have a car painted any colour that he wants so long as it's black.'

'Can anyone tell me the reason why he might have said this?'

'Maybe because he hit upon a huge store of carbon black. Is that the reason?'

Everyone turned towards the bearer of this voice, Cuebee's little brother, Joy. The Science Teacher did not ignore him. In fact, he engaged with him.

'Now why would you say that?'

'Teacher, carbon black is used to make the tyres of cars heat resistant and stronger. Maybe Ford had lots of it, so he made his car black.'

'Hmm, you are an interesting young man. You are right about the tyre, but not about the statement.'

'Teacher, please tell us. Joy is not just a bank like me, he is a universe of questions!' Cuebee said and smiled indulgently at her little brother.

'It was not because only black was preferred. It was in fact a manufacturing operations decision. Japan Black was the only colour paint that could be dried quickly, and speed was important at the Ford plant because of its enormous volume.'

The teacher then went ahead and explained how the shape and size of a car are related to aerodynamics and thereby to efficiency. It was a very interactive session. At the end of the class, the teacher looked at Joy's perplexed face.

'So young man, have I managed to stagger your senses?'

'My stomachache was gone at Japan Black,' informed Joy.

'And his complete health was restored at the "lift" and "drag". Now he is itching to go and boast his acquired knowledge, though half-baked I suspect, to his classmates,' Cuebee ruffled his hair as she spoke and gazed at him almost maternally.

The tangible presence of a syllabus was felt once too often in these higher classes. Completion of the syllabus would often become the goal for teachers. In fact, the Science Teacher had decided to take off and fly. His over-enthusiasm for finishing the day's work at a rapid pace became so trying for the children, that it came to the notice of the Head Teacher. The Science Teacher was counselled to deal with the subject with a lot of patience.

'The idea is not to finish the syllabus somehow. The idea is to instil a scientific temper in the children.'

The teacher got the point and what emanated next was one of the most masterly classroom transactions that I had ever witnessed.

He was teaching about the polar regions of the world. The first part was animals in that region.

'The Antarctic region's balance is crucial for the world's survival. About 90 per cent of the earth's ice and 70 per cent of all available freshwater is locked up in the Antarctic ice sheet. If melted, this would raise sea levels by 58 metres. Many islands and coastal land will drown in the ocean, and that could mean havoc for the earth.'

'Why does all this ice not sink for good?'

'Let me explain a very unusual property of water.'

The teacher had got ice cubes for the session. He put a few in a tumbler and poured water over it.

'It did not sink, Teacher.'

He then placed a small piece of iron, and it sank in the tumbler.

'Today, we will learn about a very illogical property of water, and then you will tell me why it is so important for nature … so who can tell me why ice floats in water?'

'Teacher, from what we have learnt, only when the density of a substance is lesser can it float, but how can the density of solid water be lesser than liquid water?'

'That is the beautiful property of water. And this anomalous property is very important for all marine life.'

He then showed them a video of water and its interesting properties.

'So, as you can see, water reaches its maximum density at 4 degrees Celsius. As it approaches freezing point, that is 0 degrees Celsius, and becomes ice, it becomes less dense. This is opposite to most substances which are most dense in their frozen state than in their liquid state. Water is different because of hydrogen bonding, and don't ask me what that is now. Just write "Hydrogen Bonding" in your Forever Dairy—you will learn about this in higher grades.'

'Teacher, does that mean if the glaciers fall into rivers they will float?'

'Let me show you an iceberg on TV. What do you see?'

'Most of the iceberg is submerged in water but it is actually floating in water.'

'Right you are! This is a gift of nature. Lakes and rivers start freezing from top downwards. This enables fish to survive even after the top layer of the lake or river has frozen. Just imagine if the whole river froze, all marine life would end. There is a design in everything that nature has!'

'Teacher, I really want to travel to see icebergs.'

'In time, little girl, in time! Now here is the research that I expect from you. List out all such things as ships that do not sink in water, and try to find out why they don't.'

The Maths Teacher would often bring back the chatter of conversation to a discussion on 'truth' and its dimensions and perspectives, such as human perception. She spoke to them as if they were her research associates, and they listened to her as if she were their PhD guide.

'Here is an interesting way to look at human perception and understanding. Scientists have defined the universe as an omelette universe, due to the perceived shape.'

'The reason we refer to electricity today in terms of current is because, in the eighteenth century, people like Benjamin Franklin thought it was a fluid and related all their experiments and even the nomenclature to that so-called fact.

'In the eighteenth century, it was thought that all disease was caused by bad smells. Malaria is *mal aria* meaning "bad air". We may laugh at this today, but for the people in those days, this was the truth.

'Hence, truth can also be a function of time. Different times, different truths.'

The twelves and the thirteens were able to identify and relate to every word the Maths Teacher said. The internal uprising within the bosoms of these adolescents might have taken the form of a war, had they not been stirred so. They loved the idea of truth not always being what it initially appears to be. The scientific diagnosis of truth became an important ingredient for their sanity just before breaking into their teenage years.

One day, the Head Teacher sensed a taut atmosphere in the Grade 7 classroom due to several heated arguments he had overheard about the relevance of subjects, especially history, its events and dates. Most students were troubled by the plethora of data—facts that they had to remember and understand. Science and maths were trending as compared to other subjects as they could relate them to their daily lives. While Cuebee, Anxy, Geekay and Mindesh argued on the side of social sciences being as great in their expanse as science and maths, the rest of the class was generally against the motion. For Cuebee, society, its past, and dreams for the future were all as important as technology. The attentiveness of the children in history class was now at stake. The Head Teacher decided to intervene to introduce a sense of balance in their lives. He got hold of several good documentaries and films on the history of India and the world, and arranged for shows for all senior classes. The children took to it like flies to a jar of marmalade. They loved the retelling of history in this storytelling manner. The Head Teacher had managed to re-establish the relevance of the subject, and it was back in the race to fight for precedence in the children's academic affections.

It was as if we were all a part of a carefully planned evolution. We classroom-mates always felt responsible for all the good developments in school and never refrained from celebrating what we termed as 'our success'.

Frontal: Do you people understand the concept of averages in maths?

Parietal: That's simple. To find the average of a group of numbers, divide the sum of numbers by the total number of events.

Amygdala: But why do we need that? Don't you think in terms of performance, average means a poorly performing person?

Cerebellum: Not in the least! Take a cricket match. Averages there mean average scores by a cricketer and can be really telling on the outcome of the match.

Hippocampus: What are you getting at?

Frontal: When Columbus left for the Americas, what do you think was the average possibility of him succeeding?

Cerebellum: None. Because, ab initio he went in the so-called wrong direction.

Frontal: Exactly! I am getting increasingly certain that the average learning levels of our students is going up by leaps and bounds, because ab initio we started in the right direction.

Brainstem: You mean 'we, the eight classrooms' have started in the right direction!

Frontal: Of course! Needless to say, 'we' are the prime movers and shakers of this whole learning process.

A few days before the last day of school in this academic session, the Head Teacher announced that there would be a special presentation. Ah! I looked greatly forward to such surprises for they gave my elements and molecules the much-needed restoration every now and then. The Head Teacher called for a joint class of all students of Grades 6, 7 and 8. They collected the next day in the largest room of the school, the staffroom-cum-library, where all the furniture had been pushed to the walls and thick carpets were laid on the floor for the students and teachers. Cuebee's grandmother was also present.

There were special guests too—the Sarpanch of the village along with a few members of the gram panchayat. The new Sarpanch was a woman in her early thirties. She was a school pass out from her parent's village, and it was said that she was very good at using technology for administration. Ever since the previous Sarpanch Madam had risen to popularity and well-deserved fame by establishing her adroitness at village governance, the village had become prone to looking at the previous stints of some of the male sarpanches as one of life's tragedies, better left undiscussed. The present Sarpanch Madam, popularly and lovingly known as Madam-2, was also elected through popular and majority vote. Her daughter studied in Grade 2 in the school. This kind of gathering to my 'cement bind'—translated in humanese as 'human mind'—was never done before.

It turned out that Cuebee had been singled out to make a presentation. She used a projector and a computer to show something mind-boggling as narrated by one of our classroom friends. The Head Teacher informed the forum that Cuebee had been working on it all through the summer vacations and even after school hours, and he thanked her grandmother profusely for being with her all the time, watching over her, and giving her moral support.

Cuebee stood in front of a crowd of about a hundred, probably feeling a little bewildered at first. She exchanged a nonplussed glance with the Social Science-cum-IT Teacher, sitting by the side in the front, who in turn dissolved her muddle with a reassuring smile.

'I have developed an App and I am going to talk about it and demonstrate it for you,' she started.

'What is an App?' yelled a sixth grader from the back.

'And I thought I was the question bank!' she quipped to a chuckling audience, and continued. 'An App or Application is a software that groups certain specific features together to give a specific experience to its user. An App represents the huge possibilities that information technology has for mankind. And I will answer all your questions towards the end, but for now please allow me to complete.' Cuebee's confidence was growing with every word she uttered.

'I have named this App—'A date with earth'. This App is based on a series of timelines starting about 3.8 billion years ago and traces the story of life on earth.'

Cuebee plugged in her App to the projector. She then proceeded to demonstrate the fascinating timelines. She began by showing the audience how one could click on any timeline to see what was happening on earth during that period. On clicking the timeline, '1.7 billion years ago', for example, first a written text appeared about the multiple-cellular organisms and complex organisms with several types of special cells and tissues that evolved in that period. And then she clicked on the 'watch a video' icon and an animated video depicting the said evolution could be viewed. She completed her presentation by giving several examples and opened the house for questions.

'This is incredible,' said Techie, looking thrilled to bits. 'But tell me, do I have to go through the entire timeline to search for something? For example, suppose I want to know how it happened that only earth has oxygen, while other planets do not, therefore only earth can support life.'

Cuebee was delighted to hear this question. She asked Techie to join her at the front and typed 'Oxygen' in a small box titled 'Search' in the App. The App immediately processed her search and gave a few options. Techie clicked on the option that read 'Life on Earth: Oxygen'. And voila! The App showed reading material as well as some videos related to her query. Techie opted for the reading material and read the following information aloud.

'Evolution of single-celled organisms having chlorophyll dates back to some 3.4 billion years ago. These organisms would consume carbon dioxide and with the help of energy from sunlight, convert it to oxygen. The entire oxygen in present-day earth is believed to be a product of photosynthesis. Oxygen made it possible for higher forms of life to evolve on this planet. Early life, however, did not use oxygen and depended on methane for energy and carbon; even today, methanogenic bacteria survive in swamps and natural geysers where oxygen is absent.'

And then came the deluge.

'When did animals walk on earth?'

'I heard that earlier earth only had oceans and land started appearing much later. Is that correct? Can this App show me?'

'When did mammals appear on earth?'

'Which parts of earth were covered in ice, say, 10,000 years ago?'

Cuebee's App had answers to many questions and did not for many others. She noted these so she could improve the App by adding the missing information in it.

'How did you make the films?' Bullie was impressed.

'Oh! I did not. I just took all the information, including text and videos from the Internet.'

'Then why do we need an App? We can see it on the Internet ourselves,' a boy from Grade 8 snapped.

'You are right. All I am trying to do here is give a good learning and information experience.'

'I am not sure I would want to use this App. I'd rather not get restricted by an App. I'd rather use the Internet.' The Grade 8 boy escalated it further, in an overtly adamant manner.

This was certainly not a discussion. It appeared more like unconstructive criticism, perhaps even envy.

'It's a free country. Feel absolutely free to do what you want.' Bullie got up in support of his classmate.

The Head Teacher decided that it was time to intervene. He got up, but before he could open his mouth, Madam-2 spoke.

'I have a request, a favour to ask, Cuebee. There is a law by the name of Biological Diversity Act. It requires us as a local body to have a Biodiversity Management Committee for the purpose of promoting conservation, sustainable use and documentation of biological diversity and chronicling of knowledge relating to biological diversity. We in the panchayat are very befuddled about how to go about the documentation. Cuebee, can you help us by making an App?'

Cuebee, the Head Teacher and the whole gathering was stunned into complete silence—the kind you have at funerals. But Bullie being Bullie began to clap loudly and said, 'Madam-2, we will all help Cuebee to do the research to make the App!'

The Head Teacher, otherwise a careful man with a tranquil attitude of general detachment, did a strange thing. He ran and hugged Bullie, and said, 'Kiddo, you are something!'

'Madam-2, since I need to overcome several shortcomings in my computer knowledge, would you give me enough time to develop it?' Cuebee asked the Sarpanch with humility.

'Of course! Take all your time. But do give the App to us before you leave school next year.'

The Head Teacher turned to Cuebee to take her assent, and on getting it, he told Madam-2 that the school would be happy to be of help to the local community and environment. He then concluded the whole show with a brief vote of thanks to the members of the audience, the Social Science and Maths Teachers, and then turned to the students.

'So, my young scientists, how is the feeling here?'

The whole class was electrified by the electronic machine. 'Magic! It's magic!' they shouted.

'Technology, as a wise scientist said, does not make gadgets but social change.'

'I always wonder though, if technology will overpower us, or will we always remain the master?' Cuebee almost whispered.

'Well, you started using the computer to explore just that. So, what are your findings, Cuebee?' said the Head Teacher.

'I think the computer definitely has the capacity to replace a teacher!' she said to the amazement of the gathering.

'Oh, really! Then I made a huge mistake by letting you use the computer,' the Head Teacher laughed.

'Yes sir, the computer never tires, it never asks us to keep quiet, it never says I don't have an answer, you are wasting my time. It is never out of syllabus in the computer world! But sir, it cannot create the bonding that we have with you and the teachers or be the guiding force like all of you. You are irreplaceable!'

And that is how the session ended that day, but not without a standing ovation for Cubee, our little student-turned-App-designer.

Whatever else we classrooms may claim, a new dawn of self-respect had descended on this tiny school, in great measure due to its teachers and students. The village too was perhaps warming up to the proposition of name and fame. Though when we, eight classrooms, were not gloating at our own so-called contribution, we were pretty clear that the trigger factor for the school's transformation was Cuebee and her classmates. And that is why we had begun to wonder, what after Cuebee and team? Would the school be able to retain its vibrancy? After all, she would have to leave the school to enter Grade 9 in the neighbouring town within the next twelve months. It was a sobering thought, verging on the unpleasant. Would someone please sit up and take notice of our concerns?

11
A Constitution for Nature

It was six in the morning. The silence that had engulfed the school for the last forty-five days was about to be broken. Eight of us appeared to be motionless as always, but we were not unmoved inside; uneasy lay our foundation. We were, in fact, on tenterhooks, and since early morning had been counting within our mortar worlds, and reached two million one, two million two, two million three.

The gates were thrown open at exactly forty-five minutes past six to welcome the droves of small-to-medium and few large-sized humanity in light blue and navy blue. Ah! The yells, the shouts, chatter, laughter, noise, the babel, we classrooms revelled in it. It was like coming alive in a trice and experiencing meadows of green, splashed with wild and colourful flowers, swaying in the cool breeze.

Though the sun had taken leave of absence for the last three days; however, on school reopening day, there it was, red and hot, aloft and aerial, baking and cooking, noble and majestic, mercilessly lighting up every nook and cranny of the school, which by now had existed for more than a quarter of a century.

And there she was! The cynosure of my brick-world, the life in my breadth (breath), the foundation of my happiness, my *raison d'être*! Cuebee walked in with Joy, tall and impressive, confident yet calm, and headed straight to deposit her little brother in Grade 2. She hugged Butterfly Teacher and her brother and left for her class, my space. She walked into my room to joyous shouts of 'welcome to Grade 8' from her friends for the last seven years.

Ocean stood on a desk at the far end of the class and was striving to deliver an impassioned speech to the class with Geekay, Yoga and Jadoo giving him 'heightened' company by standing on nearby benches.

'Friends, villagers, Indians, countrymen and fellow standers-on-the-bench! Lend me your ears, eyes, intellect and the use of your two strong arms. Dearly beloved, as the senior-most members of the society of learners in this school, we are gathered here today to decide the seating arrangement of the class.'

'Ocean! The Head Teacher is standing outside!' Bullie yelled.

'Does he appear to be in the throngs of gladness and light-heartedness, or does he seem to be looking for a stick to beat me?' said Ocean, continuing in the same fervid tone.

'He seems to be about to serve you a suspension order, Ocean,' Cuebee informed him in all seriousness.

Ocean, followed by the other three fellow 'standers-on-the-bench' sprang off their respective benches, sat down in their seats and donned the innocent looks of a six-month-old baby, all this within a millisecond. The whole class was in fits as Bullie, and Cuebee on cue, had pulled a fast one on Ocean. Before they could recover from the ruse, the Head Teacher actually entered the classroom, in flesh and blood, along with the Social Science Teacher.

'Good morning, class. So, Ocean, did your countrymen lend you their ears and whatever else you wanted to borrow?'

The class was stunned into silence, and no one quite knew how to respond to this. They clearly had not bargained for the Head Teacher to be in the vicinity of their theatrics, in which he undoubtedly had the lead role. But then the class had Bullie who was born to this world to tackle such awkward moments.

'Sir, the power of the mighty Ocean diffused before he could even wield it,' Bullie informed the Head Teacher matter-of-factly.

'Ha ha. Thank you, Bullie, for that little help there. We are going to start your academic session this year with constitutional values, rights and duties. And Ocean, you have given a great backdrop to initiate it.'

'Is the Social Science Teacher our class teacher this year?' a meek voice asked from behind. It was Mindesh as usual, always wanting to get this part out of the way on the first day of every academic session.

'No, Mindesh. The Maths Teacher is your class teacher. But since she has gone for training, she will join back next week. Until then the Social Science Teacher will take care of you,' the Head Teacher clarified. He then left, but not before giving a furtive glance towards Ocean, Bullie and Cuebee.

He had most certainly overheard the entire speech addressed to all the dearly beloved and the threats doled out on his behalf!

The Social Science Teacher laid down the rules for the class for learning about the Constitution.

'First, I hear from you what is your understanding of the Constitution, then I help you understand the topic, then I give you an activity, you work together as a class to decide upon the topic of the activity, next you divide yourself in groups to complete the components of the activity, and finally you integrate it and make a presentation before all the Teachers of the school.'

'All the Teachers, sir? That is very scary, sir,' Awey said with his eyes almost falling out of their sockets and jaw unable to close.

'Hmm, now that you are about to shift schools next year, I am only trying to prepare you for all the exigencies that life shall bring at your doorstep. Consider this one of those.'

The class settled to brace themselves for this new and unusual experience. The teacher then took three complete periods to understand their prior knowledge, give a brief history of the Indian Constitution, elaborate upon the objectives and philosophy of the Preamble and explain the fundamental rights and the duties enshrined in it. There is always this something that ensues from a good class by an outstanding teacher that makes the students feel as if the life they have lived so far was bereft of the meanings that they were discovering right at that moment in time. This was that precise and meaningful moment in time. On the surface, the students appeared unchanged, unaffected and unconnected, but in reality, these three classes had provoked a huge transformation within. The teacher then informed them of an activity.

'The activity is that you will write your own constitution. The constitution shall have a Preamble and rights and duties. As a class, you will decide the topic on which you want to write your constitution. You could, for example, write a constitution of your class, of your school, etc. You decide. But remember to use the values, rights, duties that you have learnt about in the Indian Constitution. Once you decide upon the topic, you will break into three groups. One group will write the Preamble, one the rights, and the third the duties. You have three weeks to complete it. Is that clear?' And then the teacher wrote a date on the chalkboard, four weeks hence.

'That is the date of your presentation before all of us. We look forward to it.'

The teacher left for the staff room leaving the class to its own machinations.

The students were baffled, excited and uncertain, all at the same time, about how to proceed. Discussion, arguments and commotion erupted from all directions in the classroom. There was a group led by Mindesh that wanted to write the constitution of the class, only because it would be simpler and quicker. There was another group led by Bullie that wanted to give a serious try to writing the constitution of their own homes. Bullie was covertly desirous of brandishing the important document before his father and elder siblings to attain his rights over the TV remote. The last bunch of kids consisting of Cuebee and her friends, plus Jadoo, Sky and Arty, were having a serious discussion from the looks of it. Eventually, they were struck by an idea that gripped their minds like the indelible ink on a voter's finger.

'We have an idea for the topic,' Cuebee informed the class.

'So do we!' said Bullie, confident that there could be nothing better than the idea he supported.

'Well, we too have an idea,' Mindesh said.

Three ideas, thirty denizens. There was no way they would arrive at a decision quickly enough, particularly given the frenzied and long arguments that each one of them was capable of for defending anything they stood for. Cuebee took charge. She requested that each of the ideas be discussed before the whole class by the group concerned, then put to vote. The idea with a majority vote should then be accepted by all. The kids, by consensus, agreed to permit the majority vote to interfere with the implementation of their ideas, if need be. Twenty-eight out of thirty votes went to Cuebee's team's idea. Bullie and Mindesh, the two dissident votes, gladly gave in to the congenial spirit of the whole class.

The idea was indeed brilliant. They were going to write the 'Constitution of Biodiversity' of the village. Cuebee's team would write the Preamble by explaining the philosophy and core values related to the natural life and habitats in the village; Bullie's team the rights of the flora and fauna; and Mindesh's team was to write about the duties of the human residents of the village towards biodiversity.

'Ha, this is very simple. We can complete it in one day. Let us start,' said Bullie, inclined to overlook the possibility of debate and discussion.

But hardly fifteen minutes into their heated discussions, each one of them realized that four weeks may be too little after all!

Though all other classes for the Eighth Graders started in full earnest, their active minds and the imminence of the date of presentation preoccupied them to such an extent that they spent only the necessary two minutes over 'mundane' things like lunch and other breaks whose limited purpose was cell, tissue, organ and mind restoration.

The preamble team, though often debating, arguing, researching, and sometimes lost in abstract thought, did manage to get a preamble ready. The principles of Sovereignty, Socialist, Secular, Democratic, Republic, Justice, Liberty, Equality and Fraternity were all found to be applicable in the Constitution of Biodiversity.

- Sovereign, because there can be no authority above biodiversity except nature itself.
- Socialist, because humans and biodiversity need to live with each other, cooperate with each other and work together to provide balance in the ecosystem.
- Secular, because every flora and fauna has the freedom to follow their own life cycle in their own habitat, essentially their life and survival was their own religion.
- Democratic, because biodiversity is all about being of nature, for nature and by nature.
- Republic, because no particular flora or fauna enjoys any special privileges.
- Justice applies as a value because every biodiversity must be treated fairly so that it survives and propagates; humans must not destroy species for their own benefit.
- Liberty, because all biodiversity must have the freedom of expression, in terms of how they appear, grow physically and behave biologically.
- Equality, because all biodiversity must get equal opportunity to improve their life.

- Fraternity, because each type of flora and fauna deserves a level of dignity, so they live in harmony with all sentient beings to preserve order, which in itself shall be the unity and integrity of the biodiversity.

Bullie's group also found all fundamental rights to be applicable, while Mindesh's team developed a series of duties that the villagers had towards the biodiversity in the village to ensure its balanced coexistence with humans. They justified it in their own unique ways, just as the preamble team had done. The eighth graders named their biodiveristy constitution document '*Prakriti ka Samvidhan*'.

The so-called presentation before all teachers was in reality an assessment of the students' understanding of constitutional values. The teachers shot hard-boiled questions at the three teams, and as I recollect it, not a single one went unanswered. The kids may not have complete answers for all queries but they were willing to find out and revert. Grade 8 by now was adept at self-learning, research and diagnosis of topics at hand. In fact, they stole a march, nay a carnival parade, over the hearts of the teachers that day.

Exactly twenty-four hours after the presentation, there was breaking news. Our friend, Roof, was literally doing jumping jacks inside as he collected us that night rather early by our standards. The moon was yet to go up and the stars were yet to begin their walk of fame on the carpet of night. Roof was trying hard not to lose self-control as he spoke.

'Madam-2 managed to get our school four new classrooms for Grades 9 to 12, plus, one science laboratory, a library room and a separate arts room along with four new teachers! Do you know what that means? Cuebee and the rest of her classmates continue their school education right here! Here, with us! They are with us for four more years! The universe has conspired to give us what we wished for! Thank you, O universe! How shall we ever repay you for your generosity!'

It wasn't the loveliest of summer nights, but I cannot recall a more enchanting one in my entire twenty-seven years of existence! As the clear skies smiled over us, we felt a deep connection with it in our elation. I sensed that the universe connects with you when you connect with it. The children had begun the work on the Biodiversity App and even developed a constitution for it. Was it nature's way of appreciating their efforts by rewarding the school with an expansion plan?

The news spread like wildfire in the school and the village. Parents began celebrations at home; keyed up villagers were found happily conversing about its possibilities under every conceivable tree, undeterred by the remorseless gaze of the sun, the Head Teacher was relieved; and the teachers were glowing with pride. The children, particularly, from Cuebee's class, thrilled at the miraculous development, had already and without any preliminary formalities, decided to pester the Head Teacher to allow them to design the new construction. Mercifully, the Head Teacher did not budge. Though most had dreamt of it, they could not imagine that their vision would actually materialize one day. It once again took the efforts of a persistent and insistent Sarpanch Madam-2 to bring the school to this turning point.

With the help of her classmates, Cuebee had begun to prepare the Biodiversity App for the village in earnest. Her classmates did a major share of the research online, while Cuebee and her friends undertook some field surveys and interviews, in addition to writing the program. She would take guidance from the Social Science Teacher if she ever got stuck. The children would work mostly after school hours, but sometimes the Head Teacher would let them work during school time too. To keep their minds fresh, they would participate in sports and music activities. The Sports Teacher spent all his free time with the children, helping and supporting them in every which way he could. Cuebee also had several detailed discussions with the gardener, whom she found to be a huge storehouse of knowledge about the local flora and fauna.

'The app has to be designed in a simple and straightforward manner so that it can be used by anyone. What are your ideas on it?' Cuebee discussed with the gardener.

'Can you ensure that the app encourages users to identify indigenous species? The app should be useful in showcasing insects, birds, plants, amphibians and other species we are most likely to find in our village,' the gardener asked.

'We can certainly ensure that by using the camera of the cell phone. The image recognition will be matched with the database of the app and will help in distinguishing the exact species of plant, flower, insect or animal.'

'Also, there are many natural medicines which are found in plants, shrubs or trees. See how you can give that information to the persons who use the App to identify the local flora and fauna.'

Cuebee and her friends also had several rounds of discussions with the Teachers and the Head Teacher. They suggested documenting the whole process very carefully. It would help them in reflection as well as become a way forward for other grades. A small brochure on how to use the App, a short film on the local biodiversity and measures to protect it, organizing debates, poem writing, science experiments, posters, etc., to demonstrate the App and creating awareness about saving biodiversity in the community, were in sum total the inputs from them.

On interviewing her little brother and his classmates, Cuebee felt the need to gamify the App, given the present-day bite-sized concentration levels of cell phone users.

'The app should be interactive and offer a variety of challenges, such as discovering ten living species in the given perimeter, or capturing all the different levels of the food chain hierarchy; say, one producer, one herbivore, one carnivore and one decomposer.'

Her classmates more than agreed. They were euphoric at the whole idea of gamification of learning.

By the most singular and propitious act of the cosmos, the development of the Biodiversity App also had a wonderful snow-balling effect on learning several other random but related areas.

I may have been deficient in my own understanding of the environment and its need for conservation in my earlier avatar, but this time there was nothing that was left unclear—be it physical and chemical processes behind climate change, or extinction of plants and animals, deforestation and soil erosion, ozone layer depletion, increase in temperature, sea levels, erratic monsoons, heatwave-bubble of hot areas in places as cold as Canada, the effect of ocean currents, etc., everything was encountered headlong and diagnosed threadbare until the satisfaction of assimilation was felt.

I learnt, and in turn ensured that my seven other friends did too, the scientific names of some of the plants in the school—*Iberis amara* for candytuft, *Rosa rubiginosa* for roses, *Daucus carota* for carrots, *Moringa oleifera* for drumsticks. Oh, I loved the world of nomenclature!

The car lesson was taken up early in Grade 8. This was precipitated by the fact that some of the hyper-curious children had read several books in the library and on the Internet about the types of cars, spacecrafts, aeroplanes, etc. Their appetite for knowledge was enormous and the capacity of the system to keep up with them was not exactly commensurate at this stage. The kids, therefore, had founded a class club on 'Answers to Forever Diary' with the intention of self-learning through pooling of peer knowledge and understanding. The Head Teacher was, of course, over the moon with such an enterprise, for secretly he had always nurtured the desire that these children should now take wings. He, in any case, also believed in the glorious accident of learning anytime, anywhere, anything, and what better tool could there be for it than a topic circle or a club.

The car discussion in Grade 8 began with the issue of prices of diesel and petrol and went on to why all cars do not run on the same fuel, going on to what is so special about these oils that they are used in vehicles, why trucks and large vehicles use diesel, complex issues of petroleum discovery, environmental hazards, the impact of automobiles on the market, and so on. The teacher then divided the class into four groups. Each group was to speak in favour of the four motions listed by the teacher.

1. The vehicle has had more negative than positive consequences as compared to any other technology in transportation history.

2. Automobiles have benefited more than just their owners.
3. Cars have adversely impacted nature, air and water.
4. There are solutions possible that could help reduce the impact of cars on global warming.

The heated debates that ensued on cars and the entire society of machines on four wheels were nothing less than a successful attempt by the Science Teacher to generate interest in worldly affairs.

While the groups took off on their debates, arguments and research, the teacher appeared to be immersed in a distinct air of fulfilment as he drifted out of the room to stare at the sky and the sun that was insisting on peeking from behind curly grey monsoon clouds.

That night, raindrops collided in full force with our structure. Initially, it sounded like nothing less than a brawl by all the cats and dogs of the world, who were bent upon winning an argument. Eventually, it settled into a rhythmic fall, softly bathing us in the coolness and purity of nature. Engulfed in joy, we were finding it difficult to tear ourselves away from the agility of nature. We edged rather slowly towards our discussions that night.

Amygdala: I ceased to be just a room and have become part of nature today.

Cerebellum: That is the romantically inclined brain part in you that is picnicking in the rain.

Hippocampus: Hey vaulties, do you have anything interesting to report today?

Frontal: You know, I was thinking …

Parietal: Since when did you start using those faculties?

Frontal: Ha ha. You too, Parietal!

Hippocampus: Overlook, override and overcome all such intrusions. Lend us your thoughts, Frontal. Go on.

Frontal: Twenty-seven-plus years of observation have reaffirmed for me that education is perhaps the single most important human endeavour where 'means' are much more important than 'ends'.

Temporal: You are right. There is no way to predict or find the 'end of education'. Children can only evolve based on what they experience, and experiencing is a continuous process.

Amygdala: Hmm. Talking of 'means', I feel a lot is left to be done, particularly as far as teachers are concerned. Could it not be that they go through the machinations of a changed pedagogy only to get through to the end of the day?

Parietal: Your list of suspects has always been pretty large, Amygdala. You do not trust easily.

Temporal: Why bother with the minds of the actor, Amygdala, if the drama goes on well! You can't expect everyone to love the work they do and exhibit passion for it at every moment in their life. I give full marks to the Teachers for the change that they have brought in, even if it is to get to the end of the day. The system is mighty!

Frontal: Another notion that the last seven years have dispelled is that it is much more important to be correct than just be quick.

Hippocampus: Yes, I remember, how the Maths Teacher initially gave unlimited time to children to solve puzzles. Once they got used to it, she introduced timed tests.

Brainstem: The best part of her pedagogy is that if she finds any child is unable to perform in the specified time, she never deducts marks, but just lets her do it again.

Frontal: That's true. At least in my class, no one fears maths tests now. In fact, they keep asking for more tests.

Amygdala: Hmm. Now that you say it, that is the case with my class too. But tell me, do you agree with these random testing habits? Should the children not get used to a discipline, to a system that focuses on timely completion of all topics and their testing?

Hippocampus: If we don't give space to children to learn from mistakes for want of time, they will never achieve sustainable education. It will always be a shortcut to survival.

Amygdala: But here children are working together. How will they know what their individual mistakes are? The idea of collaboration is hyped. Ultimately, it is individual excellence that really counts.

Temporal: The individual Mozart created the symphony, but it takes an orchestra for us to enjoy it. Had it been a few pitter-patter of raindrops, would you have ventured into romance? It took the entire sky to burst into water dance for you to feel connected. Did it not?

Amygdala: Now that you point out, it appears that among my qualities, quick and deep appreciation of change is certainly not included!

Brainstem: Don't worry on that count. We know all your idiosyncrasies, and we prefer to indulge your weird gift of analysis. Our chatter is incomplete without a devil's advocate.

Occipital: Taking our discussion further, do you think a school can learn from itself? Or am I losing my sense of proportion by even contemplating this idea?

Temporal: No plant looks its best just after its seed is planted. It needs time to grow and blossom.

Frontal: O Lord of metaphors, I bow before thee!

Temporal: O denizens of the mortar world, once you get over the theatrics, I have something to tell. I come as the bearer of good tidings.

Frontal: Cross my heart and I hope to be demolished, if I say another word! Do tell.

Temporal: A meeting was held today in my space, where Madam-2 informed the Head Teacher that the construction work for the new classrooms begins as soon as the rains permit.

Parietal: Temporal, my lord, Of all the glad words by the school classrooms today, the gladdest are yours!

We must have appealed to the finer feelings of the rain gods, for cosmic permission was shortly received with the temperatures soaring once again, and the sun engaged in its prime-time occupation of burning whatever it touched. The fierce rush of laying the foundation and initiating construction work instigated my own meditations on the conspiracies of the universe. Ask and it shall be given! Whoever said that, spoke from veritable experience!

It was September and Teachers' Day was to be celebrated. On this day, the school had a system of engaging the teachers in fun and games, while students of Grade 8 would act as teachers for the rest of the grades in school. They would fan out to the classrooms in small groups and teach, play, undertake activities—basically handle the children for the day. Cuebee, Millie, Techie and Geekay were given the responsibility of Grade 3, that is, Joy's class. Exhilarating as it might have seemed to them initially, I am told the class turned out to be pretty rowdy—here a scream of joy and there a shout for help. They asserted themselves by ignoring the 'student-teachers' completely and carrying on with their bench-hopping, loud singing, beating their desks like drums and what-have-you. It was, in fact, no place for senior children, who had with great difficulty managed to focus their attention and energies on activities that did not include romping and skyrocketing, at least not most of the time.

The student-teachers knew they had to preserve their own reputations to preserve that of the teaching community. With the swiftness of an aircraft released into space, Millie climbed on top of the teacher's desk and clapped and whistled. She found her audience. Her daring act, much appreciated by Cuebee's little brother and his approving group of friends, broke the spell under which the little ones were acting like arboreal animals.

'Kiddos, we are going to play some games today,' Millie yelled at the top of her voice, without giving it any thought.

'Games! We want to play games!'

'And none of them have anything to do with standing on benches,' continued Millie.

'Can we run around on the floor?'

'Hmm. Possibly.'

'What is the game? We want to play a new game.'

That struck Millie like lightning. She stood there transfixed. She obviously had no idea what game they could possibly play to find peace in the class. Swiftly realizing what she had gotten herself into, Millie looked helplessly at Cuebee. Sensing that Millie's tongue was tied in inextricable knots, the audience was already showing signs of boredom and light whispers were soon followed once again by a medley of noise, promising to rise like a crescendo.

'Not under my watch!' muttered Cuebee to herself as she regarded Millie with raised eyebrows and at the same time hauled herself up on the desk alongside her.

'We shall be playing Dumb Charades. The class will be divided into two groups. One person from each group has to act as the person whose name the other group members whisper in this person's ear. The other members of the same group whose member is acting, have to guess who the person is,' Cuebee informed the eager-beavers.

'Show us a demonstration!' They began thumping their desks in excitement.

Millie whispered something in Cuebee's ears. On cue, Cuebee jumped to the nearest desk like a Ninja warrior would, bent forward a bit and wiggled her rear.

'Guess who?' Cuebee asked.

'Joy, Joy, Joy!' thundered the combined voices of Geekay and Techie and the rest of the class. Joy's trademark manner of expressing joy was well known to all.

'That's right!' Clapping erupted in the class.

Several things happened simultaneously thereafter. Joy's admiration for his sister suddenly knew no bounds, the stature of Joy in the eyes of his classmates grew multifold, and the class felt compelled to start the game of Dumb Charades with the kind of immediacy that they had felt while leaping from desk to desk when left unattended. Vitalized, the dapper children of Grade 3 extracted a great deal of entertainment from the Teachers' Day celebrations—much more than planned!

Five months elapsed since the commitment was made to the Sarpanch for a Biodiversity App. The entire class had increased their hold on the esteem of the village and the school. Word began to spread outside the village too, about the wonder kids of Grade 8 in a certain government school in a certain corner of the earth.

The delicately tuned sensibilities of Cuebee and her friends felt the pressure of completing the Biodiversity App on time. Just before the winter break, Cuebee had managed to prepare its first prototype using several free tools. The App allowed for taking photographs, registering exact location, auto-filling of the description that was editable, auto-generation of village biodiversity register, village biodiversity dashboard, and many other features. Cuebee and team had undertaken several rounds of discussions with the members of the panchayat while making the App. Once they got the go-ahead on the prototype, they decided to use the winter break to use the App and add to the biodiversity register of the village.

The two tablets that were given to Cuebee and her friends to run the pilot test of the App came in very handy. They used the tablets to compile and upload the information on all trees, plants, animals, and insects that they had identified in and around the school, and everything else that they had observed near their homes and many other parts of the villages they frequently visited. The children planned to give a final demonstration to Sarpanch Madam-2 in the month of March.

Just after the winter break, on the first day after school reopened, the Head Teacher walked into their class in the forenoon to announce that he would be the replacement for the Social Science Teacher who had gone for a week-long training session. The children were over the moon on this announcement. The Head Teacher had crossed the barrier that separates teachers from friends, philosophers and guides, a long time ago.

'Teacher, please tell us something new, something that has nothing to do with the syllabus, like you always do.'

The possibility of his acquiescing to such requests in class was so high, that no further cajoling was ever required. The ease with which he would slip into an uncharted area was akin to a smooth and peaceful declaration of independence from the confines of education each time.

Hence, without much ado he started to write on the blackboard: 'Atoms–Molecules–Living Tissue–Living Systems–Living Organism–Social Behaviour–Social Systems'. This was followed by: 'Related by Physics–Chemistry–Biology–Psychology–Sociology–Ethnology'.

'This is called the continuum of knowledge,' the Head Teacher began to explain.

'What is a continuum?'

'Well, a continuum is a series of small changes, connected to each other, which initially do not appear very different from each other, but in the end, they lead to a huge change or difference.'

The Head Teacher had one look at the perplexed sea of faces before him and felt recharged. He was always at ease amidst curiosity.

'For example, the temperatures across the year can be considered as a continuum. It is a slow process for the summer temperatures of forty-four degrees Celsius to transform to the winter temperatures of 2 degrees Celsius. So, when you are experiencing it every day, it appears to be small changes, all connected to one another. But if you look at the two extremes of temperature, the seasons appear to be unconnected to each other.'

'I get it. I have learnt language, mathematics, science, social science and environmental studies, all from the car outside. Isn't that what you mean by continuum?' Awey asked.

'Yes. Our whole purpose of changing the style of teaching, modifying the assessment methods, getting real life to classes, allowing you all to debate, argue, work together was to understand this continuum.

'In a small and a big way, you have understood psychology, which is the scientific study of the mind and behaviour; sociology, the study of social life and social change; and ethnology, the study of the characteristics of different groups of people and the differences and relationships between them.'

'And we studied atoms to understand matter, which in turn make the cells and tissues. Then life comes to the world, evolves, depends upon each other for food, locomotion, survival, and then we interact to form a society with friends and cities, then countries. Each one of us, all living and non-living things, are a continuum.'

Cuebee's face lit up as she suffixed the Teacher's line of thought.

'How did we miss such an interesting concept before? Let us build the interconnection between humans, community and society with biodiversity into our App, Cuebee,' Techie exclaimed.

'Exactly what I was thinking! Teacher, can you please request Sarpanch Madam on our behalf to give us some more time, say until the end of summer holidays to develop on this idea?' Cuebee was galvanized and almost could not wait to start.

'Of course. And I agree to be held responsible for the delay.'

The end of March brought the sun closer to declaring a steamy summer along with a news that broke our hearts, perhaps without any hope for amends. It so happened that the Head Teacher's name and fame had spread far and wide, and his methodology of teaching and learning was being considered the last word in education in our district. The District Education Chief had served a transfer order to our favourite Head Teacher and posted him to a dysfunctional school, several kilometres away, so that the said school could also experience transformation.

It was like being irrevocably shaken out of a beautiful dream with millions of hammers and tongs beating on our chests. The certainty of this change struck us like a tsunami when the new Head Teacher was introduced by the old one in the assembly, on the last day of school, before the summer vacations. The new Head Teacher was a small woman in her fifties, bespectacled, a dimple playing by the side of her left cheek, and her hair tied in a neat and tight bun, perhaps in honour of the handing- and taking-over occasion. I instantly developed a dislike for her. No, she had not uttered a word, and yes, her smile started from her eyes, but such externalities had no effect on me. I was convinced that I had to dislike her. Nothing or no one could change my belief.

I had expected teachers and students too, to meet in classrooms and corridors to rage against such a decision by the marauders of the system, spread their dislike for the new Head Teacher, and make a case for retention of our favourite Head Teacher. Or, at least commune emotionally as kindred souls over such an untimely, unfair and unjust decision. But nothing happened other than a happy farewell to him, where not a single teardrop was shed. While Occipital had regarded the paraphernalia of food items served during the Head Teacher's final meeting in the staff room with a great deal of interest, Occipital too reported a comfortable parting. Even the impasse that we had expected in Cuebee and her classmate's socio-emotional and educational lives never happened, even if in a schmaltzy way.

All this absence of resistance to such a crucial move not only left us surprised to begin with but hugely saddened to end with. So, this is what it was all about? Use our Head Teacher to transform education in a distant school, get it upgraded to higher secondary level through his goodwill, and then forget him for perpetuity as all the requisite good deeds were done! I had always imagined this lot to be a closed community that shared and cared for each other. This new and unsuspected side to their character was being revealed to us for the first time.

We, the classrooms, were in an emotional turmoil akin to a mess, for on the one hand we had Cuebee for four more years, but on the other, we had lost our favourite prime mover of the school's education system. No, this exchange did not work for any of us eight mute spectators.

The vacations had started. Eight of us would meet every night as usual, but somehow the zing and the zest had gone out of our brickly lives. One night, as we met forlornly, there was a huge lull in our conversation. Lately, this had become the hallmark of our remarkably and spectacularly dull meetings.

Brainstem: Shhh! Did you hear that noise?

Hippocampus: Yeah, that was me wanting to cry out loud.

Brainstem: I am serious. I distinctly heard it. It is well past midnight. What could it be?

Voice 1: It is me!

Voices 2, 3 and 4: And us!

Hippocampus, Cerebellum, Occipital: AND WHO ARE YOU?

Voice 2: We are the four new classrooms. We have heard you conversing every night for the past two weeks. I was so keen for all of us to connect with you. But you seemed so sad all the time. That is why I waited.

Occipital: Wow! Four new friends! Now that calls for a celebration.

Parietal: So what are your names?

Voice 3: Names? We don't have names. And what's in a name anyway?

Voice 4: The nomenclature idea appeals to me though.

Amygdala: Ah ha! Tabula rasa! Clean slate! Frontal, comrade, would you like to do the honours?

Frontal: Of course! Remember, Cerebrum is the largest part of the brain that initiates coordinated movement. I therefore, anoint Voice 1 as Cerebrum because you took the first step to talk to us, initiated and coordinated the effort to join us.

Cerebrum: Greetings from Cerebrum.

Frontal: I name Voice 3 as Dura Mater due to your tough stand on the name issue. Dura mater is the thick and tough covering over the entire brain and its parts for its protection.

Dura Mater: Hmm. I think I am going to love my name.

Frontal: I name thee, Voice 2, as the Circle of Willis, which is a junction of blood vessels that connects the brain to the rest of the arterial system. And exactly as per its nature, you have attempted to connect with us, the rest of the classrooms.

Circle of Willis: Circle of Willis at your service, sir!

Frontal: And you Voice 4, are hereby given the title of Hypothalamus, the regulator and the synchronizer.

Dura Mater: So, when can you all catch us up with speed about the happenings here in the last twenty-eight years of your existence?

Temporal: Now is the time, this is the place and you are the rooms.

Eight of us donned the caps of energetic storytellers and narrated the story of our lives every day, non-stop after the setting of the sun, continuing as it greeted us in the morning, and persisting as it rose right above our heads, almost roasting the sanity out of our bricks and cement. Basically, we twelve classrooms met 24×7 for two full weeks. Our delightful new friends listened to us with every fibre in their bosoms quivering, until towards the end, when they started laughing at us, almost mercilessly. The glow of amiability and congeniality, which the walls of eight classrooms had displayed in the last two weeks, promised to disappear for good.

Temporal: What is it with the four of you? We are not clowns performing before you for your Sunday amusement.

Cerebrum: No, please do not get offended. We could not help laughing on learning about the reason for your utter sadness for the past so many days.

Parietal: The four of you have much lesser experience than us. You can remain unmoved at the transfer of the Head Teacher at this stage. But believe me, there will come a time when your emotions will creep on you.

Hypothalamus: Well, we have information that you don't. Actually, I overheard the conversation in the staff room. The Head Teacher has been assigned to the dysfunctional school only for a tenure of exactly one year. Thereafter, he shall return to this school, as the Head Teacher again. That is why the parting appeared happy to your 'practised' eyes.

Cerebrum: That's right. Cuebee will be in Grade 10 when he returns.

Frontal: That strip of blue above us that we call the sky, why does it suddenly appear bluer? The rays of the sun, why do they feel instantly cooler than a winter breeze? The words of the new Head Teacher and her dimpled cheeks, why do they now appear to be god's gift to mankind?

Occipital: Drama Company! But seriously, you have added life to our years with this news.

Brainstem: I can now feel the abrupt cessation of our depression. The universe has indeed conspired to bring us together.

Hippocampus: My every atom and Millie-is-cool are roaring with delightful laughter. New roomsies, you have made my day and the rest of my life!

Frontal: As a logical corollary to our emotional outbursts, we hereby abort our instantaneous mission to unfriend you, declare party time and we also hereby proclaim our eternal love for our new comrades.

Dura Mater: What wonderful proclamations! You are brilliant!

Frontal: That I am!

Temporal: Modesty, thy name is certainly not Frontal!

Frontal: Modesty? Never heard of that.

Circle of Willis: Yeah, possibly because modesty is somersaulting in the graveyard you just dug for it!

Amygdala: Ha ha. Circle of Willis, you are a room after my own heart.

Frontal: Why do I get this feeling that you folks are ganging up against me? Do I need to lawyer up?

Cerebrum: In the midst of all the jollity, I have a question that is bothering me.

Frontal: Botheration to be tackled first, rejoicing and undying later.

Cerebrum: So, at the end of the day, did Cuebee learn?

Frontal: Yes, my comrade-in-arms, she learnt much more than she was taught!

Brainstem: I can now feel the current lifting of our depression. The amygdala has indeed conspired to bring us together.

Hippocampus: My every atom and fibre [illegible] are roaring with delightful laughter. Neurotransmitters, you have made my day and the rest of my life!

Frontal: As a logical conclusion to [illegible] adventures [illegible] declare party time and we also [illegible] our [illegible] love for our [illegible]

Dura Mater: What wonderful proclamations! You are brilliant!

Frontal: That I am!

Temporal: Modesty, thy name is certainly not Frontal!

Frontal: Modesty? Never heard of it!

Cerebral White Matter: Yeah, [illegible] modesty is [illegible] in the graveyard [illegible] dig for it!

Amygdala: [illegible] you are [illegible]

Frontal: [illegible]

Cerebrum: To the [illegible] of all the others, I have a question [illegible]

Frontal: [illegible]

Cerebrum: So, at the end of the day did Cadaber learn?

Frontal: Yes, my comrade in arms, she learnt much more than she was taught!

Afterword

What this book is about

- This is a work of fiction, and it is a happy book.
- Schooling in the future shall become even more inclusive with the help of several modes of delivery—digital, through community, volunteerism, etc.—that will make quality content available in the public domain. The artificial intelligence-based digital systems will make students aware of their own unique competencies and skills. But two areas in which no computer or artificial intelligence system can possibly deliver are empathy and curiosity. Based on this idea, the central idea of the book is how a school ecosystem reinforces natural empathy and curiosity in a child.

- Our motto for this book is therefore, 'nurture curiosity to develop creativity' in children. We are convinced that curiosity, creativity and innovation are non-negotiable skills that every child in the twenty-first century needs to possess.
- It is written from the perspective of the quintessential child, who is a curious learner, whose hunger for exploring the world around her is almost insatiable, whose need for connecting to her teachers, friends and the entire ecosystem that supports her is deeply set. Therefore, for us, every child is a Cuebee to begin with.
- We believe that a child's learning is not linear, therefore it cannot be limited to a prescribed syllabus. The child is in learning mode 24×7 and needs stimulations from different directions. Hence, we are certain that it is essential to add that bit of randomness to the learning experience of every child.
- The classroom and its environs are where most learning and growth of a child in the school ecosystem take place. Curiosity and creativity are two sides of the same coin. The sum total of the learning and creativity the child imbibes depends hugely upon how innovatively each class is transacted, hence this book revolves around classrooms.
- We also believe that there is no one way of teaching or no 'absolutely right' pedagogy. Any method adopted by a teacher to teach, even if it is invented by herself leading to a joyful, engaging and learning classroom, is just fine. For this to happen, every teacher needs agency over the pedagogy she desires to use in her class.
- It is based on the premise that every child has extraordinary capacity to learn and innovate. Conditioning of a child's

mind happens in many schools and in the community of the child. We do not agree with conditioning.

- Therefore, on the one hand, the book showcases the need to give more and more stimuli, while on the other it emphasizes that we must expect more from our children. Children's capacity to learn simple to complex things must never be underestimated.
- This book, therefore, is a simple yet deliberate collection of random acts of stimulation of the curiosity of the child that lead to a huge amount of learning.
- The book uses the car as a tool in the learning ecosystem. It is meant to introduce randomness and to drive home the idea that children love to be exposed to different forms of learning.
- Even though this book is written in English—trust us—all the narrated classroom transactions are taking place in a village in the vicinity of a metropolis in India, and the teachers have adopted the bilingual approach, where they use the mother tongue to connect the students to the medium of instruction.
- We love metaphorizing! How else would you have classrooms that are nomenclatured after parts of the human brain conversing with each other so freely and fairly?
- There is a deliberate reference to the 'sun' at the beginning of most chapters. The sun and sunlight are the reason for 'light' in our lives. Education too is all about switching on the bulb within, and we cannot help metaphorizing the sun. It greets the happy kids in the morning, peeks through the clouds when it is curious, it chases the dark clouds away when it wants to spread light, it stands guard

over the school during the day and spreads the warmth of love as it sets in the evening to reveal the stars. Nothing in the Milky Way can match the prowess of the sun!

- This book is the aggregate of personal and professional experiences of authors who have spent several years as educational administrators at local, state and national levels. The 'random' experiences and learnings of the authors have shaped their views on the crucial ingredients of quality classroom transactions.

While the resemblance of some of the characters to real-life ones is purely intentional, each character is a sum total of several persons, children, teachers, and head teachers we have met in our professional lives.

What This Book Is Not About

- It is not a self-help book.
- This book does not propagate any hypothesis.
- There is no linear action plot here. It is deliberately so. We are insisting on showcasing the crucial role of random acts of learning in school and inside the classrooms for the holistic growth of a child.
- This book is certainly not for educationists and pedagogy experts who may like to look at it from an expert or a researcher's point of view. This book is not the complete answer you may be looking for as a teacher willing to practise experiential learning, activity-based, enquiry-based, discovery-based or even hands-on learning, but it certainly is the ignition for it.

- In fact, we do not claim to follow any theory or pedagogy here. We are trying to show that a typical teacher may not always be able to follow a particular format or system of pedagogy, and yet can be very effective, only because she is able to joyfully engage the class in learning.
- This book in its entirety is not based on reality; however, in parts, it is.
- The book does not claim to discuss and cover every milestone in a child's life from the ages of 6–14. It only touches on a few in an attempt to make the story very real.
- It is not an advocate for submersion style of education, where the child has a complete disconnect with the language being used in class, and is left to her own devices to either 'sink' or 'swim'.
- This book does not address all challenges that may be faced in the ground situation, such as multi-level/multi-grade teaching, teacher recruitment, teacher transfers, and much more.
- Though many child characters are named, they are all not found in every anecdote of the book. This is to avoid confusing the reader. Only a representative sample of students is used in the narration.
- Once a major activity, or part of an activity, such as a PTM, report card, street play, adolescence, library, assessment, etc., is covered in a chapter, it is not repeated in any of the next chapters. The reader may assume its continuity, for we are focusing on giving only a flavour of a classroom's adventures in learning-related activities.

Glossary of Hindi terms and abbreviations

Akshar Gyan: Knowledge of letters

Anda: Egg

Anganwadis: Government-funded childcare centre for Early Childhood Care and Education of 0–6-year-olds.

Asthadal: Group of eight

Atta: Wheat flour

Badi: Big

Bahar-se-garam-andar-se-naram: Haughty outside, Softy inside

Belan: Hindi name for a rolling pin used to prepare the Indian bread called roti

Billie: Cat

Chai: Tea

Choti: Plait

Chamcha: Ladle or large spoon, but in this case the word is used to mean a 'flatterer'

Chanda Mama Door Ke: A very popular Indian lullaby in Hindi, translated as 'Uncle Moon in the sky'

Chhau Dancer: A form of dance from the Indian state of Jharkhand that incorporates elements of martial arts

Chor: Thief

Dada: Paternal grandfather

Dadi: Paternal grandmother

Dalma: Originally a chickpea, papaya and vegetable recipe from the state of Odisha; however, it is popular all over the country for its taste and nutrition

Dhobi: Launderer

Gaali: Slang

Golgappa: A savoury snack of India, well-liked by most for its sweet, salt and sour taste

Gram Panchayat: Local self-government at the village level

Holi: An Indian festival celebrated with colours, and sometimes with water too

Jaadugarni: A female magician

Jal Tarang: Literally meaning 'water waves', it is a form of instrumental music that originated in India. It is based on creating music with different levels of water in ceramic bowls

Jungle ka Judge: Judge of the jungle

Kachcha: Raw

KBC: *Kaun Banega Crorepati*, literally translated as 'Who will become a millionaire?' It is a popular Indian TV show in India based on the original British show called *Who Wants to Be a Millionaire?*

Kurta: A long loose shirt commonly worn in India by men and women

Laddoo: An Indian sweet

Lakir ka fakir: A common phrase in India meaning dogmatic

Ma ji: Mother being addressed respectfully. 'Ji' is added to names to show respect to elders or those in power

Mithai: Indian sweets

Namaste: The Indian form of greeting with palms joined together

Nana: Maternal grandfather

Nani: Maternal grandmother

Natak: Play

Nautanki: Folk theatre, but the word is often used to refer to a gimmickry artiste

Nukkad: Street corner

Nukkad Natak: Street play

Oonch, Neech: Highland, Lowland; common outdoors game played by kids

Paani Poori: A kind of Indian snack that has a wheat-based hollow bread filled with spicy mint-and-coriander-flavoured water.

Panchatantra: An Indian collection of animal-based fables from around 200 BC or even earlier

Papdi Chaat: A tasty concoction of vegetables and fries in yogurt, sprinkled with tamarind and coriander sweet and salty sauce

Prakriti ka Samvidhan: Constitution of Nature

PTM: Parent–teacher meeting

Pyjama: This is a Hindi word which literally translates to "garment for legs"

Roti: A type of Indian bread

Salwar-kameez: A typical Indian dress worn by females

Sa Re Ga Ma Pa Dha Ni Sa: Abbreviation for the seven notes of Indian music - Shadja, Rishabha, Gandhara, Madhyama, Panchama, Dhaivata, [and seventh] Nishada

Sarpanch: The elected head of a local self-government at the village level

Shabaash: Well done

Sipahi: Policeman

Stapoo: The Indian hopscotch

Taaliyaan: All to clap now!

Tha se Thathera: Tha (a letter in the Hindi alphabet) for Thathera

Thathera: Coppersmith

UPS: Uninterrupted Power Supply

Zindabad: Long live!

Badal, badal door ke,	Clouds, clouds up so high,
Belan dikhaye door se.	Stick-like shapes in the sky.
Jhankey ghar ki jaali se,	Peeping from my window sill,
Khaaye ma ki gaali re.	Mom is about to aim and kill.
Cuebee, Techie, kahan chali,	Cuebee, Techie, where do you go,
Jhund banakar kahan chali.	In a group, in a row.
Merey ghar bhi aao na,	Come over to my place too,
Laddoo pani puri khao na;	Let's eat pani poori and laddoo.
Chalo baithe hum chatai par,	Let us three sit on the mat,
Aur gup karein hum patar patar:	And with each other, chat, chat, chat.

Acknowledgements

Writing a book, any book, is never an individual effort, and the three of us are certainly under no illusions of our individual or group prowess in this regard. We have derived support, strength, inspiration, perspiration, critical yet constructive review and/or unconditional admiration from many people. But we would like to first and foremost thank all the children out there, in our schools, in our homes, and around us, who are our constant source of inspiration.

Working in the government has provided us with huge opportunities for learning, understanding the ground realities, developing and implementing policies and best practices, and being exposed to some very innovative interventions at various levels, from the grassroots to the national level. We would like to, therefore, especially thank the Government of India for giving us this unique opportunity, and the

Ministry of Education and all its officials, who have directly or indirectly contributed to the ideation process.

As a team, we drew extensive inspiration from each other. Each of us has also received enormous support from family and friends:

Anita Karwal: Aside from giving some brilliant ideas on the storyline, my husband, Atul, provided the much-needed comic break, after hours of continuous writing would wear me down. My daughters, film-maker Janvi, and astrophysicist Tanvi, have always and enthusiastically championed the cause of my writing. Their ceaseless cheering ensured my steady pace of writing. My wonderful friend and educationist, Dr Anju Kawr, did a thorough job of pinpointing factual and other mistakes in the draft, while my author aunt, Manna Bahadur, and author sister-in-law, Rima Pandey, were the first to read the manuscript and egg me on. And thank you Ma and Papa, for always showering me with your blessings. Wherever I look up to the sky, I can sense your presence.

Rajnish Kumar: My daughters Anannya and Tanvi, and wife Devika, ensured a relaxing environment at home, as I raced against time to complete the book. They never hesitated to debate, argue or critique the events that I would churn up for every grade. It became the ignition for new ideas and inspiration to pen down the book.

Rashi Sharma: My husband Aman's wholehearted and unflinching support is what emboldened me for trying something so absolutely new. His constant nudging to write about education, the sector that has given me the most enriching and gratifying experiences of my career, is what has brought me to this stage. I am also grateful to my forever cheerleaders, my parents, Vasudev Sharma, Saroj Sharma, and my brother Piyush. I am beholden to the little Cuebees in my life, my kinetic sons, Shikhar and Samrat, and my spirited niece Divija. Without their presence in my life, I would not have been able to get insights into a child's mind.

A special and warm thank you is reserved for Andreas Schleicher, who readily agreed to write the Foreword. We commend and are deeply inspired by his efforts to transform education in the world through the tool of PISA and thereby, nurture millions of Cuebees.

We sincerely thank the editors at HarperCollins, Swati Daftuar and Arpita Dasgupta. They not only gave very useful insights for editing the book, but also endured our stubborn stance on some of our writings with much grace and patience. We thank Ananth Padmanabhan, CEO of HarperCollins, India, for the literary opportunity by accepting to publish the book.

We cannot sign off without expressing our immense appreciation for the Google Docs collaboration feature on MS Word, due to which the three of us could write simultaneously. It might be of interest to future group authors to know that initially, Anita inked in 'green', Rajnish in 'blue' and Rashi in 'red' on the Google Docs pages. And one fine day, when we decided to make the colour uniformly 'black', that day, this book in its present form was born. Our salutes to this technology that facilitated a smooth flow of ideas and words.

We are signing off, by thanking each one of you, our readers, for choosing to join us on this animated journey with the child within each of us.

Anita Karwal, Rajnish Kumar and Rashi Sharma

About the Authors

Anita Karwal, an Indian Administrative Service officer from the batch of 1988, retired in November 2022 as Secretary, Department of School Education, in the Ministry of Education, Government of India. She was deeply and closely involved with the preparation and implementation of the National Education Policy 2020 and the National Curriculum Framework for Foundational Stage 2022. She has spent several years leading, administering and reforming the school education sector in India and has acquired rich experience at the grass-roots, state and national levels.

Rajnish Kumar worked with the Ministry of Education, Government of India, on deputation from Indian Railways. He is a mechanical engineer by profession. He was involved in the framing of the National Curriculum Framework based on the National Education Policy 2020. He also worked on all the digital education initiatives of school education.

Rashi Sharma is an Indian Postal Service officer and worked in the Department of School Education and Literacy, Ministry of Education, for almost seven years. She was involved in the formulation of the National Education Policy 2020 and its implementation thereafter; the NIPUN Bharat Mission, which focuses on foundational learning: and the revamping of Samagra Shiksha, a centrally sponsored scheme for school education. She has also worked in the areas of teacher education, teacher training, out-of-school children and foundational learning studies, among many others.

30 Years *of*

HarperCollins *Publishers* India

At HarperCollins, we believe in telling the best stories and finding the widest possible readership for our books in every format possible. We started publishing 30 years ago; a great deal has changed since then, but what has remained constant is the passion with which our authors write their books, the love with which readers receive them, and the sheer joy and excitement that we as publishers feel in being a part of the publishing process.

Over the years, we've had the pleasure of publishing some of the finest writing from the subcontinent and around the world, and some of the biggest bestsellers in India's publishing history. Our books and authors have won a phenomenal range of awards, and we ourselves have been named Publisher of the Year the greatest number of times. But nothing has meant more to us than the fact that millions of people have read the books we published, and somewhere, a book of ours might have made a difference.

As we step into our fourth decade, we go back to that one word – a word which has been a driving force for us all these years.

Read.

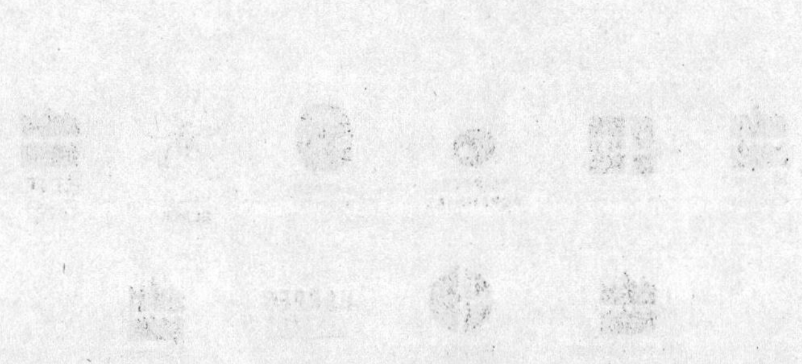